To my dear sister Val,
an inspiration to us all

and in memory of
Robert,
my one true brother

TABLE OF CONTENTS

INTRODUCTION

I had a village in Africa, in the foothills of Mount Kilimanjaro (with apologies to Isak Denison). This village, which my husband Dale and I informally "adopted" in 2007, is called Okaseni, and at that time, it had a population of about four thousand people. It was—and still is—very poor and desperately in need of help.

In 2006, after many adventures and challenges, I was working as an instructor in the Communication Department (COMM) at the British Columbia Institute of Technology (BCIT) in Burnaby, British Columbia. It was the best job I ever had. After years of freelancing as a writer, editor, and publisher, I found a steady paycheque, predictable work hours, and the freedoms of teaching to be joys beyond measure. Dale and I were celebrating seventeen years of married life, and we had recently moved to Bowen Island, a small, beautiful isle near Vancouver. I had reached a satisfactory plateau of good health, an enjoyable career, and a happy personal life.

I finally had time to devote to worthy causes or initiatives, so I began to cast about for such a cause/initiative to get involved in. I submitted several modest pedagogical proposals to my BCIT uppers (all rejected), considered a PhD (without much enthusiasm), and mused about moving abroad to teach English for perhaps six months or so. I also read a lot and stumbled one day across a 2003 article in *Maclean's* magazine about Daniel Igali, Canada's 2000 Olympic gold medal winner for wrestling. He was a student at Simon Fraser University in Burnaby at the time and trying to raise funds to build a school in his native Nigeria. A chance encounter with Milton Wong, the current SFU chancellor, led to help. Wong, well-known as a successful Canadian businessperson and generous philanthropist, was inspired by Igali's project and got SFU on board. Wong told the magazine that "there is no reason every university could not adopt a village [in Africa]. We in Canada have so much."[1]

Africa! I thought, I can do that! It was perfect for me because I had spent five months travelling Africa as an adventurous young person. That journey was one of the most difficult things I had ever done. It also changed my life forever. I was going to find out many years later that it would change my life again.

This first trip to Africa was in 1975. I met Ralph, my first husband, on the train across Canada, the first leg of my trip to Africa. We clicked and decided to travel together to Europe. We soon became an item and eventually married. Both of us were deeply influenced by the counterculture of the '60s and '70s, that grassroots rebellion against conformity and limitations. We both loved travelling, the beauties of other cultures and unusual sights, and the fine white line of the freeway.[2] I recognized a kinship with him, a fellow traveller on the same road to adventure and profound experiences.

That era was a monumental time of change in music, dress, and lifestyle, and of wanting to truly live and not just exist. The longing for freedom, individualism, and adventure was prime. It was the era of Women's Lib, civil rights, LGBT rights, the anti-war movement, the challenge to authority, and the rejection of traditional marriage, kids, and a house in the suburbs. There was a dark side of drugs and increased violence, but society in general was forever changed for the better. Many of the freedoms and inclusive attitudes today that we take for granted stem directly from that era. No need to thank us, our pleasure!

Ralph was tall and slim, with long blonde hair. He carried a kind of charisma. I, on the other hand, was short and slim, with brown hair. I was sort of unnoticeable. I was glad for this. Being nondescript was a huge benefit. Ralph was striking and so deflected attention away from me and to himself. That helped keep me safe. But times were different then, and I never felt threatened, and we never had a bad experience.

He was younger than me but far more practical and capable. He knew how to maneuver his way through new cities and foreign situations, how to delve deep for information, and how to find fortuitous people and help. I knew how to read a book and write an essay. Bookish would be an understatement. He opened up a startling new world to me, actually out *in* the world, instead of at home with agoraphobia and worthy tomes. It was a crash course in pragmatism and material competencies.

I, on the other hand, became his family and home after his several years of living alone and travelling without a base or kinfolk to return to. As the oldest child in my family, I was used to taking care of younger ones. I admired him a lot. It was a square deal.

And so we went to Africa. At the beginning of each chapter in this book, you will find a vignette of our journey in chronological order. Each is connected thematically to the chapter that it fronts.

Anyhow, back to Milton Wong's idea of adopting a village in Africa—it sounded fabulous to me. I also thought it an ideal opportunity for BCIT to pursue as well. I decided to try to persuade the powers that be of its worth by writing a report about the idea. I began in September 2006 researching and reading numerous articles and books. These books included three seminal ones: *Race Against Time* by Stephen Lewis, *Banker to the Poor* by Muhammad Yunus, and *The End of Poverty* by Jeffrey Sachs, founder of the UN Millennium Village Project (MVP). Lewis updated me on current conditions in Africa. Yunus gave me the template for running a microcredit program. Sachs gave me the idea to tackle everything in the village, such as water, agriculture, health, and education, instead of focusing on just one thing. These books were the foundation of the Africa Village Project Association.

I finished this report in December. Here is the summary:

> An unparalleled opportunity is open right now to BCIT that would bring enormous benefits to the institute, both tangible and intangible.
>
> BCIT could be the first ever North American post-secondary institute to reach out to and help the developing world. Seizing this opportunity would result in an even higher public profile for BCIT and enormous goodwill and prestige. As well, another educational offering could be added to current programs that would possibly attract more students.
>
> I would recommend that BCIT focus on Africa. It is by far the most desperately poor continent in the world and

much of BCIT's expertise and knowledge could be used there. Many arguments could be put forward against helping Africa; for example, the supposed laziness and culpability of the poor, misspent foreign aid money, Africa's corruption, and the mandate of the UN and national governments to take charge. However, these arguments are groundless. Instead, enlightened self-interest, as well as common human concern for others less fortunate, unequivocally justify helping.

By taking full advantage of this opportunity, BCIT would be seen as both dynamic and visionary.

Two possible ventures that BCIT could undertake are to adopt a village or adopt an educational institute. African villages are in need of nearly everything: upgraded food production supplies and technology, basic health care, education for children and adults, power, transport and communication systems, safe drinking water, and sanitation. Most of these requirements could be supplied by BCIT technologies, including civil, electrical, electronics, and mechanical engineering, business management and accounting, architecture and building, and health sciences.

To implement this venture, partnerships and funding sources would have to be researched and contacted. Possibilities include Vancity Credit Union, the Earth Institute at Columbia University, the Canadian International Development Agency, and the Commonwealth of Learning, amongst others.

Action should be taken immediately to take full advantage of this opportunity. BCIT should be the first to do this, but if time is wasted, another post-secondary institute might grab this chance, and we will lose our chance to be a dynamic and progressive leader and innovator.

In January 2007, I sent my finished report to Tony Knowles, president of BCIT. I received no response. A friend suggested I not wait and begin work on the project by myself. Good idea! I put together a board. Along with Dale and me, I asked my sister, Charleen, her husband Robert, and Valerie, a dear friend since high school, if they would be interested. They all said yes. Their loyalty, hard work, and dedication were invaluable throughout the years and so much appreciated.

So far so good. The next step was finding a village to help. I had no idea how to go about this, and then I thought, why not start at the top?

With unbridled optimism, I decided to get in touch with Stephen Lewis, author of the book that had been my inspiration. He had been a Canadian politician and diplomat and served as the UN special envoy in Africa for HIV/AIDS. In 2006, he started an organization called Grandmothers to Grandmothers, which called on women in Canada to support and raise funds to help grandmothers in Africa care for their grandchildren after the middle generation had died of AIDS.

On April 10, I wrote him this letter:

> A colleague of mine at the British Columbia Institute of Technology (BCIT) told me about a conference at which she heard you speak. She and her fellow BCIT attendees were inspired by your idea of "twinning" with places in Africa. She mentioned this to me because I had recently completed a proposal suggesting that BCIT adopt a village in Africa.
>
> I was delighted to find out that you had proposed a similar idea. You have been a hero of mine for many years, and in fact, I used your book *Race Against Time* extensively in my proposal. However, in my research, I did not come across your twinning idea nor did I discover any institute in Canada that had formally undertaken such a venture.
>
> I presented my proposal to Dr. Tony Knowles, president of BCIT. Although it was not formally accepted, I am working at a grassroots level to develop a program through which BCIT could adopt an African village. Would we be able to form a partnership with your foundation? We could contribute technological expertise and our distinguished

reputation and perhaps find out from you where in Africa our venture might best be accomplished.

Enclosed is a copy of my proposal. If you would like to discuss the possibility of a partnership or chat about this idea, please feel free to get in touch with me. I would be thrilled to hear from you.

A month or two later, I got a phone call in my office from a staffer in his organization. She was very kind but said politely that they were unable to form partnerships with other organizations. Oh well. I took the opportunity to ask her how I could find a village to help. She suggested trying to find someone who already had a connection with a village and advised me not to just turn up at some random village with offers to help. Great advice!

I mentioned this to a friend at work. She was taking an online course at the time on the Holocaust with participants from around the world. She suggested I write a blurb describing what I needed, and she would post it online in the class. I was delighted. Here is my blurb:

THE AFRICA PROJECT

My project is to help Africa—a place that needs oceanic help. The British Columbia Institute of Technology (BCIT) is in a unique position to be the first post-secondary institute in Canada to officially adopt an African village. This idea is based on a model created by Jeffrey Sachs, the internationally renowned economist who has worked for the UN and now heads the Earth Institute at Columbia University in New York. He is currently overseeing the adoption of approximately 80 villages around the world, most in Africa.

BCIT has a wide range of expertise. Nearly everything that an African village needs BCIT can help with. From civil engineering projects (building structures, managing water), to electronic needs (accessing power and developing new/alternate power sources), to mechanical engineering (designing simple machines for agriculture and water management), BCIT does everything.

I need your help. I am working to get BCIT to adopt a village in Africa, preferably Kenya. Do you know anyone who lives in or has a connection with a village in Kenya that might be appropriate for our project? Please let me know.

Within twenty-four hours, I had received five replies. All of them said in effect, "Please, please take my village." I sent them a questionnaire requesting information about their village. Two of them replied. One of them was a fellow called Tumaini Minja from Tanzania, requesting that we consider his village, Okaseni, and his country instead of Kenya. His questionnaire was stellar (see appendix: Questionnaire), and Tanzania seemed like a good choice. It had been a British colony, so many people spoke English, and it was easy to get to from Europe. Okaseni seemed perfect for our project: not too big, not too small, just right. I replied to Tumaini that we would be pleased to enter into a partnership with Okaseni and looked forward to working with them.

I opened an AVPA bank account at Vancity Credit Union, and the person who set it up for me kindly donated $10—our first! I decided that we would not take expenses out of our donations but would put 100 percent of the money we raised directly into projects for the village, which seemed a good selling point. I mentioned our venture to Mariana, our neighbour, who had worked for Canadian International Development Agency. She was so kind and supportive but warned us that only about 30 percent of development projects were successful. Africa was a difficult place in which to get things done, and we should be proud of ourselves if we met that 30 percent.

In the summer, I registered with the British Columbia government to become an official society. The first step was to come up with a name: the Africa Village Project Association (AVPA). I had to get this name checked by our local municipal chamber as not already in use and then approved. The next step was to apply for official "society" status, the designation for charitable and non-profit organizations and groups. It would give us credibility and confirm that we were complying with bylaws and annual reporting procedures. On July 22, I sent off our signed application, the official bylaws, a list of the board members with addresses, our objectives, and a cheque for

$100 to the Ministry of Finance in Victoria. On August 1, we were approved. We were now an official BC society and good to go.

And go we did. The AVPA lasted for ten years, from 2007 to 2017, and during those years, we went to Tanzania five times. Every trip was a business trip, not a holiday, as we were trying to get things done in the village. Every trip was difficult, and the vagaries of these difficulties never ceased to surprise me. I always came home exhausted. But we also took advantage of stopping in Europe to visit there for a spell. London, Luxemburg, Paris, Switzerland, and Amsterdam were on our itineraries and indescribably good. What's not to like? But the juxtaposition of Europe and Tanzania was always a shock. No matter how fabulous Europe was, I could never forget Okaseni. I came to appreciate and marvel at Europe more and more, but I also kept wanting to help Okaseni.

Throughout all the turmoil and struggles of these AVPA years, the one constant was my beloved Dale. Despite having a full and busy life on Bowen, he was always with me. He came to nearly every single fundraiser, presentation, event, meeting, and gathering, and on every trip to Africa. He was fine with me donating our personal funds to the AVPA and covering all the expenses related to the project. His smarts and insights into people and situations helped immeasurably when I was gnashing my teeth with frustration and dismay at the incomprehensible (to me) behaviour and attitudes of others. He was beyond helpful in every way. He lugged suitcases and bags, fixed broken things, and figured out evil computer and electronic glitches. (It wasn't just for me. Everyone we knew called on him when their car broke down or they needed help moving.) He also read a lot, was full of useful info, and made wonderful suggestions. Best of all, he was always on my side.

In joining me, however, he was sacrificing fun and pleasant times on Bowen to sweat in the African sun. I wanted to keep him happy and show my appreciation, which was why I booked those sojourns in Europe. Dale had never been to Europe or even on a jet plane. He had never been to Switzerland, home of the Alps, despite his deep love for mountains. He was quietly euphoric to get there. He enjoyed the variety of sights and always came back with hundreds of photos. It was fun for him to have a repertoire of Europe stories with which to regale the folks at home. I think it was a square deal for him as well. I was, and always will be, eternally grateful.

NOTES

My travel journals and daybooks quoted in this book were kept over the duration of our work in Africa (2007 to 2017). They have been edited for brevity and clarity.

The questionnaire has been edited for length.

Some names and identifying details have been changed.

The national currency in Tanzania is the Tanzanian shilling, written as Tsh.

CHAPTER 1

2007, MONEY

1975

On February 14, 1975, Valentine's Day, I boarded a Canadian National train at the main station in Vancouver, BC, headed for Montreal. My plan was to fly from there to Lisbon, Portugal. This trip was a long-held, cherished dream, and money *had* been an object. I had worked for months as a waitress and then as a lowly mail clerk in an insurance company, living frugally in my parents' house. I did not buy clothes or books, go out for dinner or to movies, or socialize much. I saved every penny. Now, finally, I was on my way.

My one-way plane ticket from Montreal to Lisbon (5,248 km) cost Can$700 (about $3,900 in 2023 funds). I also had about Can$700 in travellers' cheques. This money nicely lasted me the four and a half months that I travelled through Europe and Africa. I decided I would worry about my return ticket when I was ready to come home. (I phoned my parents from Togo about three months in and asked them to wire me another $700 to get me back to Canada.) When I made it home, I knew I had gotten every cent of my money's worth on that trip. For someone who was an anti-establishment, anti-materialism, idealistic young person, I knew and respected the value of money. That $2,100 ($11,700 in 2021 funds) was one of the best expenditures of my life. Money *can* get you very good stuff. Cash is queen.

2007

Throughout all the work getting the AVPA established and registered, I kept in touch with Tumaini. I mentioned to him at one point that we might be able to visit Africa next year. He sounded very disappointed, expecting us to visit much sooner. Hmm . . . I thought, why *not* go soon? I took a leave of absence for the September term and booked flights for Dale and me. Our tickets were from Vancouver to Tanzania and back via Amsterdam (14,600 km) and cost just under Can$3,000 each. (You will notice above that the price was the same as my Montreal to Lisbon trip in 1975. You will never hear me complain about the cost of flying today. We are extremely fortunate.) We would be changing planes in Nairobi so had to get visas for Kenya as well as for Tanzania. Vaccinations were required, so we went to a travel clinic where they gave us excellent info and painful but important jabs.

I was more excited than I can tell you and had nothing but honourable intentions and astronomical hopes. The joy had started . . .

TRAVEL JOURNAL
Wednesday, September 19, and Thursday, September 20
On September 19, at 6:55 p.m., Dale and I flew KLM (Royal Dutch Airline) to Amsterdam, arriving the next day at 1:20 p.m. The flight was just over nine hours. We checked into to our modest hotel and walked in the evening through the city. We saw many stylish, energetic young people. Everyone seemed engaged in their lives, aware, unpreoccupied with what everyone else was up to (unlike other places), cheerful, fairly polite. There were many African and Middle Eastern folks as well, so it was quite multi-cultural, which I love. The architecture was impossibly cute and charming, with much use of stone in buildings, bridges, streets. The city seemed très European, and the network of canals, consistency in the style of the buildings, and open atmosphere made it very appealing.

Friday, September 21, and Saturday, September 22
The next day, we rested and slept a lot dealing with jet lag and then went to the Anne Frank house and the red-light district (from the very sad to the very sad). That evening at 9 p.m., we caught the Air Kenya flight to Nairobi, arriving after about eight hours Saturday morning. From there, we flew in a small plane that appeared to have a crack in its right wing to Kilimanjaro Airport in Tanzania. We had a stunning view from the plane of Mount Kilimanjaro, a gargantuan, breathtaking monolith surrounded by flat, dry plains going far off into the distance.

Mount Kilimanjaro, taken from the top floor of Bristol
Cottages, the hotel where we stayed in Moshi.

The plane slowly drifted down and landed bumpily at the airport, which consisted of a long, single stretch of tarmac and a small, modest, one-storey reception building. Mobile staircases were wheeled out to the plane, and we all bundled ourselves down to the ground and into the building to show our visas and get our luggage.

Waiting for us was Tumaini Minja, our contact person for Okaseni, and his friend, Daudi Mavura, a dermatologist. Daudi was gracious and looked pleased to meet us. Tumaini, however, seemed a bit dismayed. This was odd and I wondered why. But no matter, we were beyond thrilled and delighted to be in Africa, with high hopes, a plan, and funds to help Okaseni as we could. It was a bit awkward though. I was so tired I kept blanking out, but Dale was great. He said, "Habari" ("greetings" in Swahili). They took us in Daudi's car to Moshi, the nearest town to Okaseni, about 40 km (25 miles) from the airport.

Moshi is situated in the foothills of Mount Kilimanjaro. Its population in 2007 was about 165,000. It was a town but had a rural feel, as Dale said, like a large, sprawling village. There were some modern buildings, banks mostly, but the majority were one and two storey, often made of stone and wood, and humble and functional rather than built to impress. The town's location was its big draw because it was an excellent starting point for climbing the mountain. Many businesses catered to this clientele. You could easily find restaurants, hotels

13

of various sizes and costs, equipment stores, and companies that provided guides and equipment for your climb. The town was also near Tarangire, Ngorongoro Conservation Area, and other wildlife parks, and there were many safari companies. Prices were reasonable. Not much was very high-end, but if you didn't mind basic and liked getting a lot for your buck, Moshi was your place.

We arrived at Bristol Cottages, a hotel I had found online. It turned out to be enchanting and only US$60 per night. Our room was lovely, large, airy, with light-coloured walls, dark wood accents, a queen-sized bed, and mozzy nets.. It was one-half of a cottage, not just a room in a hotel.

Tumaini and Daudi left with promises to return in the morning. We wandered through some streets. A closer look at Moshi showed that it was not delightful. Poverty was everywhere. Street vendors had jerry-rigged shaky-looking kiosks loaded with clothing and shoes beside the roads. The disabled and lepers sat on blankets with their donation cans and offered trinkets, pens, and such for sale. Touts prowled the town trying to sell souvenirs, sun hats, and phone cards. Few streets were paved; most of them were dirt. There were few sidewalks. The town folk looked solemn and harried. Life seemed a day-to-day struggle for them.

This sugar cane work yard is beside the Bristol Cottages hotel on a typical Moshi street.

We were especially unsettled to see soldiers with assault rifles guarding most of the important buildings in town. A couple of weeks prior, a gang of bandits had crossed the open border from Kenya and tried to rob some banks in Tanzania. Eighteen people were killed.

We bought some juice and water, and then went back to the hotel and crashed, exhausted. It was about 2 p.m. local time. We barely moved till morning.

Sunday, September 23

I got up at about 7 a.m. and moseyed on out to the dining hall, where coffee and a traditional English breakfast greeted me. After several days of travel, erratic meals, time-zone changes, and fractured sleep, I was ravenous and stuffed myself. Sufficiently revived, I started to notice where I was. I was quite taken with the covered but open dining area and the pleasant, well-tended garden in the large atrium. The dining room was in a building on the east side, along with an office and kitchen. Our room was in one of four cottages on the south side of the atrium. On the west side was a six-storey tower of hotel rooms with a huge open patio at ground level and a few stores and offices, and to the north was a high privacy wall. The complex was a graceful mix of African and South Asian elements, and its welcoming atmosphere and gentle beauty were beguiling. For years afterwards, this lovely place infused my dreams, and every time we returned, I re-entered a kind of Eden where my soul dwelt with delight.

The dining hall at Bristol Cottages taken from the patio on the west side of the atrium.

Dale appeared at about 9 a.m., and Tumaini and Melki Mushi, Okaseni's mayor, arrived about 11 a.m. We treated them to lunch at the hotel and discussed projects for the village.

"Tumaini, in your answers to my questionnaire, you mentioned the water system needed upgrading. Where does Okaseni get its water from?" I asked them.

"It is the rainwater and glacier run-off from Mount Kilimanjaro," said Tumaini. "The water goes to four villages, including Okaseni. It is the largest village, with about four thousand people. The other villages are about two thousand people each."

Melki took over: "There are about twenty-four water points (pumps) in the village. The system was built in 1974, and now many pipes are clogged. Only about half are working. But it's easy to create new branches from the main branches that are okay."

"Is it possible to buy supplies and equipment that we will need for the water system in Moshi?" I asked.

"Yes," answered Melki. "The town has several large hardware stores. We can get everything there."

"How much rain does Okaseni get?"

"We have short rains in October and November, and long rains from the end of February until about May," said Tumaini. "The rest of the year it is quite dry."

I mentioned water catchment systems for individual houses; neither Tumaini nor Melki had heard of them. Dale explained the concept, which they said sounded like a good idea.

"Most of the houses have tin roofs, even the mud houses," said Tumaini.

"Oh, that's great!" I replied. "Then all they would need is gutters and barrels to store the water in."

On that positive note, we decided it was time to head out for a tour of the village. Daudi arrived in his car to drive us there.

It was a very bumpy backroad ride but only about 10 km long. We passed a medical dispensary in a neighbouring village, then the Okaseni office, and many water points (some working, some not). We stopped at the primary school, at Melki's house, where we met his wife, and at Tumaini's house, where we met Catherine, his mother. We also passed the home of Peter Mchau, a good friend of Tumaini's who lived in Dar es Salaam (Tanzania's capital, informally called "Dar") and was a manager for Scania, the Swedish truck company. Peter had told us we were welcome to stay at his Okaseni house anytime.

There were many sturdy concrete-block houses in the village, most in various stages of construction because the villagers built them as they got money, difficult in Africa as many people lived on barely US$1 a day (2007 funds). More numerous were small huts made of mud, cow dung, and twigs, often housing a family and their livestock. The road continued to be bumpy and parts of it disappeared at times into eighteen-inch potholes that Daudi cautiously drove around. We passed many women in colourful kengas, long pieces of cloth that women wear as a kind of skirt or shawl. They were often walking with water pails on their heads, upright and strong, the backbones of the community. It was life on the other side of Pluto (the Greek god of riches) compared to home.

But it was thrilling. I felt like I had been thirsting for something like this for ages: something exotic, exciting, different, adventurous. It also had the added component of worthiness, a feeling of doing something truly useful which made it even more satisfying. I was delighted.

These village women are carrying pails of water from one of the few water points still working. The AVPA repaired the broken points, making it faster and easier to get water.

We returned to town and arranged to take Tumaini and Melki out for dinner that evening. Daudi could not come. We rested peacefully for a while in our half-cottage, bliss! Later, I checked my emails on the hotel's office computer thanks to the kindness of the owner, Mr. Aggarwal. His unfailing generosity always made our stays even more pleasant.

That evening, we all went for dinner as planned at a local restaurant called the Indo-Italian (in Tanzania, go figure!). It was fabulous. I had the creamed chicken and rice for about US$8, another wonderful meal that helped revive my travel-pummelled body. We continued our discussion about how we could help Okaseni.

"Tumaini," I said, "please tell us more about the electrical power and grevillea trees that the village needs."

"Yes, both of those projects would be very good to do. Electricity to the school means that it could be used in the evenings for studying and more classes," said Tumaini. "It would be helpful too for the office. The grevillea tree project could help prevent soil erosion and provide more income as it grows fast and is straight, which is good for construction. The village is also trying to restart coffee farming. We would need to start nurseries for both these projects, and then we'd give the seedlings to the villagers to plant on their land."

"Those all sound excellent. We would be happy to fund these projects," I enthused. "They sound very beneficial. Anything else?"

"Yes," said Tumaini. "The village needs sewing machines, bicycles, and medical equipment. They could be sent here in a shipping container. Taxes might be a problem for imported goods, but maybe not if they are donated. Medical equipment and computers are not taxed."

"Okay, we could probably get bikes easily," I replied. "The Vancouver Police Department has an annual auction of stolen bikes that we could purchase. What else could we work on?"

"HIV/AIDS is a big problem," said Melki. "We have ninety-six orphans in the village, and they need funds for school. Each child must pay school fees and buy their own uniforms and materials, such as pens and notebooks."

"A cause dear to my heart!" I enthused, a teacher born to teachers. "We are delighted to support education. Another idea we had was microcredit, like Muhammad Yunis and Grameen Bank in Bangladesh. Is that a possibility?"

"Yes, it is," Tumaini answered. "Some women in Moshi are already receiving loans through Pride Tanzania." (This microlending bank, founded in 1993, gave small loans to women, but we later found out that it only lends to those who already have some funds to start with, unlike the impoverished women in Okaseni.)

"The women in rural areas feed the families. It used to be men, who made money from growing coffee, but now, no coffee. In the 1990s, the World Bank eliminated all subsidies, and the coffee trade in Tanzania collapsed. Now the men have nothing to do. Many women have small businesses. Common ones are running a hair salon and making the local brew (banana beer). Growing and selling bananas is usual. Some women sell second-hand clothing from overseas in stalls at local markets. It is also a good business to prepare and sell food. They can buy fresh food, such as fish in town, and then cook and sell it in the village."

"Wow, that's great! Very encouraging," I said. "We would love to be able to support women in these ventures. Anything else?"

Melki replied, "The elementary school needs electrical power. There is none there now. It also needs a new dining hall."

This was great information. But a dining hall? Unlikely. My head was swimming and Dale was looking daunted. We had learned a lot today and now had a much better idea of what Okaseni needed and what was within our abilities to provide. It was encouraging. We called it a night and headed back to the hotel.

Dale and me with Melki, Tumaini, and Daudi at Bristol Cottages.

I appreciated all the many conversations we had with Tumaini, Melki, and Daudi over time. The information they gave us was invaluable.

Monday, September 24

This morning, Dale and I discussed the village's deteriorating water infrastructure and decided that it was the most immediately beneficial and so the best place to start. Electrical power and seedlings for the coffee and grevillea tree nurseries would be next. We had not done any fundraising before we left Canada, being far too busy establishing our non-government organization and planning our trip to Tanzania. But I had some money set aside and had donated $5,000 to the AVPA. It was this money that we spent in Okaseni on this first trip to Tanzania. I figured we could worry about fundraising when we got back to Canada and planned to send a quick application for funds to the Bill and Melinda Gates and Oprah Winfrey Foundations. I was sure they would be happy to give us a grant or two. (Hah!)

Tumaini and Melki eventually turned up and agreed with our plan, and we trundled off to a hardware store to buy materials and supplies.

When it came to pay, lo, they didn't take Visa. Uh oh. We tried to get a cash advance at several nearby banks. Most of them said no except for one. But its ATM would not accept my Visa card and spat it back out (which was lucky because one my travel books said that ATMs had been known to keep cards). Dale was very disappointed. He said we should cash all our travellers' cheques, move to a hotel where they took Visa, and give Tumaini and Melki all our money. I said no.

I phoned Vancity Credit Union in Vancouver about my PIN and about getting funds transferred to myself or another person in Tanzania with a bank account. It was not promising. We had to give up for the day. When we got back to the hotel, Tumaini had the nerve to charge us for the two hours we had been trucking around. Dale agreed to pay, but I thought it insulting as we were there to help, not feather their nests. Tumaini and Melki must have picked up that vibe and realized it *was* a shameless, over-the-top demand. They never tried to pull that trick again.

That evening, I called my sister Charleen to bemoan the situation. She was very sympathetic, as always, and I felt a little better. But the day had not been constructive.

Tuesday, September 25

We got the idea today to open our own bank account in Tanzania so that we could get money transferred directly there. We zipped over to the bank beside the hotel. No way, the manager said. Foreigners had to have been in Tanzania for six months to open an account. He was helpful though and suggested we go to the Chase Exchange office just down the street. They would give us a cash advance on our Visa cards, bypassing all the ATM and PIN hassles.

We hustled over to Chase. Their outlet was miniscule. Only a few people and several chairs fit in the teeny public area. The work area behind the plexiglass divider was also tiny and crowded with several desks and a few employees. They offered only money exchange transactions, no banking services. Would they give us a Visa cash advance? No prob, they said. Okay!

We went back to Bristol Cottages to wait for Tumaini and Melki to arrive, which they did two hours later. We talked about what to do today, the Visa situation, and going to Chase. I then went into a spiel about us not having a lot of money. (This spiel would become a constant mantra.)

"We are very happy to help Okaseni, but please remember that we do not have unlimited funds," I told them.

"But you will get reimbursed by BCIT," Tumaini said.

"No, I won't. BCIT may never come on board, but even if they eventually do, they will never reimburse me for anything already spent. It's all coming out of our own pockets." This was a revelation to Tumaini, and I think raised us somewhat in his estimation. But he never gave up the belief that BCIT would eventually be happy to flood Okaseni with cash. In return, I never lost the feeling that he and Melki were out to take us for everything they could get.

We beetled on back to Chase. Dale said we should get US$2,000 each. I gasped. Would they let us get that much? They did, and even more. It took ages to get the receipts, all laboriously handwritten. Then off we went to the hardware store where we ordered the supplies and materials. What a production. Again, everything was done by hand. There were no scanners, adding machines, computers, cash registers, UPC barcodes, etc. I asked for itemized receipts. It took over half an hour to get them, with the store lady writing them and adding with a hand calculator and me checking. It was nerve wracking, especially with all the money we had on us: about US$5,000, a five-inch stack of Tsh 6,230,000 wrapped up in a plastic shopping bag.

Back at Bristol Cottages, Mr. Aggarwal put the remainder in his safe for us. We treated Tumaini and Melki to dinner again, then politely retired to our room. It had been a good day, much more rewarding than yesterday.

Wednesday, September 26

In the morning, Tumaini came to pick us up to take us to Okaseni. We were to stay for two nights at Peter Mchau's house, and his son John, a kind and friendly person of about twenty, was our host for our stay. Tumaini and Melki had already been to the hardware store earlier that morning to supervise the loading of the truck with the plumbing supplies we purchased yesterday. Melki had gone with the truck to show the way to the village and would meet us there later.

Daudi's brother Issa, a twenty-something law student, was our driver for the day. I did not check his charge for driving us beforehand. Off we went to the village for a meeting with the village council members.

We found the twelve members patiently waiting outside the village office. We joined them. More waiting for Melki. Finally, the truck from the hardware store rumbled in. We couldn't have planned it better. All the stuff got unloaded right in front of the surprised and delighted councillors. We then all tromped into the office for the meeting. It went well. Melki did a great job. Tumaini translated, with contempt for me but much joy for Dale. The audience was absolutely silent but with bursts of applause at the end of our speeches and when Dale spoke in Swahili and gave them a peace flag we bought in Amsterdam. Too cool! Some of the councillors asked questions at the end, but mostly they were appreciative and grateful. It was very touching and much more fun than the sometimes-thankless job.

We were then taken to the village primary school where we met Eutropia, the head teacher, signed the guest book, and visited various classrooms where the students welcomed us in very loud voices. Some even sang a song of welcome. They were beyond cute, all in their little school uniforms with their beautiful white teeth and great big eyes. One thing struck me later: they were all quite small for their ages. I guessed lousy nutrition. We also saw a very small atrium where the grevillea tree plantings would be started.

We then went to John's place. The house was sturdy, built out of cinderblocks, and painted blue and white. It was one of the best in the village and comfy inside although small by North American standards. We were to sleep in a tiny room at the back with scarcely space for one twin bed. The house itself was surrounded by a high, formidable stone wall with cut glass and barbed wire on top. Theft was a problem. The compound was multi-purpose and about the size of a three-car garage. Beside the house was a small building with three tiny rooms: two latrines and one bathing room. The only running water was from a standalone faucet where several big, plastic pails stood at the ready for washing dishes, clothes, and one's body. On the other side of the faucet was the tomb of John's grandmother. It was large and white and had a cross on top. Beside her tomb was a shed for the family cow. We could hear moos. On the other side of the compound was a large stone and wire-mesh pen that housed about six smallish dogs, including a couple of puppies. They were not trained and were only let out at night to deter robbers. John told us never to go outside unless they were in their pen. Gulp.

I brush my teeth in the morning at John's place. This shed was the bathing and washing area of the home. On the left is the tomb of John's grandmother.

We had not brought any food with us, and I was dismayed to find that dinner was banana soup. It turned out to be difficult to get substantial food while we were there. That evening, Dale, John, Tumaini, and Melki went to a local pub and were gone for a while. I wrote in my journal. When they finally came back, Dale told me they had gone to the pub (a bit seedy) and had also visited two households, both very poor and more like the norm in Okaseni than John and Peter's house. An albino woman called Wilfrieda lived in one hut with her two kids. Her electric power had just been cut off because she could not make the payments. On top of that, she was shunned because she was albino and had difficulties seeing because the eyes of albinos lack pigment. Dale had always had poor sight until he had cataract surgery some years ago, and he was really affected by her situation. A family of four lived in the second place, a woman called Mary, her husband, two kids, and oh yeah, a cow—all together is one small hut. Dale was touched by their plights, and we decided to try to do something for them all.

Tumaini and Melki left about 9 p.m. We went to bed soon after.

Thursday, September 27

I had a pleasant cup of coffee with John and watched the BBC news. Vancouver's weather was rain (surprise). When Tumaini and Melki arrived, we left on foot to visit a medical dispensary, John coming with us. It was a very long way and I started getting tired (it was very hot). Melki said he would try to arrange a ride for us at the village office, which was nearby.

As we walked on, we passed a woman carrying a bunch of bananas. I asked John if they were bananas to eat (not cooking bananas) and how much they cost. She told him Tsh 100 for three. I said, "Okay, I'll have three." He got them from her (she gave us four). I gave him the Tsh 100, but he said, "It's okay. I paid." I was beyond touched by them both! It was the first time anyone had paid for anything or given us anything for free in Africa. I nearly cried.

We finally got to the village office where Melki asked a fellow called Juma, a local person, if he would drive us today. He kindly agreed to and off we went to the dispensary, which was in another village on the border with Okaseni and part of a small medical compound with several other build-ings. The dispensary was packed with mums and kids, lots and lots of them, including many infants and babies. We were eventually invited in to talk to the medical officer, Dr. Pascal Mkumba, and his assistant, Gregory. The clinic had an awful smell of sickness and bad germs, but fortunately, their office had a nice, healthy breeze through open windows.

I could not think of many questions to ask Dr. Pascal, but he seemed so tired and overwhelmed that I was really moved and thought him incredibly noble to be working there under such difficult circumstances. I asked Tumaini to translate for me that I thought the doctor was doing a wonderful job. Unfortunately, Tumaini was loath to do anything that might show me in a good light and refused, saying, "He already knows that."

We walked around the compound, and Dr. Pascal showed us the other buildings, including a maternity ward and housing for the medical staff, that had been built and/or renovated by a British NGO called Skill Share International (SSI). It struck me that NGOs love to build buildings. I'm not sure they are so necessary. When I asked Melki a few days ago what the primary school needed, he said, "A new dining hall." Hmm . . . I don't think so. What is it with buildings anyhow? The powers that be love them. Dale worked in maintenance at a university in the United States and told me they were always putting up new buildings. But they did not allot new funding for their maintenance, so Dale and his cohorts were overworked to the max, and the buildings in general deteriorated.

Dr. Pascal had told us earlier that the clinic needed drugs and equipment and a mode of transportation to take sick patients to the hospital. Instead, the NGO did buildings. SIGH. Ditto what the Okaseni administration was working on then: raising funds to build a secondary school. This was in a village with a deteriorating water system and extreme poverty everywhere. I'm all for schools of course, but surely funds should go to basic survival needs first. Even more disheartening in the SSI case was that the villagers had not been given the keys to the buildings, so they could not use them. We could not find out why. A lack of funds to run them perhaps? Not trusting the villagers to use the buildings properly? It was a mystery and not a happy one. Anyhow, it was all très affecting, and I really felt for that heroic, amazing doctor. I also vowed to myself that we would never, ever do buildings. (Hah again.)

We left and Tumaini asked Juma, our driver, to take us to an open-air market in Rau, a neighbouring village. Wow, what a trip, as we used to say in the old days! It was wild with colour and noise and people. There was a mass of goods: mostly food stuffs, but also shoes, clothes, knickknack things (metal, plastic, wood), kitchen and household wares, all spread over the ground on kengas and cardboard. We walked through, took pix, oohed and aahed, then went to a pub with a great view of the whole place. It was very entertaining.

Juma took us back to John's house. He refused to take any money for the ride, saying he was very pleased that we were in the village, and he appreciated it, and the ride was his contribution. WOW!!! I was very touched. Another first!

Back at John's place, Dale, Tumaini, and Melki worked on the next day's purchases, and I wrote up my journal. There was a lot to write. Tumaini phoned Issa, David's young brother, to come take us back to Moshi. Unfortunately, Issa was unsure of the concept of pro bono but very keen on the graft. A spirited disagreement took place when we arrived at Bristol Cottages, and he told us his (outrageous) price. I was furious, Dale was dismayed, and Tumaini looked scared. It eventually was somewhat resolved.

It was therapeutic to be back at Bristol Cottages, that winsome place where no one was on the make, and goodwill and appreciation for our patronage abounded. Dale and I spent the rest of the evening recuperating on the patio. Then to our surprise, in walked Daudi and Tumaini. Daudi apologized for Issa and said he should not have tried to overcharge us. He entreated us to continue helping Okaseni. We agreed and they left, all of us feeling mightily relieved. Whew.

Friday, September 28

I woke up at 4 a.m. or so, not pissed off exactly about Issa, but just remembering. We were booked today to go to the Mawella Technical Institute just out of town. Daudi turned up to drive us there, as Issa had to take their mother to Arusha, apparently. Good. I was happy not to see him again.

Daudi dropped us off at the institute, where we met the director, Gervas, who was pleasant but not very talkative Then we had a meeting with the local ward councillor, Stephen Mamboleo, a lovely guy who, fortunately, was very talkative. He told us that he felt the villagers had to be empowered and that by getting more water from the source through larger pipes (actually our plan for improving the water infrastructure), they would be able to produce more on their land and increase their income, and then be able to pay more to support the village. In general, I thought this a brilliant assessment of the situation, especially since we had to this point spent almost Can$4,000 on materials for the water system. However, he also said that they were working on a big project, namely building a high school for the village, and were trying to extract about US$6 from each household to help pay for it. Sheesh, how nuts was that? Again with the building stuff. Again with the unmet needs of the impoverished.

Steven was, however, very sympathetic to the plight of the women, saying that since the collapse of the coffee industry, they were carrying the economic burden. (I guess while the men just sat around and complained?) He also mentioned that the village was already working on improving the water infrastructure, especially installing irrigation systems and canals. Other projects included a police force and, yes, more buildings, including a medical dispensary. (Sigh.) But Steven was wonderful to talk to and realistic in most ways, but a typical bureaucrat in others: "Let's build a huge city hall! Yes!" He was, however, a highlight of our trip this first year, and I remember him fondly.

Gervas, the director, took us on a tour of the institute, which had some very nice buildings (of course). It was supported by a German church group, some of whom came to Africa every three years to teach and volunteer. The buildings were good, but the quality of the local teaching and the products themselves were very poor. I was a bit appalled, especially at the woodworking. The metalworking techniques and equipment seemed from a couple of centuries ago. On one of the porches, about ten boys were learning how to make steppingstones or patio stones from some sandy material. There was only one mold, an ingenious piece of wood with hinges, but it was laborious work for one person, and the value for the rest of the boys sitting around watching this procedure over and over again escaped me. It was disheartening. Would something like this make a difference? I asked Tumaini about this later, and he said, "Yes, it would. Boys who have a skill have a much better chance of finding a job."

Well, yes, I got that, Tumaini. But the unemployment situation was so dire that it was hard to imagine jobs for all these young (male) people. I wondered what was needed. Large industries? Toy manufacturers to compete with China? Fair-trade coffee? Specialty coffees? Industrial parks out in the boonies like in several suburbs of Vancouver? High-tech industries? Call centres? Some kind of contracting out from North America? All the above? I did know that Yunus and microcredit made a difference in Bangladesh so thought we could definitely start with that.

We finished the tour, Tumaini arrived, and we decided to do a little sightseeing. A kindly fellow from the tech institute drove us around in a big hulking truck. We first visited Kilimanjaro Mountain Lodge, a nearby resort. A big, clay statue of an elephant stood guard over a swimming pool there, so I sort of got one of my life-long wishes: to pat an elephant. We drove through a massive coffee farm, owned by the same person who owned the lodge, someone who was very successful, but who didn't give anything back to the community and so pissed a lot of people off.

Our driver took us back to our hotel in Moshi and charged us only a fraction of the amounts that Tumaini and his cronies had been charging us. I was very grateful. Again, it was lovely to be back at Bristol Cottages. Indoor flush toilets and hot showers have got to be among the most outstanding achievements of humanity.

Melki arrived and we set off to do the day's shopping. We ambled over to Chase to get a cash advance, but unfortunately, their machine was down, so we could not do as much as we had planned. Dale, Tumaini, and Melki left to do what shopping they could, and I checked out the local bike shops to see about purchasing some for the village. No luck, the shops only had rentals. I then met Dale for dinner at the Indio-Italian restaurant, where we compared notes and discussed the day. We reluctantly decided to use Western Union, which I had resisted because their rates were so high, to get more money. I phoned Charleen later and asked her to wire us some. As always, she cheerfully complied. We were so fortunate to have her as our homebase saviour. It was a great day all round, interesting and informative.

Saturday, September 29

Today was memorable for three things. First, we plowed into the full English breakfast at Bristol Cottages this morning—heavenly after the sparse food offerings in the village. Second, the money Charleen sent us through Western Union arrived. Third, a large village meeting was held to welcome us to Okaseni. Tumaini and Melki came to get us in a taxi driven by Matthias, a friend of Tumaini's, oh dear. He agreed to drive us around for the day. We went first to the Western Union office where we had the money within half an hour, then to the hardware store where we ordered the rest of the plumbing supplies, and then to Okaseni where we picked up John and headed for the meeting. We were very late, but many people were patiently waiting for us. Obviously, people had heard about us.

The meeting began.

Melki started by introducing us. A fellow called Dominican was the translator this time instead of Tumaini. He was wildly enthusiastic, yelled, gesticulated, practically jumped up and down. The crowd was getting whipped up like crazy. Wild applause all round when Melki told them about all the things we had done (mostly buying stuff) and all the things we were going to do (get malaria nets, run power to the school and village office, get sewing machines, jobs for all, save the world . . . !!!). Ack! I was getting a little nervous, hoping their expectations weren't getting unrealistically raised. Anyhow, more wild applause.

Then I had to speak. I kept it simple and thanked them very much for the welcome, especially from the women, who were most loud and enthused when Melki said I wanted to help them specifically. I did emphasize that the AVPA was very small and very new and that things might take time, but we were pleased to be there and hoped to be involved for a long time. More applause!

Melki told us that we were now part of the village and could consider ourselves villagers, that their land was our land. They moved chairs for us into the crowd in places of honour beside two elders, a man and a woman. The man was definitely an elder (late seventies), but the woman looked only about fifty or so. She had a big mess of teeth in her mouth—all haphazard and not resembling a row of teeth at all. I think she was quite embarrassed about this because after the ceremony was over, she held her hand over her mouth at one point and looked longingly at my teeth (I had recently gotten veneers). Then she pointed to the woman next to her who had pretty good teeth except for a very wide gap between her two front ones. Then she covered her mouth again and kind of pointed to me. It was quite touching.

Melki announced that they were going to give us traditional robes, a great honour. One of the village council women came over to me with a kenga, the colourful cloth that women wear that often has a saying along the border. The saying on mine was, "My hope is the Lord." The word for "hope" in Swahili is "tumaini." So my kenga said, "My tumaini is the Lord." Hah. The woman put it on me and fixed it nicely then gave me a big kiss on the cheek. They put a robe on Dale, with the Masai colours of bright red and black, which looked dazzling. They gave him an intricately carved cane with two figures on it, a man and his wife. I think Dale was touched. He certainly looked thrilled.

Melki announced that we were now honourary elders of Okaseni. Some of the women formed a circle around us dancing and singing a song of welcome. It was loud and joyous and heartfelt. Had we suddenly landed in a *National Geographic* television show?! John motioned to me to start clapping too, which I did although I could not get the rhythm exactly. One sees these things in documentaries and here it was happening to us in real life—WOW!

It made me feel a lot better about the AVPA and made me forget, at least temporarily, about Issa, Tumaini, Melki, and the appalling feeling that we were just being taken advantage of whenever possible. As Charleen pointed out in a recent email, we were there for the villagers, not Tumaini, so we should carry on. (A couple of days later, I read a newspaper report about corruption in Tanzania that said there is a direct correlation between corruption and poverty. That made me feel a bit better, that all the scamming wasn't personal. As well, by trying to alleviate poverty, we were doing *something* to combat corruption.)

The women rearranged my kenga so that it was more like a skirt than a shawl. They moved us back to the table, and Melki continued the meeting with other village business. It finally wound up. About a gazillion people came up to shake our hands. One villager told us that he had been praying to God for help and that God had answered his prayers by sending us. Tears stung my eyes. The gratitude from these people was palpable.

Tumaini then gouged us for more money for Matthias.

After the meeting, we visited Tumaini's cousin in Okaseni, a nice fellow called Renatus who did metalwork. He had his own small foundry and a couple of helpers and created all manner of things, including scales, frying pans, and irons. It was a real cottage industry but very basic. The workplace was small and not well organized, with no dedicated spaces for any of the steps in the process. A huge, finished piece of metal was plopped down on a random pile of dirt by the door, completely unprotected. Tumaini touched it for some inane reason and started back in pain. It was hot!

But the work was beautifully done. As Dale said, the guy was an artist. He was also incredibly graceful, and as he moved around putting the molds together and pouring the metal, it was like he was performing a dance. But it was all so much effort. It was demoralizing to think that the West could produce a practically infinite number of identical items, probably better quality, provide many well-paying jobs, and ultimately put someone like him out of work. Hmm . . . there surely had to be a way to resolve this Africa/rich world conflict/dilemma.

Renatus removes a medallion from a mold in his small foundry in Okaseni village.

We went back to John's place where we would stay the night. We hung out for the rest of the afternoon although we did bestir ourselves to pack for our return to Moshi tomorrow and put together little care packages for Wilfrieda and Mary. I wrote up my journal. In the evening, Melki came to get us, and we walked with John to Tumaini's house for dinner. Catherine, his mother, was very gracious, but none of us were great talkers and with the language barrier, there were long but not uncomfortable silences. Tumaini turned up eventually. He had been to Moshi. After a scrumptious dinner, we talked more about the AVPA projects. Tumaini and Catherine mentioned their neighbour Anna, a woman with several kids, no hubby, and minimal income. Her oldest boy, about fourteen, wanted to stay in school, but she did not have the money to pay the fees. Tumaini and Catherine asked us if we could help. Yes, we probably could. But I wondered why it was always Tumaini who got the goods. It was *his* mum who benefited from us doing this. She and Tumaini were worried that the kid might go bad if he could not stay in school and cause trouble for *them*. Sigh.

Tumaini did do something nice. He had bought us some presents: a cloth bag for me and a mask for Dale. How kind. It didn't change my opinion of him though.

It got on to 9 p.m., and we headed back to John's place. The walk through the village was unexpectedly pleasant. It was completely black (no moon, very cloudy) except for the lights in the distance of the few houses that had electricity. We passed near to a house that had a kind of (kerosine?) lamp on a table and saw a young couple sitting together close to it. No TV, books, games, kids, and no other sources of light, but they seemed gently happy and content with each other. The walk itself in the dark wasn't scary or unsettling but calm and benign. There was a gentle spirit to the place. It seemed full and not worrisome at all.

Sunday September 30

It was slim pickings as always for breakfast. We were to return to Bristol Cottages today, but first we had some gifts to give to Wilfrieda and Mary. John came with us to translate.

Wilfrieda was very nervous when we arrived. We gave her some sunscreen, my big hat, and a pair of sunglasses. I wasn't sure how she felt about the gifts because she hardly said anything. But Dale had read in a guidebook that the Chagga don't make a big deal out of thank-yous because they attribute everything to God. Maybe that explained it. Dale took a pic of her and me, and I put my arm around her. I could feel how scared she was, practically trembling. My heart went out to her.

Wilfrieda and I at her place in Okaseni village.

Then we went to Mary's place and gave her and her husband a mosquito net, some cooking pots, cans of salmon, and a wind-up flashlight (no batteries required), all of which we had brought with us but did not need. Again, there was very little enthusiasm. Thanks be to God, I guess. We asked John to take a picture of us with Mary and her husband (but no cow). Again, it was very affecting. The hubby looked like he wanted to run away. He was dressed in the shabbiest of clothes—a jacket that was practically ancient—and I felt that he was embarrassed to have his picture taken. But I gently asked him to stay and gave him the pots to hold. His fingers went to the lapels of his jacket, and he pulled them together to try and spiff himself up a bit. It was a most touching gesture of vulnerability and shame and dignity.

The picture turned out beautifully. Dale was gesturing towards the hut because the cow was in there bellowing away at not being included, and all of us looked pretty happy. When we left, John told us they were overjoyed about the gifts. Could have fooled me. Anyhow, it was all painfully touching.

Anna, Catherine's neighbour, was waiting for us at John's house when we got back, sent to meet us as planned last night. She had her son with her, who looked about ten or so but was actually fourteen. He was a real sweetie and looked so shy and scared. She was small and thin. She said her husband had died (of AIDS probably) and that she had four kids to take care of. She raised bananas and sold them: that was her income. John told us that on that little money, they probably often went hungry.

We talked with them about trying to help send the son to school. I asked John to tell him to study English so that next time we visited, he could talk to us. He blushed and ducked his head down and would not look at us. We asked the mother what she thought would improve her income (John's suggestion). She said growing vegetables. I said we might be able to give her a loan to get started, but that it would take some time. I didn't want her to get all excited about this but felt we could eventually set up a microcredit program for such women.

She didn't seem very excited about it all. But John took her out to the gate to let her out of the compound and told us when he came back that she was very happy. She said we were angels sent from heaven. *Very* affecting. We were pleased to help her although it wasn't exactly our mandate. Our primary goal was to fund projects that would help as many people in the village as possible, not just scattered individuals here and there. However, as I mentioned, Tumaini always got the goods.

We packed up our stuff and waited for Tumaini and Melki to arrive as promised. I had earlier prepared a contract between Okaseni and the AVPA about our funding for the village, most especially, what the money could *not* be used for. They eventually turned up, and we sat outside in the windowed porch of John's house. John joined us. I gave them each a copy of the contract.

AFRICA VILLAGE PROJECT ASSOCIATION
AGREEMENT WITH OKASENI VILLAGE

The Africa Village Project Association (AVPA) of Vancouver, Canada, will try to help, as it is able, Okaseni village of Moshi District, Tanzania.

The AVPA will provide funds, as it is able, to Okaseni for general projects to benefit the village. These projects must be approved by the AVPA.

These funds are not to be used for

1. Ongoing administrative tasks for the village, for example, phone costs
2. Inflated costs for services provided by friends

3. Personal expenses
4. Political expenses
5. Travel expenses, for example, taxis, buses, dala dalas
6. Anything not approved by the AVPA.

If the AVPA funds are mismanaged in any way, the AVPA will immediately stop aid to Okaseni.

We, the undersigned, agree with this statement.

I went over the contract with them and got their signatures of all the copies. John agreed to be the witness. Afterwards, there was a long, very solemn silence on the porch. Both Tumaini and Melki seemed deep in thought and far away. I think they had finally realized we were not rich, not corrupt, not representing or using the funds of a large institution with no morals and deep pockets. Hard reality had presented itself. It was only Dale and me, two humble, modest, not-rich people whose only agenda was to help. I sensed a huge disappointment and uncomfortable disbelief. Their expectations of easy street, a gravy train, the life of Riley was slowly evaporating before their eyes.

We gave them funds to pay for Mary's contribution to the school fund. I told them this was a one-off, that we wanted to be fair to all the people in the village, but that we were willing to do that for her. We also gave Tumaini the money for his mother to give to Anna for her son's school fees and expenses. Melki seemed pleased with the money for Mary, and Tumaini was his usual sneery self. These payments were our personal funds that we would not get reimbursed for from donations, so we did not ask for receipts for this money.

We went back to Moshi with Matthias, the same friend of Tumaini, alas. (Another rip-off/exorbitant overcharging ensued.) It was sad to say goodbye to John, what a sweetheart. I hoped to stay in touch with him. It was heaven to be back at Bristol Cottages. I had a shower, which was wonderful. We then went to meet a local tour guide about going to Tarangire Park on a day safari. Tuesday would work well because the driver could drop us off after the safari at Kilimanjaro Airport, nicely in time to catch our flight that evening to Amsterdam. We put down a deposit for the excursion. The rest of the evening we spent in blissful quiet at our peaceful Bristol Cottages.

Monday, October 1, 2007

We took it slow this morning and had a leisurely breks. Tumaini and Melki were to come about 11 a.m. We sauntered over to Chase and got another Can$700. I felt sick this morning with tummy woes and cramps, but I did feel better by evening.

Melki arrived nearly on time. Dale gave him the money for the final purchases, including the list of things they had agreed on yesterday for the grevillea and coffee nurseries. He told us he had arranged for someone to take over from Tumaini, who could not be our AVPA liaison anymore because he was trying to get a job with the UN or a peace organization. (He was not successful this year but was eventually.) The new guy, a government employee who worked in animal welfare in Moshi, arrived on a little scooter. His name was Venance, and he seemed great: good English, articulate, taking science courses through Open University on the internet. He told us he was willing to be our contact person for free after I explained that we were a very small organization with limited resources. I was happily surprised and very grateful.

Tumaini arrived. Melki, Dale, and I chatted while Tumaini and Venance had a long conversation in Swahili, which I finally realized was about us and what we had done. Tumaini seemed to be explaining what our purpose was and that we had bought all sorts of stuff for three projects. Venance looked very moved, like he could not believe it. He asked if we were married. (How could he not tell?!) Tumaini eventually included us three in the conversation, and at one point, we showed Venance the estimates that we had received from a local electrician about getting power to the school and office. Again, he looked quite emotional and said that this would really be something if we managed to do this. Of course, Tumaini said nothing at all. Heaven forbid that he would do or say anything positive while I was in earshot.

Venance eventually left, again looking choked. Tumaini said he and Melki would come by in the evening to let us know about the day's shopping for grevillea tree seeds and supplies. Dale gave them some extra money as a contingency fund, and I had the pathetic hope that they might actually bring some back. They finally left. We went to pay for our safari trip tomorrow at the travel company, fortunately close by.

We had an early dinner and loafed about some more. Tumaini and Melki arrived to say goodbye, and surprise, they did not have any money left over!

(Dale was surprised that I was surprised.) Tumaini uncharacteristically made a gracious little speech about how Dale and I could have gone on holiday to the Bahamas and spent our money drinking mai tais on the beach, but instead we chose to come to Africa to help the poor. He even thanked us. I managed to not fall off my chair. Daudi also turned up too, which was kind of him. By this point, I had had enough and went back to the room, saying they should stay and drink more beer. They left soon after, goodbyes all round.

Tuesday, October 2

I was ready to go at 8 a.m. Zeribu, our safari driver, turned up with the owner of the safari company who collected the rest of our payment.

Off we went to Tangere Park. It was quite the drive (bumpy, very fast) to get there but terrific when we did. The Land Rover had a huge sunroof that let us stand safely inside the truck but with our upper bodies out in the open air for a panoramic view of the park. It was savanna country with vast expanses of open grasslands dotted here and there with small groves of trees. We drove around and saw a lot of predator food, impalas, wildebeests, zebras, and as well several elephants far off in the distance. Zeribu warned us not to get out of the truck or we would become dinner. Alas, we weren't going to see any big cats because they sleep in the day and only get active at night. Disappointing!

We drove down to a river where we saw a lot of giraffes, and then slowly, slowly, we saw a family of elephants plodding along the riverbed towards us. There were three very large adults and two babies and one slightly older one. It was glorious to see them! They ignored us (we were safe in the truck and high up on the riverbank) and were concentrating on their progress along the river. One of the adults rubbed itself against the riverbank: sides, head, then bum. One of the babes plopped down in the mud and wallowed a bit. Right in front of us, they came to a deeper pool of water and spent some time drinking. It was a familiar sight, from television of course. It was a shock to realize that I was actually seeing it in real life, not on TV. I love elephants and was transported beyond words.

During our time in Moshi and Okaseni, I saw many people doing futile things that to me seemed a complete waste of time. For example, the gardeners at Bristol Cottages spend their days picking up by hand fallen leaves on the grass. A rake might have worked better. Women in Moshi spent a lot of time sweeping the ground in front of houses and stores. The family that took care of John's family house seemed to live extraordinarily little lives: drying maize then plucking it manually from the ears, washing and washing and washing the same dishes after a meal four or five times in different pails and with different cloths, sweeping the yard, watching a lot of television. It was depressing. I began to think that I was just imposing Western values onto them, thinking in my ethnocentric way that my lifestyle was better. But it did seem like all that energy and work was either misspent or without any worthwhile outlet, and if there were more valuable work to do, the whole society would be much more productive and infinitely better off. We saw so many people who were doing literally nothing because there was no work to do, so all they did was sit around. As I said, it was quite depressing.

But the elephants, the elephants! They were utterly themselves, completely with purpose, which was to walk the riverbed to where they wanted to go. There was absolutely nothing futile about them. They were so sure of themselves, completely without doubt, totally on their way. It cheered me up immensely. I'm not sure what the lesson was to be learned about the situation in Africa, but I felt a lot better.

We left the park at about 3:30 to get to the airport by 6 p.m. for our 9 p.m. flight. We got there about 5:40 p.m. after another very fast drive. Our driver was okay but feeling the need to atone for my first-world life, I gave him a very large tip.

We waited for the plane in the airport lounge. The lights kept going out. This did not inspire confidence. The plane was late arriving but was quickly ready to board. We walked out over the tarmac to that enormous KLM flying machine and up one of the two mobile staircases and into its tummy. It left almost on time. The flight was not non-stop as the plane always made a regular stop in Dar for refueling and a crew change. We had to wait there for clearance from Amsterdam because of some electrical problems on the plane. One of the three electrical systems was down, yipes, but they finally got clearance and we left Dar about midnight.

Wednesday, October 3

The meal was good. I slept well considering it was a plane ride and then had to listen to a truly obnoxious person behind us, an American missionary in Tanzania, berate his wife. We arrived in Amsterdam at about 7:40 a.m. local time after a flight of about eleven hours total.

It felt liberating to be back in Western civilization, such as it is, where most people don't look at you as their own personal ATM and where sellers post the prices of goods and services and then stick to them. What a concept! It was too early to check in, so we left our stuff at the hotel and wandered around a bit. It started to rain, and we got very wet. Dale began to look glum, so I took us into a nearby café where we had some delectable apple pie, actually more like cake. Revived somewhat, we went back to the hotel where they kindly let us into the room early. We crashed, then had dinner nearby. I wrote madly in my journal trying to catch up. Dale read. Then we crashed again. It had been a glorious day!

Thursday, October 4

I had an unbroken night's sleep and woke up refreshed and thrilled to be in Amsterdam. We sallied forth to the Van Gogh Museum.

The collection was sublime. It was a complete retrospective of his career, and of his life of course, so closely interwoven with his art. Looking at his paintings was like seeing the elephants, so familiar, so well known, yet here for the first time, we were seeing them in person. The paintings were astounding, intense, and vibrant but a bit scary. It was like looking at the world on high alert with way too much adrenalin surging through you. Being there with Dale (also an artist) was instructive. He would go off by himself randomly looking at the pictures while I systematically did a circuit of each room and then go on to the next one. Suddenly, Dale would appear at my side and make some salient comment about the work I was viewing. He pointed out things that I had completely missed.

What I found was most affecting about Van Gogh was his life. Such suffering and despair, and yet such idealism and dedicated hard work were beyond heartrending. I could scarcely bear it. He was close to his brother Theo, who was a stalwart support to him throughout his life. I didn't know that Theo passed away six months after Vincent lost his life to suicide and I think Theo probably died from a broken heart. They were buried together in the town in which Vincent died. I also didn't know that it was Theo's widow who was instrumental in promoting Vincent's art and who published their letters. She doesn't get much credit for doing that—I had never heard of her. It was an extraordinary exhibit. I was in tears by the end of it.

We needed food after that and got lunch from one of the booths on the street. Then it was on to the Rijksmuseum where we saw many Rembrants and some Vermeers, although unfortunately not *The Milkmaid*. I bought a print of that painting in 1976 and have carefully taken it with me through every move to every new living abode and different country. But apparently, she was sojourning in Japan at that time. Too bad. I would have liked to tell her she was my favourite painting ever.

We went back to the hotel where we read and rested mostly, with a brief foray out for dinner. It was very companionable, and our hearts were happy together. Africa seemed very far away indeed.

Friday, October 5
This was the last day of our trip. Our KLM plane left Amsterdam at 3:30 p.m. local time and arrived in Vancouver at 3:15 p.m., a flight of almost nine hours. Exhausted, happy to be home, we were pleased with what we had accomplished on the trip. It had gone well with only a few mild hiccups. I was excited about the future but was completely unprepared for what was going to happen to the AVPA.

THE HISTORY
As you have seen in our interactions with Tumaini and Melki, there was an underlying and very unexpected current this first trip that continued unabated for years. Being from Canada, known for its politeness and civility, I was astounded by the rude, hostile, and outright harmful behaviour I at times faced. I was well travelled and had encountered mostly kindness, good cheer, and generosity from the world. On this trip I brought immense

goodwill, respect, and cash. To say it was disheartening to meet the opposite was a pitiful understatement.

It started early. On the Air Kenya flight from Amsterdam to Nairobi, the bad temper of the flight attendants was a shock, especially as one of their planes had recently crashed, killing all 114 people on board. You would think they would be a little nicer to people who were still willing to fly with them.

When we arrived at Kilimanjaro and met Tumaini for the first time, I was taken aback by the disappointment and dismay in his face as we walked towards him. What was he expecting? We were just a middle-aged couple of humble origin and means. Was he expecting rock stars? Multi-millionaires? What ever it was, we were not it. That disappointment never left him. In fact, it got worse. As our visit wore on, he—every day—managed to let me know he held me in contempt. He expected us to pay for everything at exorbitant prices, was very aggrieved at my simple requests, and made snide and sarcastic comments. He had quite the repertoire of mean actions. He got his friends and taxi drivers he knew to drive us around, for which he unfailingly charged us sky-high rates and then got us to pay for gas, other costs, and surcharges. He also wanted money for accompanying us on a two-hour tour although he realized immediately how inappropriate that was.

We were not using him. We bought him, Melki, and Daudi many meals and even more beers as we discussed projects, purchasing, timelines, costs, hiring, and such. We expected goodwill on their part for our endeavours on their behalf. Their rudeness was personal and always directed at me. Often during our discussions, I would say something to them. There would be dead silence. Both Tumaini and Melki would seem preoccupied by some important male thought and studiously ignored me. I finally gave up talking directly to them and instead would turn to Dale and say in my normal speaking voice, "Dale, could you please ask Tumaini and Melki to meet us at the hardware store tomorrow at 10 a.m. to buy the water pipes." Dale would turn to them and ask the question. They focused on Dale as he spoke and then nodded and smiled and said, "Okay, Dale, we can meet you there at 10."

The biggest insult happened in the early days of our visit. I guess Tumaini and Melki could not believe that I, a mere woman, could possibly be responsible for running the AVPA.

Tumaini told Dale in confidence, "Melki and I know that it is actually you in charge of the project. We know you are doing all the work and that Sheena is trying to take credit for everything."

"No, that's not true," said my beloved Dale. "This is all Sheena's project. I'm just here as her helper." Unfortunately, he was not able to convince them of this, and Tumaini repeated his opinion often to Dale for the rest of our visit.

It was hard. But my passion to help the village was enormous at this point, and I mainly just got on with things. I did not fight back or retaliate or get mad (mostly) at them but tried instead to let this stuff slide off me. Perhaps this was not the best idea. But I can tell you why I did.

Tumaini had once mentioned to us in an offhand way that the policies of the Western world had been very detrimental to Africa. That is true, of course. The history is dreadful. Africa had, since 1400, been a mecca for procuring slaves to export, primarily to the Middle East and India.[1] The trans-Atlantic slave trade, however, was by far the most voracious, exporting more than twelve million slaves, with untold numbers dying en route. It was a vicious enterprise. "Theft, bribery, and exercise of brute force [and] ruses"[2] were standard operating procedures. Tribal members kidnapped and sold people from other villages, and from their own.[3]

The slave trade was formally ended in 1801, but by then the damage was done. Good will and cooperation between villages was shattered, normal trade and commerce was ruined, political and judicial systems were weakened, and large stable states as well as nascent smaller ones were destroyed.[4] By 1850, the population was 50 percent less than would have been expected otherwise. This devastation is reflected today in tribal warfare in Africa, and lower economic and social development correlates with the countries that were most affected by the slave trade.[5]

European colonization, from 1885 to 1960, continued the destruction that slavery had begun. Portugal, France, England, and Germany, eager to exploit the resources they assumed Africa had, rushed to grab as much of the continent they could. No one seems to have questioned the legitimacy of waging war against and then mistreating a vanquished people. These colonizers did try to justify their actions, invasion, and conquest with a self-serving and arrogant moral imperative: Europeans were superior culturally, politically, and technologically and therefore had the right—indeed, the obligation—to bring these fruits of Western civilization to the Africans.[6]

No one, however, seems to have thought to ask Africans what they wanted or to have treated them as equal partners in this high-minded venture. The arrogance and self-righteousness of the Europeans were immutable. In theory, however, this plan might have worked. But unfortunately, the actual colonizers were often the worst of European society: "ruthless armed bandits"[7] who did nothing to improve the lives of the colonized. Instead, they plundered resources, forced natives from their lands, and perpetrated genocide.[8]

The continent was then summarily divided up by the European monarchies into random countries that exist to this day. The borders slashed through tribal territories, integrated ecosystems and areas rich in natural resources, disastrously affecting cohesion and unity, and resulting in stymied economies and weakened security.[9] It was a mess.

In the 1950s, African countries began the fight for independence, which was for the most part a fairly peaceful process. The 1960s and '70s were decades of optimism and improvements in the standard of living.[10] But the Cold War era brought another vicious kind of colonialism. The countries were treated like pawns, and the US perpetrated "meddling," included offing promising leaders and/or supporting thugs.[11] Western governments knew Africa needed help, such as the Marshall Plan which rebuilt Europe after World War II, but lacked the political will to do it.[12]

You might think things could not get worse. Nope. Welcome to Reaganism and Thatcherism. In the 1980s and '90s, the next iteration of colonialists and slave traders turned up in the guise of financial institutions: the World Bank (WB) and the International Money Fund (IMF). They brought in the era of the Structural Adjustment Programs (SAP), in which "a simple, even simple-minded view of the challenge of poverty [prevailed]. The rich countries told the poor countries, 'Poverty is your fault. Be like us and . . . you, too, can enjoy the riches of private-sector-led economic development.'"[13] In practice, however, the mission of the SAPs was to "curtail and decimate the public sector [and] enhance, at any cost, the private sector."[14] This era was another disaster for the continent.

"Enhancing" the private sector meant, in practice, opening up closed market systems and eliminating subsidies. As Tumaini wrote in his questionnaire, Tanzania could no longer compete internationally, and the coffee industry—a major source of revenue for the country—collapsed (see appendix: Questionnaire). As Stephen Mambalao told us, the men had no work and no income because growing coffee was their work, and so the burden of supporting the family fell on women. Men deemed fetching water, growing bananas and vegetables, and setting up small businesses beneath them. That was what women did, said Stephen.

I saw on our drives along the highway to the airport many, many young-ish men hanging out in the small villages we passed. They weren't selling things or staffing the small stores that lined the road. I noticed idle young men everywhere: hundreds of them, sitting on benches or hanging out on the streets in Moshi, milling around in the evening at the town's central bus depot, lounging at the village office in Okaseni. They were handsome, strong-looking guys, energetic, and likely very capable. But there was nothing for them to do, no work, few companies or corporations to hire them, scanty entrepreneurial opportunities, and not enough small shops or businesses to give them work. There was barely an economy, except at the very lowest level, the level of women.

It was a tragedy, and one of the saddest things I saw in Africa: the tragedy of unused dynamic male energy, of their talents and smarts, their vitality and motivation. It was a kind of lost generation. It was dangerous too, as the prevalence of young males in a country can lead to civil unrest and violence. To Tanzania's credit, it has remained a peaceful and stable country and hope-fully will stay so (see appendix: Questionnaire).

I felt an oceanic compassion for Africans and sorrow and guilt for what the Western world had done to them. "Little surpasses the Western world in the cruelty and deprivations that it has long imposed on Africa."[15] I also felt a huge need to make recompense, although my funds were limited, my influence miniscule, and my power weak. It was, however, dramatically more than they had. This imbalance was most obvious in the financial exchanges between us and came to symbolize for me the injustices they had suffered from our hands, although the unpleasant irony was that Dale and I were there to help as we could.

So I held my tongue, did not retaliate beyond the occasional mild admo-nition, and tried to keep the big picture in mind. I reminded myself that behind Tumaini and Melki was a whole village of grateful and appreciative people, who welcomed us and applauded what we were trying to do. I tried to do the same: acknowledge what we accomplished and the difference we made in the lives of the villagers, humble though it was. I even allowed myself a small surge of pride now and then. I also tried to remember that even though money was important, it wasn't everything. Cash may be queen. But it is not a trump card. It is not the ace of spades.

CHAPTER 2

2008, SHIPPING CONTAINERS AND MAN TRUCKS

1975

When Ralph and I arrived in Europe, we were considering a stay of a few months. But a plan soon evolved of traversing the Sahara Desert. Not one to be conventional and trendy, I wasn't keen on doing the tour of the day, hanging out on a Greek isle or volunteering at an Israeli kibbutz. What more exotic place could we possibly find but Africa? It was tantalizingly close, just across the Strait of Gibraltar from the southern tip of Spain. From our arrival point of Lisbon, we hitchhiked to Tarifa, Spain, surreptitiously spending a night there in one of Franco's unused train cars, then took the ferry to Tangier, and we were in Africa!

We ventured south into Morocco, where we spent several weeks in Fez, an ancient city about 300 km south of Tangier. We stayed in the medina, the old section of the city. The streets were cobblestone and narrow, too small for cars, and lined with stalls and tiny shops selling everything: food, spices, shoes, dishes and household stuff, clothes, materials, rugs. Buildings were short, made of stone and beautiful, many with mosaics and other decorative details. It was a busy place, with an abundance of boys in their late teens holding hands or with their arms clasped tightly around each other. I hardly saw any women, and we heard later than wives were usually kept at home in a single room with no freedom. My fierceness for women's rights at home took a hit, and I realized the West had indeed come a long way (although of course, there was still work to be done). We got a tiny room in one of cheap, rundown hotels for travellers although we saw no other Caucasians. The room was miniscule and the sheets unwashed perhaps since Fez was founded in the 9th century. A small peep hole had been scratched into the paint on the door window so that the staff could peek in and watch what you were doing. Ugh.

We were excited to be in Africa, however, and decided to explore further, aiming for Kenya on the other side of the continent. It seemed easier and probably faster to head south to Nigeria and then go east from there. So we departed Fez, and as we left, we went through the newer part of the city, which had high rises, wide streets, cars, and buses, and was much more like home, so it was a big yawn compared to the medina. Back up north we went to the Mediterranean and across to Algiers, the capital city of the country.

We then headed due south, down one of the few major crossings of the Sahara Desert. We got three rides over several days to Tamanrasset, the starting point of the hardest part of the trek across the Sahara.

Our first ride was with three Algerian guys who were driving a vehicle that looked like a bread delivery truck. They were friendly and chatty. The road was paved and good, and there was other traffic. They dropped us off outside of a small town called El Golea (now El Menia) with a population of 7,100 at the time. It had once been an oasis town and was at the beginning of the desert. We slept by the side of the road and in the morning waited there for another ride. The guys in the bread truck came trundling towards us, but they did not stop and drove past, carefully ignoring us. Hmm . . .

Our second ride was in a huge tanker truck with another Algerian guy. The road was still paved and good, and there was little other traffic. We were on a high plateau of rocky outcrops and mega boulders and pockets of swirling sand from the dunes. The view was great from way up in the cab of the truck. The driver said to Ralph that he would do well in Algeria (being blonde and tall I guess) and that he should stay and find a nice Algerian girl to marry and send me back to Canada pronto. Nice.

He dropped us off in In Salah, an even smaller town, where we were well into the desert and at almost the exact centre point of the country. There were dirt roads and no sidewalks. We were almost out of cash and asked where there might be a bank. Oh dear. There was no bank. This was not good. We were told that Tamanrasset was the next stop south and that there was a bank in the town. Okay, good. But how we would we get there?

In Salah was filled with young Europeans, all heading south in various kinds of vehicles. There was a young couple in an older model Jeep, stylish and unfriendly. Guys in twos and threes drove beat-up retrofitted cars and vans that looked pretty iffy. I think there was even a chap on a motorbike. Ralph started asking for a ride. Everyone said no. Space and weight were at a premium at this point in the crossing, and no one wanted extra people. Then he talked to three British guys driving an ex-ambulance. It was roomy and tank-like and perhaps our only hope. They said no. Ralph clamped his hand around the arm of their rearview mirror and literally begged them to take us. They finally said yes, albeit reluctantly. I did tell you Ralph was resourceful.

We clambered on board and off we headed for Tamanrasset. The road was still a road, but just barely. It was piste at this stage, unpaved, rocky, with sections of wavy ridges that could destroy the axle of your vehicle quite handily if you went too fast. We now were deep into the desert. Ralph and I slept outside on the ground looking up at a sparkling hemisphere of dense starry, starry night skies. Light pollution was zero, and stars reigned supreme. It was bedazzling. I had never seen such beautiful skies ever and never have since. I also wish I could thank those guys now for the great favour they did us, which I didn't truly appreciate for many years.

We arrived in Tamanrasset, and thank goodness, there was a bank. We cashed some traveller's cheques and were good to go. From this point on, you could not hitchhike so you had to have your own vehicle or pay someone to take you across. No one would give you a ride gratis from here because it was the most dangerous part of the crossing. Fortunately, there were ways to get across, such as on commercial truck carrying loads south. Twelve Caucasian travellers (most from Europe and Australia), including us, paid a driver $5 each to ride on the back of his enormous MAN truck carrying huge sacks of dates.

For two nights and three days, we bounced and thumped along on this truck across the Sahara. There was no road, no towns, no landmarks, just infinite sand in every direction. The ride started each morning at sunrise (6 a.m.), stopped at noon for a break in the hottest time of the day, and then continued for another two to three hours before stopping for the night. Ralph and I slept in the open where again I was enraptured by the brilliant stellar display above us.

Ralph and I got shipped across the Sahara Desert on a truck a bit bigger than this one.

The truck was not a camel for sure, commonly called the "ship of the desert." But we were definitely being "shipped" across the Sahara and down to Niamey, the capital city of Niger, where we would continue our African adventure.

2008

The second year of the Africa Village Project was eventful and exciting. We did one of our biggest projects ever that year: sending a shipping container to Okaseni. The idea crystallized after our meeting with the villagers in 2007, when they told us they needed bikes and sewing machines especially. Shipping a container with such items sounded just peachy. What could go wrong?

At our monthly board meeting in April, my loyal and supportive board okayed the shipping venture and the major collection blitz that I proposed to do at BCIT. I loved my teaching job at BCIT, and, fortuitously, it also gave me access to a vast number of employees, instructors, and students who kindly and enthusiastically supported the AVPA over the years I worked there.

To publicize our collection blitz, I first held an information session on May 22 in the Great Hall, the major campus thoroughfare and meeting place near two cafeterias and the administrative offices. It got a lot of traffic. I gave out fliers and brochures to let people know how they could help. I also sent out emails, posted blurbs on the BCIT e-bulletin board, and hung posters around the campus.

I booked two classrooms to accept and hold donations for two days in June. They were staffed by BCIT folks who had answered my call for volunteers. To accommodate people who wanted to donate but could not make these days, Dale and I offered to come to their BCIT offices or homes to pick their stuff up. (We later spent one day driving all over the Lower Mainland, picking up mostly bikes.)

The response was tremendous, and we got tons of stuff. Lara, a friend at BCIT, arranged for storage on campus. She contacted Jim, who was in charge of the campus warehouse. Jim got the donated stuff moved from the drop-off rooms to the warehouse and stored it there until June 20, the shipping day. He was an easy-going and pleasant person, and Dale and I bought him a bottle of Scotch as a thank-you.

Here is what we sent to Tanzania in the container: thirty-four bikes, fourteen sewing machines, fifteen boxes of kids' books, six boxes of school supplies, four boxes of teaching supplies, about forty-five boxes of toys, seven boxes of balls, four boxes of backpacks, three boxes of soccer uniforms, and six boxes of medical supplies. Most came from BCIT folks, and our board members, friends, and acquaintances. Bowen Island neighbours also donated.

A wonderful man called Tunde was referred to us by his wife, Melanie, a BCIT employee who was interested in our project. He had a small business handling shipping to Africa, so he knew what he was doing and offered to help us pro bono. He was a gift from the gods. He arranged for a trucking company to drop off an empty container at the BCIT warehouse shipping bay on June 18. He also gathered and donated numerous toys and other goods. I had put out a call for volunteers to help with the loading, but only one person turned up. She, Dale, and I moved all the stuff to the bay, while Tunde organized and stored it in the container. It took several hours, and by the end, the container was still not quite full (it was very big). The truck picked up the container about 3 p.m. and took it to the train station for transport across Canada to Halifax. Again, I thought, what could go wrong?!

The next afternoon, I got a call from Tunde that the wrong container had mistakenly been delivered to BCIT. Oh dear. He arranged for an exchange. Both the right and the wrong containers were delivered at 9 a.m. on June 20, to the BCIT parking lot near the warehouse. Tunde, Dale, Gou (a friend of Tunde), and I moved the stuff from the wrong container to the right one. The right container was trucked off at about 11:30 a.m., on its way to Africa, halfway around the world. The voyage would take about three weeks.

Besides the shipping container, we had many other ventures on the go this year. I worked on contacting people, organizations, and businesses that might be interested in helping the AVPA. Ever hopeful that BCIT might formally work with us, I reached out to folks in the upper hierarchy of the institute, sending memos to deans and vice-presidents, amongst others.

In March 2008, BCIT got a new president, Don Wright, an erstwhile government official and business executive. I immediately sent him a package outlining the AVPA and suggested that BCIT consider joining us. He phoned me at my office one afternoon! I was overjoyed and grateful for his call. He wanted to acknowledge receipt of the package and kindly suggested that BCIT might get involved sometime in the future. But not now. I was pleased to hear he was interested in Africa and would lend his moral weight to our venture.

I did a presentation/workshop at the BCIT annual Professional Development Day in February that went well. My goal was to introduce my work colleagues to the AVPA and invite them to join us. I did a PowerPoint presentation and then broke the audience into small groups and asked them to brainstorm ways to help. The feedback was positive, and the presentation netted two people who became dedicated supporters of the AVPA.

In April, I hosted a small lunch meeting for these folks and other interested BCIT employees. About twelve people attended. We discussed an eventual fundraiser at BCIT and the collection blitz for shipping. They were amazingly supportive. I also gave a presentation/update to my colleagues in COMM on our 2007 activities and accomplishments. Their kindness and encouragement helped bolster me through the many AVPA events I put on at BCIT, which I greatly appreciated.

Off campus, we reached out to many other groups and individuals, including two Rotary Clubs, one in West Vancouver and the one on Bowen. Rotary has an international program which supports ventures like ours and seemed like a possible source of funds. Hoping for some publicity, I contacted Don Cayo, a local journalist at the *Vancouver Sun* who wrote on international affairs. He was encouraging and interested, which was nice, but we did not get a mention in his column. I also put together five packages for possible local businesses suggesting they help us with the shipping expenses. Lara kindly delivered these five packages, but we received no replies, and I was too busy to make follow-up calls.

We held one fundraiser this year: a presentation/silent auction on Bowen Island one Sunday afternoon in June. The venue was held at Cates Hill Chapel, a small, pretty church in the woods with a soaring Alpine ceiling. I did a major publicity blitz beforehand, putting out posters and sending emails. Coffee and tea were donated by the Snug Café on Bowen and handled by the daughter of the café's owner. We also sold baked goods, granola, preserves, and note cards, all donated.

Many people attended. I showed my AVPA PowerPoint presentation. A special guest was Daudi Mavura, Tumaini's friend whom we had met last year in Moshi. Fortuitously, he was visiting us that weekend on Bowen. He gave a short speech thanking everyone for their support for Okaseni. He was a hit!

The silent auction was officiated by the minister of the Bowen United Church. She was stellar. Fourteen auction items had been donated, including gift certificates for a massage, a café, a chiropractor, a restaurant, and a freezer pack from the island butcher. There were three books from local authors (including Dale), a cord of wood (also from Dale), four pieces of art (one also from Dale), a tea set, a giraffe runner, and a wine gift basket (from Valerie). Six door prizes were also donated, including flowers and chocolates. All were from Bowen businesses and friends, and all were greatly appreciated.

Twelve people helped out that day, including some who made the trip over to the island from Vancouver. It was one of best fundraisers ever and so much fun. I was gobsmacked by how generous everyone was with their time and donations and was grateful beyond measure. We raised $2077.

After our success with the auction, I pondered what next to do for fundraising. Doing a big event like that frequently was daunting. Happily, at our October board meeting, Valerie and Sarah suggested that we do a lot of little events instead of big, expensive extravaganzas. Even if we raised only several hundred dollars or so, every little bit would help. They suggested a pancake breakfast or lunch at BCIT and a garage sale. They had a lot of stuff to donate as did Charleen. Putting out a call to BCIT for things to sell seemed a good idea since folks there had donated generously to the shipping container.

I was convinced; a lot of little events might be very good.

We welcomed two guests from Moshi this year. As mentioned, Daudi was here for the Bowen fundraiser, where his quiet and grateful speech delighted the audience. He stayed only a day or so, but we were happy to see him and held a party in his honour.

Tumaini visited us for a week in June. We had a party for him too on Bowen to introduce him to our island supporters and another party in Vancouver at Charleen and Robert's to introduce him to our Vancouver friends and colleagues. Both he and Daudi had made a big effort to visit, perhaps wanting to check us out. I was pleased for them to see that we did not have a mega-mansion, lavish lifestyle, or high-powered friends and acquaintances. We were just regular people doing our best to help them.

Our help, however, did not always work out the way we hoped. To our dismay, we discovered that some of the Okaseni finances were a bit dodgy. Tumaini and his mother had asked us last year for Can$120 to pay the school expenses for their neighbour's son. They told us that school fees were Can$35 and that the rest of the money was for school uniforms, supplies, and materials, and such. We later found out that school fees were only Can$17 CDN, twice the amount he and his mother had told us last year. They had obviously given us an inflated cost for everything, but in my chronic naïveté, I thought it must have been a mistake or misunderstanding. Either way, we decided from then on to pay $35 each for all the needy children for their fees and materials and dispense with the lottery. Over time, it did occur to me where much of the money we gave them for their neighbour might have gone.

In the spring, we applied for official charity status from the Canada Revenue Agency (CRA). This designation would give us legitimacy and the right to issue tax receipts for donations, so it was worth the time and trouble to apply. I put hours of work into it. Six months later, we received a letter from CRA rejecting our application. They took issue with our objectives and gave us ninety days to resubmit the application. I revised the objectives and other sections as well. The reply had to reach CRA by December 29. It was nerve wracking and time consuming, but we did it. Then we waited . . .

The Africa Village Project Association
Fall Newsletter: September 5, 2008

Habari (Hello in Swahili)

Welcome to the first **Africa Village Project** newsletter! I am delighted to be able to communicate with you like this.

Trip to Tanzania

Dale and I are leaving on Thursday for our second visit to Okaseni in Tanzania. We are thrilled to be going again and looking forward to seeing the villagers.

We hope to accomplish the following:

- setting up a microcredit program for the village women
- running power to the primary school and village office
- enrolling six girls in school with specific donations we received

It will likely be a very busy visit. Please send us your best wishes!

Financials

We raised $2077 at the Bowen Island auction fundraiser in June and were delighted with the support the AVPA received! Thanks to the folks who donated items, the helpful volunteers, and the Snug Café for the coffee and goodies. The expenses were approximately $70.00. Dale and I covered this, as we do for all other AVPA expenses, including. our trips to Tanzania. We do not take a salary. You can be sure that every penny raised goes to projects for the villagers.

A friend, me, Dale, and Tunde in front of the container we shipped to Okaseni.

Book of the month

If you'd like to learn more about the positive effects microcredit has on the lives of impoverished women, check out Muhammad Yunus's book, *Banker to the Poor*. Microlending seems one of the best things we can do for Okaseni.

Summer thanks!

Thank you to everyone this summer who supported the BCIT collection blitz, the Bowen fundraiser, and the shipping container. You are the best!

We made our second trip to Tanzania this year. Our departure date was September 11. I also booked a visit to Luxembourg on our way to Africa and to London on our way back. I arranged to meet an old friend, Saul, who had made a tremendous difference to my life when he helped me get over agoraphobia back in my twenties. We had been friends for a while but lost touch years ago. He recently sent me an email and was now living in London with his wife. I was excited about seeing him again. I was also excited because the shipping container had arrived in Dar. I hoped it would arrive in Okaseni while we were there. Again, that fleeting thought floated through my brain: what could go wrong?

TRAVEL JOURNAL
Wednesday, September 10

At about 2 a.m. the day before we were to leave, I was nicely dozing when I suddenly got a terrible pain in my side. I woke Dale. I thought it might be a kidney stone. He phoned 911. The ambulance arrived. It took us to the ferry terminal where the Bowen water taxi met us and putt-putted us across to the mainland. No ferry at this late hour. Another ambulance was waiting there for us, and off we zipped to the North Vancouver hospital. Pain!! They gave me some meds and some tests. Then we waited. At about 10 a.m., the doc came by with the results. He said I did have a kidney stone, but fortunately it was near to popping out into the bladder, so he didn't think I needed any treatment. He said it was okay for me to fly and gave me some mega pain meds and a prescription for two more.

Hmm, great start to the trip. Charleen and Robert, loyal family and board members that they were, came to North Vancouver to get us and take us back to Bowen. (We had no car of course as we had both been in the ambulance.) I staggered to bed and slept till the next morning. Dale worked on getting everything ready in the house and jardin for our absence.

Thursday, September 11

I felt a bit better this morning but still needed the pain meds. Somehow, I managed to get all the final travel preps done in time to catch the last morning ferry. We left our car at Charleen's house, and she gave us a ride to the airport. We got in line to check in. I discovered to my horror that I did not have my passport. In my pain-addled and drugged state, I had dropped it on the floor in the back of Charleen's car. I phoned her and she whisked it back to me. Fortunately, she hadn't gone far.

Our KLM flight left Vancouver for Amsterdam at about 7 p.m. It was okay. I had not had one second to worry about it, which was good. I had mostly conquered my deathly fear of flying but still got anxious at times. The movie selection was huge, and I settled on *Sex and the City: The Movie,* on a par with the enjoyable TV show. There was not enough time to watch the ending, but I hoped the movie would be offered on the flight to Tanzania.

Friday, September 12

We arrived in Amsterdam at about 1 p.m., a nine-and-a-half-hour flight, and then left by train for Weesp, a small town 15 km outside of Amsterdam, where we were booked to stay the night. It was wonderful. The hotel was modest and reasonably priced. Our room was huge (actually two rooms), breks was fabulous, and the people very kind. The town itself was charming: clean and sturdy, with a pleasant, decidedly Dutch vibe. All was perfect. It was nice to find it so, especially because when we arrived in town, it was pouring rain, we had no idea where the hotel was, and no one we asked seemed to know. (No GPS on this trip.) We got absolutely drenched and walked around pathetically this way and that trying to find it. It was heaven when we did. When we finally got into the room, I immediately took off all my sopping clothes and went straight to bed.

I rested and napped for most of the afternoon and did sudoku. Dale watched a lot of Dutch porn. (He had discovered the Netherlands porn channel just minutes after we arrived.) We later had a delicious dinner next door, which helped revive me. But I was still weak and very tired and realized there was no way I could do our planned trip to Luxembourg tomorrow. I phoned to cancel all our reservations there. Fortunately, our rooms at the Weesp hotel was available for the next few days.

This little town, a suburb of Amsterdam, was perfect for me to stay put and recuperate. Although Weesp wasn't high end or luxurious, the quality of everything everywhere was excellent. How grateful I was that it had been our first stop on this trip and not a wee village in Africa. It was perturbing to think about the difference between the two and how easy it had been to recover in Weesp and how difficult it would have been in Okaseni. My brain could hardly grasp the disparity in the world. Surely all people in the world deserve what you can find in Weesp.

Saturday, September 13

I somewhat better today but still in pain, so I took many meds. We walked around Weesp a bit. Its down-home, low-rise buildings were appealing, colourful, and well maintained. The weather was sunny and bright and good the whole time we were there (except when we arrived). The Vecht river runs through the town, and we watched a drawbridge rise to let boats through. I had a strange feeling of time collapsing, and I was suddenly ten years old, on a journey through Holland with my parents (we lived in England for a year at that time), gazing in childish wonder at this mesmerising sight of naval variety and mechanical wizardry: yachts, fishing boats, small cruisers, speed boats, a barge, and a ferry—all chugging and zipping past a road that was pointing skyward. Back at the hotel, we had a yummy dinner of food Dale bought from a local supermarket. It was a nice day.

Sunday, September 14

I had a lot of bladder pain this morning and thought I would have to go see a doctor. I knew I could not make it to Tanzania on Wednesday as planned, but we had to leave Weesp the next day because the hotel was full. What to do? Getting myself shipped to Tanzania had become quite a mangled web, not the easy journey it was in 2007.

Fortunately, later that morning, I passed two small, bloody masses and soon felt better. The pain vanished, except for a few twinges and slight aching so I didn't need any more meds. Ta ta, stone!

It was another soothing afternoon in Weesp. We explored the town a bit more. It was quiet, being Sunday. I rested a lot, did more sudoku. Dale watched more porn. I did feel up to travelling to Luxembourg tomorrow, although not 100 percent.

Monday, September 15

The hotel bill for this gentle respite was very reasonable considering I made all those phone calls to cancel our Luxembourg reservations. We hopped onto the train to Amsterdam, then the one to Luxembourg. It was an eight-hour trip, a very long day. In Brussels, there was some confusion about a transfer and Dale got off the train, but in my dazed and foggy state, I could not get off in time. I watched as the door closed, the train slowly moved ahead, and Dale drifted into the distance. The train and I chugged off to the next station. Fortunately, it went back again, and Dale and I were reunited.

Three hours or so later, we arrived in Luxemburg and took a cab to the Hilton, which I had booked for the night. (There were not many cheap and modest hotels were to be found in this city, a banking centre of Europe and one of the richest countries in the world.) The hotel seemed okay although rather intimidating and corporate and out of the city by itself on a hill. We watched a bit of news on TV and then crashed at about 11:30.

Tuesday, September 16

I got up about 8 a.m. and went down to the breks buffet, which was beyond lavish. I was absolutely starved and packed away a huge meal before I started getting pains. Dale came down eventually and ate a lot too. Many, many suits abounded. We had seen on the news last night that Lehman Brothers, a major US bank, had gone under, and another, Merrill Lynch, almost had but had gotten bailed out by the government. AIG, the huge insurance company, was also on the verge of going under. This would have been catastrophic, apparently, because of its connections one way or another to practically every other insurance company in the world. We did not notice any of the suits in the dining room running around frantically as if they had just lost their jobs. In fact, they all looked pretty smug and self-important, well dressed, and well fed.

I'm sure they discovered the situation as the day wore on.

Our flight to Tanzania was originally booked for tomorrow, so I phoned KLM and changed it to Friday. The Hilton was sold out for that night, so we moved to the Best Western across from the railway station, which was convenient as we would be leaving the next day by train for Amsterdam.

We wandered a bit about the city and soon came to a gorge, a stunning, natural formation through which the Alzette river flows. We were on a wide pedestrian pathway near the top of the cliff and could see the river below. At the bottom beside the river was a flat area that sported a large building, a parking lot, and a huge field for sports and performances. Young people in uniforms were milling around and then got into a marching formation. Maybe it was a military academy. It was ant-like from our perspective, but we could watch them without feeling rude or obtrusive. An enormous brick wall went up the cliff above us and down the cliff below us. We later found out that the town had once been rich and powerful because of its strategic position vis-à-vis Germany, France, and the Netherlands, and that the wall made the city an impenetrable fortress. Walking back to the hotel, we admired the beautiful architecture and lovely streets. It was so charming and quaint that it seemed like a dream, and indeed so it became as I could not stay awake. After everything I had been through, I had also overdone things today. I went to bed and slept for twelve hours.

Wednesday, September 17

I woke up shaky and drained although not in pain, thank goodness. We spent a low-key day exploring the city on a bus tour. (I would have sneered at bus tours during my hitchhiking-across-the-Sahara days, but they are a fast and efficient way to see a city. I hopped on board.) The tour took us through the old section of town and then to the modern area, filled with impressive big buildings that housed organizations and corporations. I was especially touched by the Jean Monnet Building. I had never heard of him, but he and several others had worked after WWII to unify Europe economically to help prevent future wars. Over time, the Common Market and then the European Union were the results of their work. How wonderful that these far-sighted people built a peaceful zone in the world after so much horror and destruction. Monnet was instrumental as well in setting up the United Nations. I could only wish for similar miracles in Tanzania and other developing counties in the world.

Dale was getting low on euros, so we decided to cash a traveller's cheque. Funnily enough, there were a lot of banks in Luxembourg. We ventured into one and felt like we had stepped into a prison. The walls were concrete, the colour scheme black and grey, and the place devoid of any décor whatsoever. There were no chairs and no people. A fellow emerged from a gloomy hallway and seemed surprised to see us. We told him what we wanted. A slight smile crossed his face, and he led us to a row of teller booths. Each booth had a plexiglass barrier, bulletproof no doubt, and was several feet deep for privacy. A person emerged in one of them. Again, a slight smile appeared on this person's face when Dale gave him the US$50 cheque to cash. Were we dressed like clowns or something that we were so amusing? We realized later that it was probably an exclusive bank for multi-millionaires and that they hardly ever dealt with the hoi-polloi like us. At least they didn't give us the bum's rush.

We had lunch at a café and then ambled down the street. A woman came by walking a little dachshund nicely kitted out in a colourful, woolen sweater. So cute! Another well-dressed woman stopped on the sidewalk, looked at the dog, and started loudly laughing and laughing in the meanest, nastiest way. What an odious thing to do. Here in this country where wealth abounded and nobody seemed to want for much, it was disheartening to see such unkindness, and then to think of our poverty-stricken village friends in Tanzania. Surely extraordinary wealth and privilege should make people kinder and more generous of spirit, not worse.

Thursday, September 18

We caught the train this morning for Amsterdam. I felt immensely better than on the trip to Luxembourg and paid attention to the passing scenery. We went through the Ardennes area where Pat Moran, our beloved friend who introduced us (lo, those many years ago) fought in the Battle of the Bulge and was injured. It was very moving, and I could hardly bear to think about what it must have been like for him. I silently sent him my thanks. The rolling, peaceful hills and glens showed no signs of the battle, and I thought that a good thing: better to let life and new times take over and supplant the wretched past.

We arrived in Amsterdam about 6 p.m. and caught the shuttle to a Best Western hotel conveniently near to Schiphol Airport. We got ourselves organized and then conked out early in preparation for our flight tomorrow for Tanzania. I did feel up for it.

Friday, September 19

We took the shuttle to Schiphol, which at this point was starting to feel like home. Although the airport was crazy busy, we got boarded and the flight left only forty minutes late. I watched the *Sex and the City* movie again and saw the ending, which was quite sweet. We flew over the Alps, the Mediterranean, Libya, and the Sudan. Dale took many pictures. It was heartbreaking to think of all the misery and conflict on the ground and made me ashamed to be Western, safe, and removed. How will history judge us?

We arrived in Kilimanjaro Airport at 8 p.m. after a flight of about eight and a half hours. The gargantuan Boeing 777 landed on the tarmac of this miniscule airport and taxied slowly to the tiny terminal. We trundled down the mobile staircase, breezed through immigration, and hopped into a cab for Moshi. The drive took about an hour. It was pitch black. Every now and then, we passed through a village: lights, fires, some slow activity of people. Then back to blackness. There was not much traffic on the road, but most of it was very slow, especially the big transport trucks, so we were constantly passing somebody. Then another stretch of blackness. It was magic. You knew without a doubt you were in Africa. The fragrance of the cooking fires was everywhere, and that particular earthy smell of the African soil mixed with that of the fires to create an exotic, only-in-Africa kind of enchantment. The deep darkness only added to the ambience. I was enraptured.

At about 9:30, we arrived at Bristol Cottages. It was a busy scene: lots of new arrivals, lots of workers. We chatted with the friendly, kind owner, Mr. Aggarwal, who told us he had taken over the hotel last June (before our first visit). He had made some impressive renos and seemed pleased with life. He employed a lot of people so was helping the local economy although I was sure he was a canny businessperson. Well done him!

We had Spanish omelettes and chips at the hotel restaurant and then crashed. We had made it.

Saturday, September 20

I woke up about 5 a.m. in extreme pain with a major migraine, only minus the visual stuff. I tried to get back to sleep, dozed on and off again until 8 or so.

It was awful. (I rarely get migraines anymore after suffering years with them.) I could eat only three bites of breks. I didn't take any painkillers in case I threw up. After sleeping till mid-afternoon, I found the pain had mostly subsided, but I was completely wiped out and spent the day resting. Dale bought some cans of tuna and I was able to keep some of it down. By evening I did feel better and went to bed at 11-ish.

Sunday, September 21

This was the first day of autumn. I got up about 8 a.m. No headache. No kidney stone. Not much fatigue or jet lag. I got dressed and out for breks. Yay!

The dining room was noisy and packed with Kilimanjaro climbers from Europe. I sat awkwardly at the end of the coffee table drinking my coffee. A young, American woman called Jill joined me. She was talkative but also a good listener. We covered a lot of territory about our lives, hopes for the future, and relationships. It was a fun chat.

Dale and I hung out at the hotel for most of the day. The weather was sunny but not too hot. I wrote in my journal and rested, then sent all the Okaseni folks an email on the hotel computer saying we had arrived. I expected them to get back to us immediately, but no, nothing. It was, however, delicious just to relax, enjoy this beautiful place, and gird our loins for the pandemonium that would surely follow.

Monday, September 22

It was another gorgeous day. At breks, Jill and her group, "Women on Top," were getting ready to leave for their climb up Mount Kilimanjaro. She was worried and not feeling well. We wished her luck.

We moved to the patio, reading and in limbo, waiting until we heard from someone. All of a sudden, Melki came walking through the garden. Hugs, happy hellos, big smiles all round. Oddly, it was great to see him. He and Dale went out to find a cab and came back with a guy called Simon whose cab had seatbelts (a first in our visits here). I, meanwhile, got things organized for our trip to Okaseni.

When we arrived, we went directly to the village office. There we admired the verdant, lush coffee nursery of ten thousand seedlings and signed the guest book. Then off we went to the Okaseni Primary School. We were shown their grevillea tree "nursery." Oh dear, not so great. About twenty dried-out little plants were languishing in the tiny, hot, completely enclosed atrium that we had been shown last year. Apparently, the school had given a lot of seedlings and seeds to the villagers and grown some seedlings themselves. I had my doubts. Why wasn't there a nursery, like the one for the coffee seedlings? I began to suspect that many, many seeds had gone to waste. I thought Eutropia, the principal, was maybe suffering from depression and having a hard time getting motivated to do anything. It was very disappointing as we had given Melki and Tumaini more than enough money for seeds last year, and there was nothing to show for it. (It did not occur to me until writing this book what might have happened to those funds. I also discovered later that I had no receipts for this "purchase.")

We chatted with Eutropia and two other teachers and told them about the books that were on their way in the shipping container. We also mentioned getting electrical power for the school and village office. Their eyes widened with delight, and they thanked us very much. We warned them the container might not make it while we were here. They said they would pray! I mentioned only the books because I didn't want to raise their expectations. Alas, as I was to discover later, that did not work.

But that was later. At the time, I was pleased to be able to tell them about it. They were so appreciative and excited. It was quite the moment. I was feeling so in love with Africa this morning: this ancient, entrancing continent, our original home. It seemed so familiar and so appealing: the ramshackle array of things; the plain but functional buildings in cheerful colours; the cute little kids; the women in their bright kengas carrying various loads on their heads. It was intoxicating. My affection for it went right to my molecules, and I felt wrapped in its familial warmth.

We headed back to Moshi and on the way passed a house where a woman was seated on the patio using a sewing machine. She had kengas for sale, displayed on a table beside her. We stopped to buy a few, so pleased to support a woman's small business. Her name was Justine, and she seemed confident and capable. We were heartened and impressed. We also passed the Catholic church in Okaseni, a three-storey building with a delicate spire, by far the highest structure in Okaseni. The Chagga tribe, the native people of this area, was staunchly religious, as were most Tanzanians, and deemed prayer a universal panacea and disaster-prevention method.

Back at Bristol Cottages, Tumaini turned up. We sat on the patio, the guys had beers, and we discussed industries and manufacturing in Tanzania. I told them about Amrita, a friend who had a small clothing store on Bowen and was interested in getting her manufacturing done in Africa. Tumaini said that there were mills in Tanzania that produced cloth and clothing. I wondered if we could visit such a mill. He said that yes, we could go tomorrow.

Tuesday, September 23

I felt so much better today. A ten-hour sleep last night really did the trick. Dale and I went to Chase, where we got cash advances on our Visas: one batch each of about $2,000. Yipes! This wad of bills would look like pregnancy in our money belts, so we carried them in a grocery bag, trying to look nonchalant. Tumaini and Melki arrived about 11—as usual, very late—with Wilhelm, the electrician who was to do the electrical hook-ups. Dale, Melki, and Wilhelm went off to get electrical and water system supplies and materials.

Tumaini called Matthias, the cab driver from last year, and we left for Motex, a local knitwear mill. It made mosquito nets mostly but could no longer get the polyester it needed from India, so the mill was shut down and the employees laid off. It was very quiet. The only people there were the office manager (a nice, personable woman), an ancient guy who seemed like a caretaker, and a young guard. They were quite chatty, and I hoped they might give us a tour, but no, they did not. Too embarrassed, I thought. So I was not able to see their knitting machines to tell Amrita, but it was somewhat encouraging.

We then went to meet Dale, Melki, and Wilhelm. They had already bought the materials for the water system and arranged for a truck to pick up that stuff and then meet them at the electrical supplies store to pick up the materials for the school. When Tumaini and I arrived there, the guys had just finished purchasing US$3,450 worth of electrical supplies. Fortunately, Wilhelm was in charge. The truck trundled off to take all the goodies to Okaseni.

We also zoomed off in the cab to Okaseni, where we first stopped at the school. As we were chatting with Eutropia in her office, Julian, the head teacher, came in with a folded piece of paper and gave it to her. It was a bill for a bookcase of US$135.

When we arrived, we saw a couple of guys in the schoolyard laboriously sawing through a big log. I now realized they were likely making this bookcase. Eutropia handed me the bill with some glee, fully expecting me to whip out a wad of bills and peel some off.

Naturally, I was horrified. The items listed on the bill were construction, painting, bracing, and sanding. I realized that it would have provided work for two guys, but it was so elaborate and unnecessary. It also did not look big enough to house the fifteen boxes of books that were on their way. I said, "Couldn't they have done something simpler?" (I was thinking of unfinished boards and mason blocks, a la student bookcases.) Tumaini started arguing, saying that the bookcase actually *was* simple. I was not going to argue with him (no point in that), so I took the piece of paper, folded it, gave it back to Eutropia.

"No," I said. "I'm sorry. No."

She looked a bit sick, and Tumaini and Dale looked quite sick. But I was obdurate. It seemed ridiculous. We just didn't have that kind of money. That amount would pay for schooling for several kids for a year or buy twenty mosquito nets. I did not want to spend money on a bookcase. Also, I wasn't thrilled about being handed a bill with the expectation we would automatically pay. So I was firm, polite, but firm. We had limits on what we could spend and what we would buy, and we needed to let them know that.

It was awkward and uncomfortable. The conversation shifted to getting kids into school who might be from impoverished families who could not afford the fees. (Sally Scott, a friend in the United States, had given us a donation to pay for girls in this situation.) Eutropia said maybe we could fund the orphans who are in school without having to pay fees for six months.

But it turned out that Okaseni tries to keep these kids in school somehow. I did want to get students without *any* resources. She and Tumaini did not look happy about this (we were never able to find such kids). They also did not want it to be just girls, so I foolishly agreed that two could be boys, only remembering later that was not what Sally had requested. We held a lottery for the kids whose parents could not afford to pay as we didn't have enough money from Sally for all of them. Oh dear. It was even more uncomfortable by the time we left.

We came back to Moshi and arranged for Tumaini to come back later in the evening with Daudi. We put together some money in an envelope to give to Tumaini. He was leaving in a couple of days for England to start his PhD and had limited funds, so we had decided to give him US$400.

It was surprisingly pleasant chatting to them when they arrived: like old friends getting together again after some time apart, which I guessed it might be. We gave Tumaini the money in the sealed envelope. They left at 9 p.m. or so. Dale and I discussed the day. He supported my refusal to pay for the bookcase and agreed that we had to let them know we were not a perpetual stream of money. It was a worthwhile day and sans any great drama, even with the bookcase.

Wednesday, September 24

I woke up to an upset tum, not feeling well. Dale was also feeling poorly. Our plan for today was that Tumaini and Matthias would arrive at 10 a.m., and we would go to Pride Tanzania, the microfinance institution that Tumaini had told us about, to find out about microcredit, and then go on to Okaseni for some planting ceremonies.

Matthias arrived on time, but Tumaini, as usual, was late. When he arrived, he was appreciative of the money we had given him last night. For once! He said he wasn't expecting that much and that it would help a lot.

We decided to go to Pride Tanzania anyway, despite the lateness. The office was near to the hotel but down an unprepossessing alleyway and up the back stairs of a two-storey building. It was abuzz with energy and people, crowded with groups that had come to report and make loan payments. It was impressive.

The Africa Village Project Association
Spring Newsletter: May 26, 2009

Greetings and a Special Thank-You

Hope your spring is going well. We are pleased to start this newsletter with a thank you to the BCIT Friday at Four group for donating their March 50/50 draw of $75.00 to the AVPA. Thanks so much!

School Fees for Okaseni Children

One of the projects the AVPA is working on: paying the school fees for Okaseni kids who might otherwise not be able to go to school.

When we first visited Okaseni in 2007, we asked the villagers what they needed and wanted. (This has been our approach from the beginning. We do not assume that we know better than the villagers. Instead, we find out from them what they would like us to do.) They said many children needed help paying school fees.

"Okay!" we said. So some of the AVPA donations we have received have been spent to help keep these kids in school. When we visited Okaseni in September 2008, we held a draw to pay the fees for six girls and two boys.

The Okaseni kids draw to get their fees paid.

About 18 students took part in the draw. Each student drew a slip of paper with either a "Y" (yes, your fees are paid) or "N" (sorry) on it.

Mrs. Sally Scott

Our most regular donor for school fees is Sally Scott, the mother of a dear friend. She is passionate about getting children—especially girls—into school.

"Children are our most important resource and education is the key to their future," says Mrs. Scott. "As I read about the AVPA, it was apparent that this is a hands-on project with a minimum of red tape. So now instead of birthday, get well, graduation, and thinking-of-you cards, I send a note of how the person is being honored." Thanks so much, Mrs. Scott! Thanks to you too!!

We were ushered into a room where Tumaini convinced one of the employees to talk to us. She was helpful and explained in some detail how Pride Tanzania worked. She confirmed they did not target the rural poor because the loans had to start being repaid immediately, so the borrower needed to have some resources already. She was great, and we thanked her very much indeed.

We left for Okaseni, arriving at the village office almost half an hour late. Melki said that said that not many people had come for the coffee planting ceremony and that some of them left because we were late. (I guess it was okay for him and Tumaini to always be late and make us late, but not okay for us. Sigh.) Anyhow, it was quite the production. Dale was given the honour of taking some of the coffee seedlings from the nursery and putting them in a box. Then we were all bundled aboard a small pick-up truck, with me in the front with our driver Juma (the same nice guy who drove us around last year and did not ask for payment) and about ten guys, including Dale, standing in the back hanging onto the roll bars. We bounced along the Okaseni roads to Juma's property, where we tumbled out for the "ceremony." Dale and I had the honour of planting a seedling each into two pre-dug holes. We were each given a second one to plant.

We then stopped in at the primary school hoping to see the electrician at work, but he had not started. We chatted with Eutropia. I had talked to Tumaini earlier about how the grevillea tree project had not gone as well as the coffee one, and he had agreed, so at the school, I asked Eutropia about the tree seeds. She said that they were given eight thousand seeds and doled out five to each Okaseni student. Some seeds that they had planted at the school had been stolen, and some were not viable. Okay, fair enough, but I thought we had bought them many, many seeds. I did not trust what Eutropia told us. It was probably exaggerated and seemed a bit fishy. Melki looked a bit sick. Perhaps the health problem she might have had explained the poor results. Whatever. I deemed this project not a success.

I suddenly felt quite discouraged about our own little project and began to feel very doubtful about it. It was so much work for such small results, especially the fundraising, and in Africa, there was so much need. It was overwhelming. I always like the big picture, so I can envision factories, cooperatives, hundreds of women getting microcredit loans, and so on, which was actually distressing. How on earth could I accomplish all this?

I could not, I realized. I could not do everything. My focus had to narrow sharply. To my surprise, this realization banished my sense of demoralization, and I felt much better. I decided I would do what was within my limited power to do and focus on what would garner the best results.

We headed back to Moshi and Bristol Cottages. It was restful and quiet. I wrote in my journal on the patio and got chomped on by a mosquito. I got the adage that mosquitos operate at ankle level. One bit me about six times before I finally swatted it, slowed down no doubt by all the blood it had sucked out of me.

We had been invited to dinner at Daudi's place this evening. Tumaini was invited too and was to come for us at 5:30. At about 6:45, he finally sauntered in with his friend Edwin. We walked to Daudi's place, a couple of blocks away. Daudi introduced us to his wife Salma, a bright young woman, and gave us a tour of their pleasant but oddly shaped apartment. They showed us their wedding albums, three of them, including one of their honeymoon in Mombasa. Daudi and Edwin ribbed Tumaini mercilessly for not being married. We feasted on a delicious meal of African and American food.

Salma and I had a chance to talk by ourselves, and I mentioned our microcredit plan. She was supportive and knowledgeable and had, in fact, done something similar for a project in graduate school. She said training was key for business and money management and thought our plan might work well. I think she thought targeting the rural poor was a nice idea but probably futile; however, she was too polite to say that. She did say that ideally, loans should go to people who already had some knowledge of the business, such as raising chickens or growing vegetables.

It was reinvigorating to talk to her. After distancing myself from the project this afternoon, her enthusiasm and encouragement drew me back in and absolutely energized me. I hoped she would be involved in our project, especially with the training. She was a find, and I could hardly believe my luck. It was an unexpectedly fruitful evening.

Daudi drove us back to Bristol Cottages even though it was only two blocks away because the area was dangerous after dark. A local man had been murdered recently in the park across the street. We said goodbye to Tumaini and wished him well in England. He looked choked, as if he were going to cry. Go figure.

What a day, a ride on the AVPA rollercoaster.

Thursday, September 25

Dale looked better this morning: rested and less pale. At 9:30, Matthias arrived and took us to Okaseni. Melki had arranged for us to set up the new waterpoint at the village office, so we went straight there. Outside the office was the coffee nursery, and we were pleased to see that a sign had been posted giving the AVPA credit for funding this project.

Melki and the sign saying we had paid for the coffee nursery.

The work began. Dale mixed the dry cement, moistened it with water, mixed it again, shovelled it into the form around the water tap, and tamped it down. Several guys were there to help him, but I think it was considered a big honour to have him do most of the work.

Melki said we would come back in an hour or so when the cement had dried a bit and write our names in it. We zoomed off to the school for a tree-planting ceremony. When we got there, we checked inside and saw Wilhelm and his helper working on the power installation, too good! Back outside, the ceremony began. There were eight or ten seedlings that the school had apparently got from the village office nursery (of course not theirs since they had hardly done any). Large holes had been dug in a wide grassy area in which to plant them. Again, Dale was given the honour of preparing the dirt, sticking the seedling in the ground, and patting the dirt around it. Then they got me to do one as well.

Melki and some villagers watch Dale concretes a waterpoint.

Lots of kids were at the ceremony. They were well behaved and energetically helped with the planting. It was kind of fun but very hot. I began to feel like I was catching a cold: scratchy throat, a bit feverish, and such. It is my fate, I thought, to feel mostly rotten on this trip. I was resigned to it.

Wilhelm installs electricity in the primary school.
Safety regulations and procedures are rare in Tanzania.

Back at the office, Dale and I dutifully wrote our names in the cement. Then it was off to Kikilora, the local credit union office, where we all crammed into a tiny little room with four employees. I had asked to meet with them to talk about microcredit and explained the concept to them. I said we would like to open a microcredit account there. They all seemed willing to let us do this, happy to take our money, of course. We said we would let them discuss it and come back on Monday. All seemed okay, and Melki seemed pleased.

Matthias drove us back to Bristol Cottages. It had been an eventful day with not too many ups and downs on the AVPA roller coaster.

Friday, September 26

We had nothing scheduled this day except for a trip to Okaseni this evening to stay at John Mchau's house and go to the water-pipe installations tomorrow. We had a companionable morning sitting on the patio, Dale reading the paper, me writing up my journal. It was relaxing and soul-restoring.

At about 2:30 p.m., Melki arrived. He and Dale spent a long time on the patio working out the electrician's bill, which turned out to be a lot less than the estimate. Happy day! We left for Okaseni, had dinner at Catherine's place, and watched a TV show of an evangelist preacher and salvation. They were all spellbound. Then we went back to John's. It was a peaceful day, with no rollercoaster to be seen.

Saturday, September 27

Melki arrived about 10 a.m. to take us to the installation of water pipes near John's house. Dale helped as usual, bashing and whacking the soil to cover the pipes. About fifty people turned up to help, with varying degrees of effectiveness (that is, working). I got some great pix. Three rolls of 150 m pipe got laid in an hour or two, which was very gratifying.

We came back to Moshi and discovered that Jill and her Women on Top group had returned from climbing Mount Kilimanjaro. She had done well, and the group had lots of stories to tell about their adventure. They mentioned that the trip was a fundraiser. My ears perked up, and I asked about their fundraising. It was very difficult, they said. They had gone after corporate sponsors and gotten lots of no's for various reasons. One person, Erica, was a freelance writer and had been in charge. She said it was very humbling and that the whole experience had been hard on her. They had raised approximately US$3,000 to $4,000. When I heard that I was immensely cheered. Wow, we had raised more than $2,000 at just one event, our Bowen auction.

Another person, Meghan, gave me some good advice. She was more realistic and practical than Erica and said that fundraising from companies was a long-term project and needed to be developed into ongoing relationships. She had suggestions about specific companies to ask for money, such as Singer Sewing Machines and bike companies to help with shipping these things, ditto DHL to also help with shipping. It was great. I felt like meeting her was worth the price of the airfare to Africa. I had no inkling on that happy day how soul-destroying fundraising would eventually become for me.

It was pleasant to sit on the patio in the sun with these friendly people, chatting and exchanging info. It was odd though. They did not seem to have much idea about Africa, of the poverty, the corruption, the hardships. They seemed impatient and naïve about how things were. (Of course, I should talk.) It was a grand adventure for them, but they had taken no time to learn about the dazzling, heartbreaking continent they were visiting. Still, it was good to talk to them and I was glad to tell them a bit of what I knew about Africa and the AVPA.

I later checked my emails in Mr. Aggarwal's office and found one from Gerald Mchau, Peter's brother. He worked at the Dar port and was supposed to be getting the container released for us. His email detailed the costs for this: about US$4,000. I was stunned. Again on the AVPA roller coaster. I talked to Mr. Aggarwal about the charges. He said they were all legit and seemed reasonable, except the US$1,200 for "port charges." Yipes.

I went back and told Dale. He was very upset and wanted to abandon the goods and the AVPA, but we decided that was probably not a good idea, especially with the power to the office in progress and the sewing machines in the container sort of on their way. Yipes again. Another stomach-churning ride on the AVPA roller coaster.

Sunday, September 28

Today was satisfactory. It was cool and rainy in the morning, but the skies cleared in the afternoon and the day got warmer. It was grand that we did not do much. Being Sunday, everything was closed, so we ate at the hotel, lolled about, read, and rested. I wrote up a memo to the Kikilora credit union and village council describing our microcredit plan. Dale wandered about and into a little store in the hotel's atrium. He found the clerk, a woman of about forty, with her head on her arms, crying and crying. He asked if he could help. She said that the store was going to close because business was very slow, and she was going to lose her job. With no money coming in, she would not be able to keep her two girls in school. Dale brought me to meet her; her name was Nuria. We gave her $100 for her daughter's education. Dale told me later that we should try to help her. I wasn't too keen because I was so focussed on Okaseni and felt we couldn't handle other random people as well.

In the evening, we went again for another pleasant dinner at Salma and Daudi's house. They were very gracious. We talked more about microcredit. Salma was still enthusiastic although she did say that finding the impoverished women would be tricky because of village politics. The funds might go to friends and relations of the council members, not necessarily the neediest. She said that she would help us, however, by sending reports (she was keen on reports) and by acting as a resource person. I was very pleased and grateful and looked forward to working with her.

Monday, September 29

I slept well last night and felt much better this morning, thank goodness. I worked on a memorandum of understanding (MOU) for our partnership with Salma on the microcredit venture. Then Dale wanted me to go talk to Nuria about keeping in touch so we could help. I somewhat reluctantly did so. She was very beautiful. We talked for a while.

In tears, she told me, "My husband's family says that girls are useless and that I should keep having babies until I have a boy. They are South Asian. My father was Greek and my mother Chagga. I am Muslim. I want my two girls to get an education and not get married. Our cultures say that girls should not get educated. They are not worth it."

"I think your husband's family is wrong," I said, a feminist born to feminists. "You must just ignore them. My mum and dad had three girls and wanted us all to get an education. They never thought we were less important because we were girls."

How lucky I was that my mum and dad were on the vanguard of the women's rights movement. I was suddenly overwhelmed with appreciation for them, and the strangest feeling came over me. I felt filled with a kind of spirit, as if I were not just myself but also a voice for some deep truth of the universe. I kept telling Nuria that education was so important. This was a way I could honour my dear parents because they had given me such a gift the world could not contain my gratitude.

"We will help you although we do not have a lot of money."

"But your heart is rich," she said. I choked up and could not speak. It seemed the nicest thing anyone had ever said to me.

"You are an angel," she whispered. I choked up again. It was the most amazing conversation and by far the most wonderful thing that had happened to me yet on this trip.

Then Melki arrived.

After a few pleasantries, we showed him the email from Gerard with the bill for getting the container out of the port and told him we might not be able to do anything next year because we would have to pay off this very big bill. He looked very upset, but what could we do? It was a huge bill, now standing at about Can$9,000, and we would have to pay it. We had earlier done a rough calculation of the value of the goods we sent: about Can$7,000. At this point, it seemed shipping goods might not be worth it.

Tuesday, September 30

Oh dear, major diarrhea this morning. Last night, I had a lot of rumblings and gurgles that did not bode well.

Nevertheless, we got a lot accomplished today. First, we went to the school to pay the school fees for the impoverished children. Second, we went to the village office where we met with the village council. John joined us and kindly did the translating. I spoke about what we had done this year (the power hook-ups and kids in school) and then at some length about microcredit. They all looked so solemn and grim that I thought that they were absolutely against microcredit. (Both Melki and John said later that they were very pleased. Who knew?) Then I told them about the container, and they did look a bit happier. I also told them how expensive it was, and how we were in debt now and might not be able to come next year or do any projects. More glum looks. Then a village elder stood up to thank us, saying that we had done what they had asked us to do and that they were very pleased about that. I think they felt that we had been respectful of them. That was very sweet and good to hear, and I was touched.

After the meeting, I talked to a woman we had met last year who was in agriculture. She complained about how expensive the coffee nursery was, the fertilizer, and such. I was not sure why she was telling me this. (I realized later that she might have been working there and wanted to get paid but did not want to directly ask for payment. Alas, that escaped me at the time.) I was a bit offended (being hit up again), but this year was much better in general than last year for feeling used and sucked dry. No Issa, mostly no Tumaini. I just let Dale deal with the taxi drivers. I gave up on that one. Also, saying "no" to the bookcase was good, to let them know that we are not an eternal money fount.

The next task of the day was getting from Chase today for the school fees, the first microcredit loans, and school expenses for the eight kids and went with Melki to deposit them in the Okaseni account at a bank in Moshi. Then it was back to Bristol Cottages. As I walked through the dining room back to our cottage, one of the guests said, "You look so pretty walking towards us with the sunlight in your hair." I nearly cried. That was so kind of her. I certainly have not felt pretty on this trip or experienced much positivity, to say the least.

Lastly, Salma came by in the evening, and we went over the microcredit MOU. I was so pleased she had agreed to work with us. It was indeed a very productive day.

Wednesday, October 1

This was a low-key day for a change. My tummy was still upset. I worked on a report to give to Melki about this year's visit and what we had done. John and Melki turned up with some presents for us, which was kind. I puttered and wrote in my journal. Dale dozed, read, and watched TV.

I checked my emails in the evening. There was nothing from Gerard. The container had still not arrived in Okaseni. Very disappointing.

Thursday, October 2

Leaving Tanzania today!! I still had the runs, alas.

I finished the report for Melki and printed out copies. Matthias took us to the village office where Melki was waiting for us. I gave him a copy of the report, which detailed the good, the bad, and the suspect. He looked shocked to be having an evaluation. Again, they all seem to think the AVPA is a big free-for-all, a veritable cascade of loot requiring only a little song and dance on their part. As we went through the report, his face crumpled more and more, especially when I talked about what we would not fund, specifically the grevillea tree project which was obviously not a success. I didn't want to cause distress, but we were not Mr. and Mrs. Santa Claus.

Whew! Back to Moshi. At about 5:30, we hopped into the Bristol Cottages van for the Kilimanjaro Airport, where it was the usual pandemonium. We discovered, to my horror, that we were not on the passenger list, a screw-up perhaps from having to change our reservations in Luxembourg. That was a very bad moment. I really, *really* wanted to leave, and the thought of having to spend another night in Tanzania was unbearable. Anyhow, it did get straightened out, and the flight left with us very happily on board. We even got comfy seats together after our refueling and crew-change stop in Dar.

Friday, October 3

I managed to sleep on the plane so was not completely zonked when we arrived in Amsterdam at 7 a.m. I still had the runs. We transferred to our London flight, which left at 12:05 and landed at 12:25 local time (about an hour and a half in the air). We took an old-fashioned London taxi back to

The Africa Village Project Association
Fall Newsletter: September 5, 2008

Trip to Tanzania

Dale and I very much enjoyed our second trip to Okaseni this year. It was great to see everyone again and check out last year's projects. We also funded three new projects this year thanks to your donations!

Last Year's Projects

The water system upgrades looked great. We saw many repaired water points, and about 6,000 ft. of pipe had been replaced.

Dale and the villagers unrolling new pipe for water system upgrades

Theses upgrades have helped made the lives of the villagers easier.

The coffee nursery was flourishing. How gratifying! The grevillea tree nursery was not as successful although many seeds were distributed to Okaseni families. Thank you for your donations. Your kindness has touched many lives.

This Year's Projects

This year, we set up a microcredit pilot project for fifteen women in the village. Salma (Tumaini's friend) is overseeing the program pro bono. She is wonderful—a godsend to the project! Thanks, Salma!

Salma and I shake hands on the microcredit program

The AVPA also paid for electrical power to the primary school and village office. Children can now study after dark and women can run sewing machines to make extra income. Lastly, we paid school fees for six girls and two boys. Your donations did this. Thank you.

The shipping container has arrived in Dar es Salaam but not released. I'll keep you posted.

my childhood when my family and I first arrived in London, and I was agog at the beauty and history of this outstanding city. Oh, and the taxi also took us to Aster House, where Dale and I were booked for a three-day stay. It was an older two-storey building but deliciously updated in a charming country/ Regent style, with crown molding and delicate decorative touches. Our room was in the daylight basement and looked out on a tiny garden with a teeny pond and ducks. The room was small, but the whole house was painted mostly white, so everywhere was light and airy. The breakfast room was like a greenhouse, all windows with an arched glass ceiling like the Crystal Palace. Light and sunshine poured in. It was a beautiful hotel and one of the loveliest places I have ever stayed at.

We said hi to the ducks and settled into our room. I went out to Tesco and bought some food. Then we hit the sack.

Saturday, October 4

About 2 a.m. this morning, Dale got up and threw up. It was awful. He was very sick. He must have gotten up about six or eight times throughout the night to throw up. I finally lost count. We never did figure out why. We had both eaten the same stuff the day before (a salad from Tesco). I could not leave him although the plan was to do some sightseeing before I was to meet Saul at 2 p.m. Dale refused to let me call for a doctor. It was very distressing. I still had the runs as well.

Saul arrived early. He was instantly recognizable and, despite being a little balder, didn't looked any older at all.

We went to a coffee shop, talked a lot, and surprisingly had a great time. He was very kind and listened with great interest to the story of my life and had nice things to say. He was also quite apologetic at times because he had indeed been an extremely arrogant young person. I mentioned what he had told me when we hung out together that first summer so long ago: that he would remember nothing about me when we were forty. He looked chagrined. He said that he didn't remember too much about me, which made sense. I was so shy, not really unformed because I was always there on the inside but rather was unexpressed. He also said I was kind of cynical, which surprised me. I would never have said cynical, although negative for sure given some of the challenges I faced.

We caught up on his life events. I was struck by how unfulfilled and not very happy he seemed. He had done some amazing things—studied law at Yale, for one—but time and time again, he felt like he had taken a wrong turn or made the wrong decision. As a lawyer, he specialized in human rights advocacy and travelled around the world and had argued cases before the UN. Pretty cool. But to hear him tell it, it just was all rather mundane and just not good enough. I was shocked and rather saddened. Saul was such an interesting person and had so many advantages: brains, money, charisma (his word, but I do concur), a nice family, drive, passion, and that extra spark that I always love in people. Life laid out a major smorgasbord of choices for him, and he looked at it and discounted and belittled it. Maybe he was a malcontent, or maybe everything came too easily to him and he never got challenged much.

I, on the other hand, never felt things came easily to me, although I was certainly blessed with many opportunities. But I always felt I had to grab them and make the most of them and seriously work at them. Big difficulties befell me: agoraphobia, physical health problems, no money, no work, no career, wrong country, broken heart. But I tried to learn from them, recoup, improve, change. All *my* joys and successes seemed predicated on passion, focus, drive, hard work, and almost desperation at times. I did get a sense of accomplishment when things worked out. I also knew what a real problem was (panic disorder; worry about going to sleep because I was so sick and weak that I was afraid I would die in the night; long, lonely nights of sadness and loss after a terrible break-up). Consequently, I always acknowledged and was infinitely grateful for the humble triumphs and successes I did achieve. When happiness appeared, I grabbed it with both hands.

I was disconcerted to realize that I might have been more successful than Saul in some ways: happier, more adventurous, more profoundly aware of a few worthy things. What a stunner! He told me that I was very "positive" and seemed to marvel at that. Perhaps it *was* just a difference in attitude. But I don't think so. I was very negative, so a huge evolution had gotten me to where I was that day in London. But maybe there was something else going on as well: that desire I have had all my life for intensity and fire, for truth and beauty, for profundity and meaning.

It was all very ironic and unsettling. I always thought Saul understood that about me, that he was the only person who ever really got what I was trying to do with my life, and that he respected or at least encouraged it. But who knew? Maybe not. We didn't have time to talk about it. Wouldn't that just be beyond life's pointed sense of humor that it was all a misconception on my part? What I thought was Saul's validation of me might actually have been an illusion!

So had he understood me? In the end, it didn't much matter. I *thought* he had, and that encouraged me to continue to try to live the life I wanted. Either way, I do know for certain that but for that inner core of passion and inspiration, I would never have travelled throughout Africa as a young person or started the AVPA. Whether or not Saul had seen it, that inspiration was there. It has never left me.

Sunday, October 5

I threw up in the night, probably because of something I ate yesterday or out of sympathy with Dale. It felt like I was being poisoned. I did not feel well when I woke up this morning but managed to keep down some breks. Dale ate a little bit as well. I felt marginally better in the afternoon and did a lot of Sudoku. Dale mostly slept all day. I went out a couple of times to for food, which we were both able to eat. I phoned to book the Best Western hotel near Schiphol Airport in Amsterdam for tomorrow night.

Sheesh, what a day. But it was one day closer to getting home.

Monday, October 6

Dale felt well enough to fly this morning. Me too. We ate our last breakfast in this lovely hotel and then went by taxi to Heathrow Airport. We were in plenty of time to catch our flight to Amsterdam, which left at 2:20 and arrived at 4:55 local time, a flight just over two hours. No, just kidding! We were on our way home. Joy, oh joy!

It was leisurely and pleasant at the Schiphol hotel, and we lolled about like rescued castaways on a luxury cruise ship. I even went for a swim in the unoccupied pool. We had some food then continued our lazing till bedtime. Goll, this trip had been difficult. I felt various degrees of crappy about 90 percent of the time. I could hardly wait to get home.

Tuesday, October 7
We took the shuttle to the airport and got there early, so it was all quite relaxed and unhurried. However, when we tried to check in at the KLM counter, we discovered we did not have our e-ticket numbers. My heart sank. They were finally found, and we got our boarding passes. Good to go. But then the flight was delayed for two hours. I could have cried. I didn't just want to go home—I wanted to already *be home.*

The plane finally left about 6 p.m. Dale and I did not get seats together. There were no individual movie selections, so I did not get to watch the two movies I was hoping to see. I tried to sleep. The time dragged on and on.

We finally arrived in Vancouver about 7 p.m. after a thousand-hour flight. (No, just kidding again, a ten-hour flight). Charleen kindly picked us up and took us back to her place where we hopped into my car in time to catch the last ferry to Bowen. We drove half a block, heard weird thumping noises, and realized we had a flat tire. NOOOOO! I burst into tears. This trip had been just too much. We were almost home yet still not home, and we were not going to make it home that night.

Wednesday, October 8
It was nice to wake up not in Africa, but indeed, *almost* home. We chatted a bit with Charleen, then left to catch the last morning ferry to Bowen.

HOME! Wonderful, wonderful, and again most wonderful! The trip was done.

HOME

In November, we got disappointing news. I got an email from Don Wright, BCIT's new president, regretfully turning down our request to participate in the AVPA. That was a blow, but I did appreciate him letting me know. The AVPA was going to be just us. Onward . . . I was very glad I had not waited for BCIT to join us.

The shipping saga continued after we got home. We heard nothing for weeks, which meant that the container was still in the port at Dar. I was busy and distracted at work but eventually sent an email to Gerard on November 3. He replied that he was working on it. I sincerely doubted that at this point and began to get worried. I remembered a story that Lorna, a Bowen neighbour, had told me. She and a group of teachers sent a shipping container to Cuba full of books they had collected. They too had a hard time getting the container released from the port. When it finally was, it was empty.

I sent an email on November 5 to the Canadian embassy in Tanzania asking for help. They responded immediately and requested the contact information for Gerard and Melki. Then we did not hear anything else from them. I had had it. Beyond exasperated, I emailed Melki on November 28 and told him we would stop the project unless the container was delivered to Okaseni. On November 29, we received an email from Gerard saying that he had gotten the container out of the port. It was a miracle. (Sigh.)

On December 2, we received two emails from Melki with pictures of the villagers in Okaseni carrying and opening the many boxes from the container and admiring the bikes, sewing machines, and other goods that we had sent. Finally.

I sent out the Christmas newsletter with the news and received many kind emails from our mailing list folks about it:

- Well, what great news! Congratulations on all your hard work. The various projects sound awesome. I'm glad there are people like you and Dale in the world who put the time and effort in to make these things happen. You truly do make the world a better place!
- What a wonderful Christmas letter! So glad the container arrived and they got the goods! Wow, look at what a difference you have made! Good job!

- Many thanks for this. You are doing wonderful work.
- Thank you for the updates. I really enjoy reading them. What a WONDERFUL thing!
- Jambo, Sheena. Thanks for the wonderful pictures. I'm so delighted the village finally received your treasures. You are doing wonderful work for them.
- Thank you so much for such exciting pictures from the village! And thanks again for all your (and your team) efforts and time for organizing all of this. It is an amazing feeling to see the happy faces of the people down there and to know that you can help.
- What a wonderful Christmas present to the villagers and to you and your donors,
- Thanks so much for sharing the pictures! It's SO GREAT to see the items arrived and to see such joy on their faces. Made my day. (from Melanie and Tunde)

> The newsletter was fabulous! Is that Grandma's sewing machine I wonder? It is so good to see the results of the container shipment.
>
> –Charleen

Looking back on the shipping adventure, I wondered why Gerard did not get the container out of the port until we threatened to abandon the project. It dawned on me that he wanted a bribe. Perhaps he was hesitant to ask directly but thought I would understand and offer to pay. Too naïve to even get it and too puritan to pay bribes, I blithely went about doing my best to get the container released. Sorry, Gerard.

The whole venture was extraordinarily expensive. Getting the container from Vancouver to Dar and getting the container out of the Dar port and to Moshi each cost about Can$5,000, for a total of $10,000. The hoped-for funding from the Rotary Club did not materialize. Over this year, we had been able to pay for the shipping itself from donations, but I had borrowed from my line of credit to cover the port expenses. We needed to pay this debt off.

AFRICA VILLAGE PROJECT CHRISTMAS NEWSLETTER
The villagers of Okaseni send you their heartfelt thanks and best wishes for a Merry Christmas and Happy New Year!

The container that we sent to Okaseni this summer has arrived!! Melki Mushi, the village chairperson, sends you his thanks and the gratitude of the villagers.

The Okaseni chairperson, Melki Mushi, surveys boxes shipped by the AVPA.

We are thrilled that the shipment arrived safely, after an excruciating four-month delay in the Dar es Salaam port.

The Bikes

When we asked the villagers last year what they needed, they said, "Bikes!" Hardly anyone in Okaseni has transportation and there is no transit system, so bikes allow people and goods to move around quickly, especially in emergency situations.

The Sewing Machines

The villagers also requested sewing machines. We sent 14 of them. If you donated a machine, you might see it in one of these pictures.

Justine checks out a sewing machine.

The villagers plan to set up a sewing room in the village office building, and anyone in the village who wants to use a machine will be welcome. These machines might allow women to earn some extra income.

Did you donate this electric machine?

Helping women is a key element in improving the lives of everyone – women, men, kids – in the developing world.

Stuff for the Kids

You gave so many wonderful donations that we shipped over 70 boxes of goodies for the kids.

Okaseni children carry boxes of books, etc., from the village office to the school.

The primary school has no library and no books except textbooks. Now they have over **1,000 English books** up to the Grade 6 level. (English is required for higher education.)

Melki sorts through some of the items donated by Tunde.

Tunde, the fellow who helped us with the shipping, donated some large items for kids, including a tricycle, walker, and a playpen. Tunde's items will be given to the kindergarten

next to the primary school. Thanks for everything, Tunde!

The kids show off some of the stuff they received from AVPA donors.

If you donated notebooks, crayons, pens, colouring pencils, stuffies, soccer balls, team uniforms, baseball mitts, dolls, other kinds of balls and toys, etc., you can be sure that **you have thrilled a little child** on the other side of the world. As well, your donations of medical and/or teaching supplies will help the local professionals do their jobs.

Thank You!

On behalf of Melki and the Okaseni villagers, we **thank you so much for your generosity**. Your donations will help give them the chance to create a better future. Because 100 percent of the funds we raise go directly to the village, you can see in these photos that your funds have been put to good use.

All the very best to you and your loved ones for a wonderful Christmas and an absolutely fabulous 2009!

You might well wonder, as did we, if shipping was worthwhile. The pros were that most of the items we shipped were either very expensive in Tanzania (bikes), or difficult to get (kids' books), or of poor quality (sewing machines). Also, it was far easier to get in-kind donations from people than cash. The big con was the expense. Would we have been better off to raise money at home and buy stuff in Tanzania? I did think it *was* worth it for the publicity at BCIT, the excitement, the contributions, the plumping up of the mailing list. As well, it was almost impossible to purchase goods in Tanzania of the quality that we sent. The excellent North American sewing machines and bikes that had languished in the port put to shame any cheap foreign knockoffs, and these knockoffs were mostly all that was available at reasonable prices in Tanzania.

In any event, shipping a container to a developing country is a gamble—a big one. A straightforward financial calculation of costs/benefits is skewed dramatically by the possibility of theft, corruption, incompetence, or all three. We could have lost all the goods we sent, as did Lorna and her fellow book donors. Gerard could have held out for a bribe and ignored our threats to shut down the project, and we would have had to give up and abandon the container or pay the bribe. Melki might have not been able to get Gerard to finally comply. But we did finally manage to get all the goods to Okaseni, and that was a tremendous success.

So our gamble paid off, although we did not know at the time that we were playing high stakes roulette. In fact, as I realized only as I was writing this chapter, we were gambling with every dollar we gave to Okaseni. The thousands of grevillea tree seeds that "disappeared" and the inflation of the actual schooling costs belied our 2007 contract with Tumaini and Melki. We gave them money for Okaseni in good faith and trusted in them. It is painful to realize, as I write this account, that some of our money might not have gone to the children or purchased many grevillea seeds at all. We might have lost that gamble.

Even the trip itself was a gamble. Should I have cancelled our tickets the day I woke up with a kidney stone? I gambled that I would be able to do it, and indeed, I was able to. But it was very, very difficult, and I *was* taking a risk. However, if I had rebooked, we would not have met Nuria, who became a dear friend. I also might not have seen Saul in London and would have missed the extraordinary revelation that he had perhaps *not* blessed me in my quest. Those two people themselves were more than worth the trip. My gamble, in this case, paid off fabulously.

At a board meeting after Dale and I got back from Tanzania, we made a desultory attempt to decide if the shipping had been worthwhile and whether we should do it again. Some months later, I received an email from Tunde (that wonderful guy who had helped us with the shipping) about some computers he had for us to send to Okaseni if we wanted. After pondering for about a millisecond, I thanked him very much and said we could not ever do shipping again, now or in the future, unless we got the money donated to us up front. But if we did decide to do it again, we would get in touch with him for sure.

We never did discuss it again, we never got any money donated to us up front, and we never sent another container. Some things are only one-offs, and maybe that is a good thing. I also never again crossed the Sahara Desert on the back of a MAN truck, or a "ship of the desert."

CHAPTER 3

2009, THE FUN IN FUNDRAISING

1975

When Ralph and I debarked the date truck in Niamey, it was the first of only two rides that we paid for in Africa. We travelled south through Niger and into Nigeria, and by "travel" I mean "hitchhike." We had very little money, and Ralph was an old hand at hitchhiking (you should forgive the pun), so that's what we did for the rest of our travels.

Traffic was minimal. Most people did not have cars. But we were patient. We would settle with our backpacks beside the road and wait, usually on the outskirts of a small town. We were an anomaly. We saw no other Caucasians travellers on our route. The other travellers on the date truck were heading for South Africa. So here we were, a very odd couple indeed, landing in small West African towns.

Town folk were curious but busy and passed us by. Not so the kids. Great groups of them would gather near to us, not wanting to get too close although one little girl did come to touch my (very) white arm. The kids giggled at our noses, which stuck out so far and came to a point, unlike their elegantly flat ones. They pushed their noses up like ours, laughing at how odd we looked. They were irresistible, and I laughed too. I never did like my nose much.

Sometimes an adult approached us, usually male, and told us there was no point in waiting for a ride, few people had cars, no one would know what we were doing. One kindly fellow even paid our fare on a very spiffy bus to the next small town, where we settled in again by the road and waited. Usually within a few hours, a car would come into view, slow down, and slam to a stop. Out would climb a very surprised Caucasian. What were we doing hitching here? Where were we from? Why were we travelling? Would we like to come and stay with them (it was nearly always a couple) for a day or too?

We always answered "yes." Of course. We were treated to free lodging, delicious meals, and the privilege of being welcome visitors from the same milieu and backgrounds as our isolated and homesick hosts. Often engineers, sometimes teachers, occasionally religious affiliates, they were starved for the companionship and conversation of people from their own culture. It was an easy price for us to pay, and we did so gladly. We benefited immensely from the kindness of these (not-so-strange) strangers.

2009

As 2009 began, the AVPA was $5,000 into deficit funding for getting the shipping container out of the Dar port. I had paid this cost personally and now needed to get reimbursed.

Thus began a year of fanatic fundraising. Enthusiasm ran high. We were getting known at BCIT, and the approximately twelve thousand students and one thousand employees at the Burnaby campus were a huge source of support and participation. We decided last year that doing many little fundraising events would likely be worth it even if the returns were modest. We were going to throw as much spaghetti at the wall as we could and hope some of it stuck.

Our first fundraiser of the year was a book and bake sale at BCIT. I booked a seminar room through the Student Association for Thursday, February 12, from 11 a.m. to 8 p.m. This room was beside the Great Hall, that central meeting place on campus, so we hoped for a lot of customers. I publicized the sale on the BCIT e-bulletin board with requests for books, baked goodies, and volunteers. I also put out a call for help using the email addresses I collected during the collection blitz for the shipping container. These efforts were very successful.

We got a huge number of donated books and rented a storage locker for two months near to BCIT to store them. It cost $80 a month (Dale and I covered this expense). The locker was worth it and excellent for sorting books beforehand. We trucked them over to BCIT on the morning of the sale.

My wonderful board members, Dale, Charleen, Robert and Valerie, and her daughter Sarah, arrived at BCIT at about 10 a.m. on the day of the sale. I had gotten parking permits, but when we arrived on campus, we discovered the approved areas were very far away from the room. So we unloaded everything in a much closer lot and took the books in from there. Valerie brought an enormous dolly, wider than a hospital gurney and with several shelves, that was fabulous for transporting the books. (She borrowed it from the library where she worked as a librarian.) The vehicles we then moved to the approved parking lot.

When we arrived at the room, we found there had been a mix-up on the dates and the room was double booked. Yipe. But fortunately, another room nearby was quickly found for us, and in we trooped. Many volunteers turned up to help us unload, sort, and place the books and baked goodies on tables.

The room was crazy with energy and excitement. Even glitches were tackled with glee and resourcefulness. There were ten tables already in the room, but these were not enough. We had so many books that we could have used twenty. Two volunteers tore off to find more and came back twice with large round ones they had found in a nearby alcove. They helped save the day, bless them. (Even so, many books were still in boxes on the floor.)

We set up signs and a sandwich board in the hallway outside the room and promotional displays about the AVPA inside. They were super although we could have gotten them up earlier. Charleen made smaller signs for the book prices, which were eye-catching and helpful. Someone had left an easel in the room, so we commandeered it and stood it in the hallway advertising the sale. A couple more would have been good.

We started off at $1 per book, then dropped the price to fifty cents in the afternoon. The baked goods were $1 and a hit with students. We had set up a cashier table with a cash box at the exit of the room, but the table itself was much too small for all the activity. It was a madhouse: customers trying to pay for their purchases, volunteers taking the cash and giving change, answering questions, trying to hand out fliers. The donation and draw boxes were also on the table but got lost in the shuffle.

Nonetheless, the day roared by with activity. I had created a schedule for volunteers to staff the room throughout the day, and everyone turned up to for their shift. They were all fantastic. Instructors and staff came from all over the campus to help, donate goodies and more books, and buy stuff as well. They were the majority of the book purchasers, the students not so much, being more interested in sustenance for the tummy than for the brain. Lunchtime was excellent and the busiest time, but business throughout the day was steady and we were delighted with the sales.

In the evening, we found out that night-school students were at BCIT, so we kept the room open for their break at 8:30. Charleen walked through the Great Hall and nearby cafeterias several times and handed out fliers to the students. She said simply, "We're having a book and bake sale. All books and baked goods are going for one dollar. All proceeds go to help a village in Africa." It was very effective. Each time, we had a surge of customers.

At the end of the day, we still had a lot of books. I had booked the room for Thursday only, but the day had gone so well that we decided to extend the sale to Friday. Fortunately, we were able to keep the room until noon. One dollar got you five books on Friday and we sold a lot more. Three door prizes were given out: gift certificates for Home Depot and Indigo bookstore and a box of truffles.

Both days were very good. We made a total of $1337. I was filmed and interviewed by some broadcasting students and hoped for world-wide coverage, but alas it was only a class assignment.

We learned a lot.

Publicity needed to start much earlier and be more consistent over time. Lack of time on my part meant the BCIT e-bulletin board postings were very late. A COMM colleague contacted the editor of the staff/faculty newsletter but was told that they needed at least a month's notice. (The editor did forward our information to the BCIT blog person, and we got a posting there.) We also should have gotten into *Link*, the student newspaper.

We needed a cut-off time for book donations and should have not accepted any on the day of the sale. It was way too much and impossible to sort them. A bigger baked-goodies table with room for the donation and draw boxes would have relieved the pressure on the exit table. We also needed a specialty table for the higher quality books, which should have been priced higher. Gene, my wonderful office roommate, told me at the sale that we should have culled the books beforehand. He said older travel books, almanacs, and *Reader's Digests* would not sell, and that hardcover fiction must be very recent and in excellent condition. He offered to help us next year.

The quantities for the baked goods were not consistent, which made selling them a little awkward. They all needed to be about the same for the price. We also could have done better at making sure everyone who came into the room knew about the draw and got an AVPA flier.

The Africa Village Project Association
Early Spring Newsletter: March 11, 2009

Our First Business Donor!

We'd like to thank Cates Pharmacy on Bowen Island, our first business donor. We received a $200.00 donation from them—we were thrilled! Thanks Bud and Elaine!

The Book and Bake Sale at BCIT

On Thursday, February 12, we held our first ever fundraiser at BCIT: a book and bake sale. It was a great success, and we send our heartfelt gratitude to everyone who donated books and baked goodies, handled the room booking, set up the tables and the offerings, staffed the room during the sale, and bought stuff, THANK YOU!!

Kathy sets up the baked goods table using African kangas as tablecloths.

We had a delicious variety of baked goods that sent folks back for more! The fudge by Lara in the Math Department was a particular hit. Over sixty people entered the draw for three different gift certificates. The winners seemed very pleased.

Jean and Patricia wheel another table into Town Square B.

We received over sixty boxes of books and didn't have enough tables in the room for them all. Two resourceful volunteers scrambled to find more and fortunately did!

Deidre sets up books on the non-fiction table for the grand opening at noon.

We raised a grand total of $1,337.35. Your generous support of this sale means that we can continue the power project in Okaseni village.

Valerie and Charleen, Africa Village Project Board Members, set up the entry table where customers entered the draw to win cool prizes.

Charleen did a great job of bringing in the night-school students on Thursday, who were getting a break from classes in the early evening and hanging out in the eateries and Great Hall close by to our room. She let them know what we were selling and why and invited them to come check the sale out. Many did! Thanks Charleen!

(Here's a quick update. Last week, we received an email from Tumaini Minja, our Okaseni contact. He said, "Electricity has already been connected to the school. This really is good news. Okaseni Primary School has been in operation since colonial times and . . . electricity is a milestone to the Okaseni community.")

This is wonderful news! Your donations have made this successful project happen and your ongoing support will continue to improve the lives of the Okaseni villagers. Thank you.

Brenda checks out the good reads at the children's book table.

We were beyond thrilled with the success of this fundraiser. As always, we thank you for your generosity. The Okaseni villagers send their thanks to you as well.

All and all, however, this fundraiser was successful and a lot of fun. New philosophy: the spaghetti is rocking!

Our second fundraiser was a garage sale in June. We were picking up fundraising momentum and were keen to do anything that might work. A garage sale seemed worth a try. We spent some time hunting for locations. I checked out Willingdon Church across from BCIT, but it was not available. The Shriners Hall also near BCIT wanted $800, way too expensive. I contacted the Centre for Peace in Vancouver, but it cost $300. We decided this was still too expensive and that the max should be $75 to $100. Charleen checked out local community centres, which were cheaper but did not do garage sales. Then a friend told us about a Lions Hall in Burnaby, near where she lived. I checked it out. It was a small, older, humble building comprised of a theatre/banquet hall with a stage, a tiny kitchen, and not much else. The location looked promising, in a busy neighbourhood with lots of pedestrian and vehicle traffic. It was $75 for the day. I booked it for Saturday, June 27.

I put out a call at BCIT for donations and held drop-off times there twice before the sale. We got several truckloads of stuff, which we stored in the locker we had rented for the book and bake sale. All the board members and Sarah also brought things. At least one person dropped off items on the day.

The publicity worked well. We put flyers on neighbourhood telephone poles the night before and morning of the sale, postings on Facebook thanks to Sarah and Clara (one of my loveliest BCIT students ever), and postings on the BCIT e-bulletin board.

I had booked the hall from 11 a.m. to 3 p.m. We got there at 9 a.m. to set up, unload stuff, and get organized. It was a good thing we did because when we arrived, we found that the hall had been double booked. We were bounced. Not again! It was a few bad moments, but then I had an idea. Could we hold the sale in the parking lot? Fortunately, they said yes and even more fortunately, they charged us only $20 instead of $75. The lot turned out to be great. It was actually much better than inside the hall because we were highly visible, and people could easily stop to take a look. But the day was very hot, and we of course were not prepared for that. (We later made a note for next time to bring sunscreen, hats, long-sleeved tops, parasols, and water, just in case.)

The sale went very well. The volunteers and helpers were fabulous. All the board members turned out, as did my nephew Jess and his girlfriend Nadia, Sarah and her boyfriend James, several of my wonderful Medical Laboratory students including Clara, and an instructor from BCIT. We had so much person-power that even though the sale itself was a lot of work, it went quickly and smoothly, and nobody got totally exhausted.

We sold a lot of stuff, but the sales were quite random. The very good stuff went right away, of course. The books left over from the book and bake sale also sold well. Some stuff, mostly small kitchen things, did not sell at all. The rest of the stuff was hit and miss and completely unpredictable. The oddest things sold, and other stuff that seemed okay we could not even give away for free.

We received many donations of articles of clothing, which were not hot sellers. Two women spent a couple of hours going through everything and only bought about $20 worth each. But they looked thrilled, so it was nice to have made someone so happy. We decided that clothes were worth doing because I could take any leftovers to Triage, a homeless shelter in downtown Vancouver that always needs them. It was a double benefit.

At 3 p.m., we closed shop as the number of customers had tapered off.

Getting rid of the unsold stuff turned out to be amazingly easy, which made me very happy. Dale and I took all the acceptable remaining stuff in our truck to Value Village (about a five-minute drive away). They were exceptionally efficient. We drove into a drop-off bay and simply handed the stuff to an employee, who took nearly everything except two ratty bar stools. The leftover books were taken by Jess and Nadia to a Learning Tree drop box nearby—again, fast and convenient. The bar stools and a few other very junky things Dale took to the city dump near to Charleen and Robert's place—again, très convenient.

We got a very nice compliment when looking for a garage sale venue. A church receptionist mentioned *Fierce Light*, a movie about spirituality and doing good and whether they are, or should be, inextricably joined. She said that we were obviously way ahead of the curve on that question. Aww thanks!

We made $740.

We learned a lot.

Publicity was the main thing that could have been better. As with the book and bake sale, we should have started sooner. We could have put ads in the local community papers and the *Vancouver Sun*; posted information earlier and more often on craigslist, Used Vancouver, and Facebook; and put the fliers up in the neighbourhood two days before the sale. We could even have improved the date of the sale, holding it in May instead of June, because most BCIT people were still at work in May. By the end of June, they were mostly gone.

At the end of the day, we evaluated the actual sales. We realized that we should have rejected any junk at the time of collection. For example, the two ratty bar stools that Dale and I accepted had not sold at the owner's own garage sale. They did not sell at ours either, and we should not have taken them. We also should have priced things higher. Dale said that some of the tools he donated could have sold at twice the price ($10 instead of $5). We did want to move stuff, but on the other hand, a garage sale is a lot of work, so we should have tried to make as much money as possible. We could always have reduced the prices later in the day.

We could have also improved promoting the AVPA itself. The flyers should have been offered directly to the customers because they did not take them voluntarily. I eventually started to hand them out, and most people were polite and mildly interested. We had brought materials for an AVPA display board but did not have time to put it up. It was an excellent idea however, and we decided we should always have one but that it had to be prepared beforehand. The donations box was a good idea (we did get some), but the draw for gift certificates was not worth it. Only four people entered.

Finally, we realized that we should have brought cameras. If you can believe this, nobody did, so we did not have any pictures of the sale itself. (None of us had phones with cameras at that time.)

New philosophy: the spaghetti rocked this summer!

Our third fundraiser this year was a brunch in August to celebrate the AVPA becoming an official Canadian charity. Yes, we were approved! On December 20, 2008, I had sent off our multi-page response to their rejection of our original application. In January this year, I got a phone call from them requesting more information, which I sent off right away.

The Africa Village Project Association
Summer Newsletter: July 21, 2009

Summer Greetings!

Isn't summer the best? We are enjoying gorgeous weather after a long, cold winter.

Official Charity Status

Great news: we are now an official Canadian charity! In April, Revenue Canada notified us that we were approved. Happy day! It took about a year and a half to complete the process, but it was worth it. We are beyond delighted.

You can now get an official tax-deductible receipt for your donations to the AVPA. We can now apply for grants and get publicity so that we can do even more work in Okaseni.

Garage Sale

Our first ever garage sale was held in June 27 at the Rumble Street Lions Hall in Burnaby.

We discovered when we arrived that the hall had been double booked. Yipes! For a moment, we thought we might have to cancel. But then we asked if we could hold the sale in the parking lot.

Yes, we could. So we set up tables there and got on with the sale. We probably got more attention in the parking lot than we would have in the hall. The sale went very well and we raised over $740.00.

Most of the donations we received for the sale came from BCIT staff and faculty. Thank you! Many items sold, and the buyers looked thrilled with their purchases (including AVPA board members, who unknowingly bought each other's donations).

Robert, AVPA board member, shows off some of the treasures he found at the AVPA garage sale. Cool hat, Robert!

Thanks to everyone who helped on the day, including my nephew and his girlfriend, Sarah, her friend, a BCIT colleague, my students and their friends. Many thanks as always to the AVPA board: Dale, Charleen, Robert, and Valerie.

Thanks to you too. We could not do this without you.

In April, we received word that CRA had granted us official charity status. After waiting one and a half years, submitting stuff and more stuff, making changes as requested and waiting some more, we were finally vetted, approved, and good to go! We could now give tax deductible receipts, which we hoped would open up doors for us to get publicity and funding. CRA gave us a fiscal year-end date (July 31) and sent us information about submitting tax statements. We were to send in our first annual financial report by January 31, 2010, six months after the end of our fiscal year. With pleasure! We were also advised to spend no more than 10 percent of our income on fundraising. This seemed a fairly easy concept to grasp, I would have thought, but events in the future were to belie my nonchalant assumption.

To celebrate, we held a brunch in August. Charleen and Robert offered their place in Vancouver as the venue. They owned a beautiful, older home that they had lovingly renovated in an updated Victorian style. On the top floor was a large, open, central room with several smaller rooms off it. The house itself was on a double lot with the remnants of an aged fruit-tree orchard and a huge grassy area that they had converted into a large vegetable garden. They had also installed a Mediterranean garden on the sunny side of the house with a fountain, sun dial, grapevines, and charming benches. At the back of the house, they put in an al fresco patio near the trees with a table, comfy chairs, and a large parasol. The setting was heavenly and perfect for the event.

We decided it should be a private brunch with personal invitees and set the date for Sunday, August 9. Charleen and I both invited a lot of friends. I also sent out a special invitation in my July newsletter to our general email list, which included our BCIT contacts, and did a special posting on the BCIT e-bulletin board. We also did targeted invites for the most likely attendees.

Charleen booked Valerie, a friend who played crystal bowls, to perform for us. She also got a bluegrass band called 5 on a String. They both seemed fabulous. Charleen and I covered the cost of the music, and she and Robert supplied the food for the brunch.

About thirty people attended, including our sister Val, her husband Art and daughter Alicia, my nephew Jess and his wife Nadia (who was a wonderful help), Robert's daughter Adina, her kids, and many friends of Charleen and Robert. A few of my invitees attended. The weather in the morning was gloomy, a concern because of the outdoor part of the program. We started off upstairs where I made a short speech, and the guests kindly made donations, for which I was thrilled, for the first time, to write official government receipts. Then we tucked into the amazing brunch. So far, so good.

Then, amazingly, the weather cleared up. We all trooped down to the Mediterranean garden where we sat on the grass amidst the grapevines and filtered sunshine and listened to Valerie beguile us with her crystal bowls performance. The surroundings were beautiful, the music enchanting, and the ambience magical. Then we tromped back upstairs where the bluegrass band had us rocking and dancing and cheering up a storm. It was fabulous too.

Yet underneath all that fun and excitement was a sad, tragic story. Charleen told me while we were listening to the band that one of the members had just lost his adult daughter. I think it was from cancer. Charleen said that another child of his also died several years ago. I could hardly catch my breath. He was up there singing with abandon and putting his all into the performance, seemingly without a woe. I felt my heart would break into pieces for him. I knew not what to do except send him a silent thank-you above the music.

By 3 p.m., we had all had a splendid time, and the guests started to depart. There was little to do afterwards except clean up from the brunch and move the furniture upstairs back into place. We had made $886.69, which was double the expenses ($450 for the band, Valerie, and food). This income/outgo ratio seemed fine to me at the time, and indeed became even more so after an extravagant fundraiser we would hold in the future. We had boogied our boots off to the band, been charmed by the bowls performance, and chowed down some fabulous food. Best of all, the support for the AVPA was heartwarming.

We learned a lot.

At the next board meeting, we discussed doing an event like this again. We were all pleased with it and had had a lot of fun. There were, however, some concerns. The first was that the event was weather dependent. If it rained, we would need a Plan B. We could get a pop-up tent for the garden or move indoors if possible. We could also hold the event at a different venue, such as a local community centre or the communal party room at a friend's condo complex.

The Africa Village Project Association
Fall Newsletter: September 28, 2009

Happy Autumn!

We are still enjoying fabulous summer weather and hope your autumn is going well.

Official Charity Status Celebration

On August 9, we held a musical garden party fundraiser at Charleen and Robert's house in Vancouver to celebrate getting official Canadian charity status. It was fabulous! The morning was unpromising with clouds and rain, but by noon when the party started, the sun popped out and the weather got glorious.

We had two musical performances. The first was a bluegrass band called 5 on a String, which got us all dancing and bopping. They were fantastic, and we loved them! The second was a crystal bowls performance by Valerie outside in the Mediterranean garden. The heavenly tones of the crystal bowls transported us all to a blissful state.

We were also blissed out that the party raised almost $900.00 and want to thank the performers, everyone who came, and everyone who helped. Your support is much appreciated, and your presence made it a very special day.

Valerie, crystal bowls player extraordinaire, performs at the AVPA garden party fundraiser in August.

Bake Sale and 50/50 Raffle at BCIT

It's time to get some yummy baked goodies! We're having a bake sale in the Great Hall on Monday, October 5, from 11 until 2:30. Come by and have a delicious treat or six. If you'd like to donate to the sale, we'd be thrilled! You can drop off goodies to the booth in the Great Hall at 10 a.m. on the day. Hope to see you at the sale!

We are now holding our first ever 50/50 raffle. Half the ticket sales go to the winner and half go to the AVPA. Buy a ticket, or two, or ten. You could win big and help the African villagers. The draw is on Thursday, October 8. Get your tickets **now!**

The Okaseni villagers send you thanks, as do we. We appreciate you to the max.

Charleen had several personal concerns. She found it too nerve-wracking waiting for guests to arrive and was disappointed because the number of people who came was far fewer than had been invited. She was also uncomfortable with having a lot of people in her home, many of whom she might not know. We decided that if her home were not an option, we could find a different venue and come up with a theme. If we had the party at a condo complex, it could be a pool, Hawaiian, and/or barbeque theme. For a local community centre, it could be a western theme with the bluegrass band. If Charleen were okay with doing it again, we could invite fewer people and sell tickets beforehand. This would help with the food estimates and not lead to disappointing numbers because guests would likely come if they already got tickets. We would also be able to screen the guests, but we would probably have to charge a high price for the tickets depending on the number of people we invite.

However, it was one of the best and easiest fundraisers we ever had.

New philosophy: the spaghetti continued to rock this summer!

Our fourth fundraiser was a bake sale at BCIT. We held it on Monday, October 5, from 11 a.m.to 2:30 p.m. and tied it in with a 50/50 draw. I booked space in the Great Hall and put out a call for goodies at BCIT. Valerie said that she and Sarah would make some baked goods and might as well. Charleen and Robert also volunteered to help.

The location was excellent, just at the bottom of the ramp in the Great Hall. It cost us $50 for the booth (non-profit rate). Not very many people donated baked goods, but the ones who did came through with a lot. We prepared and brought the sandwich board and display board, both of which worked well. Charleen, Valerie, and I staffed the booth, with Dale as a backup. We sold tickets for the 50/50 draw. We also had AVPA fliers that we tried to give to people but not many took them. Charleen did a great job of selling the 50/50 tickets, and Valerie was expert at selling the goodies.

The sale itself went well, and we made $257.

We learned a lot.

Although the sale was modestly successful, the publicity could have been much better. Announcements on the BCIT e-bulletin board for the book sale and the 50/50 draw were supposed to be posted on alternate days but were not. I decided to ask a different person next time to help. Also, we needed various supplies, including plastic wrap, little plastic gloves for handling the goodies, tape, scissors, and plastic baggies of various sizes.

But the biggest gaffe for this sale was the start time: 11 a.m. was far too late. Our customers that day were mostly students on their way to class, and they were hungry before lunch. But after lunch, hardly anybody bought anything. We would have done much better by starting at 9 a.m. when the students would have been starved. If we had, we probably could have closed up shop by 11 a.m.

New philosophy: more rocking spaghetti!

Fundraiser number five was the 50/50 draw at BCIT planned for Thursday, October 8. The manager of a BCIT department had the original idea and was very keen to help us. She got in touch with five or so people at BCIT to sell tickets. Charleen created the tickets and flyers. The two of them did a super job of organizing it, which made it a dream for me. I arranged for a posting on the BCIT bulletin board every few days for about three weeks before the draw day. This time it went well.

The tickets were one for $1, five for $2, and ten for $5. Sales were good. We made $230, half of the $460 total that we raised. There were no expenses. The winner was an instructor in the Natural Sciences department. I delivered a card and the cash to him the next day. He was very pleased.

The A/V manager told me later that she was very disappointed with the BCIT response and had hoped to raise at least $500. However, this might have been the norm for BCIT. Charleen raised almost $100 herself not at BCIT. I was very grateful to both of them. For me, this was the easiest fundraiser ever thanks to these two wonderful people. It was, on the whole, a success.

For our sixth fundraiser, we got a booth and sold little goodies at the annual Christmas Fair on Bowen Island. This venture was the idea of Brooke, a Bowen friend who became one of the most enthusiastic supporters ever of the AVPA. She was a volunteer at the Island Discovery Learning Community (IDLC), a local alternative school on Bowen, and wanted her students to get involved in the AVPA and learn about Africa and its challenges. She was also keen to get them to do some fundraising for the Okaseni primary school.

She wanted the kids to create something tangible that they could sell. The kids wanted the funds that they raised to buy goats for the villagers. I sent an email to our Okaseni contacts asking if goats would be acceptable but received no response. No worries, I assumed they would be over the moon. The students went ahead and reserved a booth at the fair.

The plan was to sell luscious bars of natural soap in small pottery holders made by the kids. Each bar would cost $10. The purchaser would be buying not only the soap but also a goat for a family in Okaseni. These goats would help improve the health and income of the villagers. The kids called the fundraiser "Soap an' a Goat."

The students and their parents were alight with enthusiasm. They made dozens of the small pottery holders for the soap, which were fired by a Bowen artist and painter. The bars of soap were made and donated by two sisters, one of whom had a small speciality shop on Bowen. Phoenix Photo, the local bookstore, donated the tissue paper that the kids used to wrap up the soap and holders to make cute gifts. A little tag line was included in the holder that said, "Hey pal! Merry Christmas! I got a soap for you and a goat for them! (The Africa Village Project)."

Other things were donated to us to sell at the fair, including plant holders and beautiful Christmas wreaths. Some kind soul created cards that people could use to donate to the AVPA to help pay the school fees.

Almost thirty people contributed in some way to the sale, including making the soap holders, painting t-shirts, creating the tags, and staffing the booth on the day of the sale. Brooke, our amazing AVPA saint, was in charge of everything. Lori, her fellow teacher at the IDLC, organized the donations of soap. Both Brooke and Lori were brilliant at chatting up the visitors to the booth and made many sales. Allan, the principal of the IDLC, was a huge support. The school paid for the booth at the fair, and he encouraged all the kids to get involved.

This sale itself was fabulous. All the soap and holders were sold out by early afternoon. Over $1815 was raised. Bowen unexpectedly turned out to be a huge support, and we were elated. I was so grateful to all the people who helped us and sent out thank-you cards to everyone afterwards.

It was a year of rocking spaghetti!

Aside from the fundraisers that we put on, we received over the year random donations from unexpected sources. We received $75 from the BCIT Friday at Four, a social event held every Friday afternoon for staff and

How to Adopt a Village in Africa

instructors. We got a donation from an elementary school class in North Carolina for US$1,765, whose teacher had found us online and used the AVPA to teach the kids about village life in Africa. What a stroke of luck. I facilitated a letter exchange between her students and the Okaseni primary kids. As well, one or two donations per month came through on PayPal.

This year also involved some indirect fundraising, also known as publicity. I took every opportunity to speak to groups, organizations, classes, fellow instructors, and such. I did not usually make a direct request for donations at these events, but we did at times receive some. Mostly, they helped raise our profile, plumped up our mailing list, and encouraged participation in our various events.

I made the second annual AVPA presentation for the BCIT community in February. Four people turned up. Two door prizes were given out (a box of chocolates and a gift certificate), a fifty percent chance of winning.

In June, Dale and I went to Anacortes, Washington, USA, a small town on the northern tip of the Olympic Peninsula, just across the strait from Victoria, Canada. We had been invited to make a presentation at the town library by Jackie Boss, a long-time friend of Dale. The library hosted talks throughout the year, and the theme for spring was *Beyond Three Cups of Tea*, a reference to a book by Greg Mortenson about a small aid organization he founded. Speakers from many small grassroots organizations came talk about what they were doing to help around the world. Our presentation went well, and we were pleased that several of our American friends attended. We received US$305 in donations at the event and an honorarium of US$75. You might think it was a long way to go for such a small amount, but we saw friends, did a relaxed amble through Anacortes, and enjoyed the ferry rides to the US and back with splendid views of the Olympic Mountains. It was well worth it.

This year, BCIT announced a new initiative to replace a long-standing event in the fall called "Shinerama," which raised money for cystic fibrosis research. The new event was called the "Volunteer Fair for the BCIT Peak Leadership," and its purpose was to encourage students to get involved in volunteering. I got in touch with the coordinator about speaking at this event and was approved. I was given a booth and presentation space in the Great

105

Hall, that prime location where we had held the other fundraisers. It seemed like a great opportunity.

The event was held on a Thursday in October. It was just me this time, staffing the booth and doing the presentation. I set up the booth with a sandwich board, display, and flyers with amazing help from the Student Association staff. They were all dears, moving me to a better spot in the hall and getting the audio/visual equipment hooked up and working. Patricia, my COMM colleague, kindly volunteered to staff the booth while I did the presentation. I was good to go.

What I thought was a great location turned out, alas, not to be. There were many other booths and presentations in the hall, and it was overwhelmingly noisy. The din while I did my presentation was nerve-wracking, and only about twelve people paid any attention. As well, the overall attendance at the event was poor because, unlike Shinarama, it was not mandatory to attend. Perhaps twenty to twenty-five students stopped by the booth itself, a miniscule number, but some were interested and took fliers. One student volunteered to help.

I was not allowed to ask for donations or do any fundraising. However, one of the students looked absolutely rapt during my presentation, and I was charmed to talk to his lovely, beatific self. Ian, one of the helpful staff, gave me a very sweet compliment: "You have a Buddhist thing going on." Patricia told me that she thought the students seemed quite interested and that it was touching to see their enthusiasm. These heartwarming things made up a lot for the disappointment of the event itself.

Another presentation, which unfortunately I was not able to do, was held on Bowen in November. Brooke again was the primary mover. She wanted me to make a presentation about the AVPA to the kids at IDLC. She organized everything and scheduled it for early November. Alas, I was sick that day and could not do it. I gave Brooke my PowerPoint presentation so that she could just read it to the audience. She bravely did the presentation and did pull it off. I gave many thanks again for her. She was one of the best people ever to get involved with the AVPA.

The next presentation I was healthy enough to do, but it was inadvertently scheduled on November 11 at 1 p.m., almost exactly the time Dale and I would be heading to the airport for a holiday in Hawaii. Brooke was again in charge and had arranged for a young man called Jeff Torres to speak. Jeff was about twenty years old and, after some challenges in his teens, had become passionate about helping people. He was most concerned about the needy in Africa and began fundraising for them. His outstanding efforts earned him a spot as a World Vision youth ambassador. Brooke had seen him at a previous event and thought he would be an excellent presenter/speaker for Bowen.

The event was held at Collins Hall, a small building beside the local United Church, perfect for a presentation like this. Again, I gave Brooke a PowerPoint presentation I had prepared, with a skeleton script cobbled together for her to follow. She had not done a lot of publicity for the event and was unsure about doing the presentation herself. No worries, it was a huge success. Several families with lots of kids turned up, and $520 was raised. Jeff was fabulous, the kids were rapt, and as Brooke said, "Our hearts all opened up a little more." As did mine, in gratitude to her.

New philosophy: the spaghetti is rocking, albeit a tad slowly!

These were the successes. Needless to say, there were many things that were not. The no-go's, the things that remained in abeyance, the defunct attempts that did not come to fruition still took time, thought and energy. Sometimes possibilities were in the works for a while but never actually materialized. A neighbour on Bowen asked if we would give a presentation to the Bowen Rotary Club in the fall. They were the new president at the time and said they would like to form a partnership with us. Then we heard nothing. When I followed up, they said that they were booked until December but that the secretary would get in touch with us. Still waiting . . . We also received an email from the minister of a church on Bowen, asking if the church could help us. But after several attempts at contacting them with no response, I gave up on that too.

Sometimes a project appeared that seemed a godsend. The School of Business at BCIT had a program called Students in Free Enterprise (SIFE), which accepted the AVPA as a possible project. The students were to research the feasibility of getting cheap coffee beans from Okaseni/Tanzania for the Union Gospel Mission, an NGO in downtown Vancouver. Shipping would not be a problem as UGM had its own shipping contacts. Unfortunately, the project was eventually cancelled because the students said they were unable to get a local sponsor. SIFE resurrected it later in a more modest form, which they called a mini-project. We were accepted for the September 2009 term, but no students picked our project. Alas. This would have been great.

Grants were another no-go. Jackie Boss, who had organized our Anacortes presentation, sent us info about grants for American cities to create sister relationships with cities in Africa. We could apply, but it seemed unlikely for us in Canada. Valerie checked the Canadian grants directory and found all of them required official charity status. When we finally became official, I looked into applying for regular and matching grants. The requirements, forms, paperwork, and stipulations were onerous and applying for even one of them quickly slipped to the bottom of my massive to-do list.

A modest idea was to sell baked goodies at the weekend Farmer's Market on Bowen. I got in touch with the manager and was told that the market already had a baked goods vendor. But if we wanted to sell something else, they would consider giving us a booth. Nope, another no-go.

The amount of work that these fundraisers, presentations, and ultimately failed ventures required, plus keeping up with my 50-hour-a-week teaching job, meant that I had no chance to attend to some of the smaller ventures we had started. I had no time to follow up on the five businesses packages Lara delivered requesting funding for shipping, or contact any BCIT orga- nizations and departments, including the BCIT Foundation, or post info on the CharityVillage and Imagine Canada websites, or find funding for the dispensary Stephen Mamboleo wanted to build. The immediate and fast projects took precedence always over the long-term ones, especially fast ones that brought in cash. I had to eschew anything that required patient networking, the establishment and cultivation of ongoing relationships, and repeated follow-up. Understandably, no one else willing to take on this dif- ficult, long-term task.

Back in Okaseni, things were inching along. We received receipts for the power project and school expenses by snail-mail from Melki in January. I sent him a reply of thanks but reminded him that we could not continue the AVPA until we got the receipts for the shipping as well. Lo and behold, we finally got these in March. I also let him know that we were still paying off the shipping expenses, and until we did this, we could not take on more projects.

Early in the year, we received emails and documents from Salma, our microcredit program manager, with updates on the program, as well as receipts and pictures, some of which we used at the book and bake sale. It seemed to be going well, although we later received an email from Salma that some of the women were having trouble maintaining their businesses because they had chosen to sell bananas. There was always a surplus of bananas in the area, so it was an obvious choice but perhaps not the wisest. In May, we got word that the women had received training on how to expand their agricultural repertoire. This seemed practical and beneficial and was encouraging. By the end of the year, the program moved to the next phase with a second round of loans. We were very pleased about this. We also sent funds directly to Salma to get a knitting machine for Happy, one of the women in the second round of loans. She wanted to knit and sell school-uniform sweaters for the primary students. It would be a lease-to-own arrangement under the microcredit umbrella.

By October, we had finally raised enough money to get out of debt. The board approved reimbursing Dale and me for the money we had fronted the AVPA for the shipping container, as well as the power hook-ups, electrical installations, and school fees from the September 2008 trip. Happy day!!! We celebrated with wine and more wine.

Being back in the black meant we could move forward with projects in the village. I sent an email with the news to Tumaini, Melki, Peter, John, and Gerard Mchau in October. This was our first contact with them in months. I told them we were ready to go again, and again asked them about goats. We got no response.

In the fall, Robert, our wise and beloved board member, suggested doing a five-year strategic plan for the AVPA. We had a separate planning meeting in October at Charleen and Robert's home with wine and cheese. Robert did a superb table of contents. We created an ambitious plan. I gave a report on a book called *The Blue Sweater*, which was excellent especially on the limits of aid. I also brought an article about Elinor Ostrom, one of the winners this year of the Nobel Prize for economics. Ostrom researched and developed a theory that credits small groups and grassroots movements with solving serious social, economic, environmental, and other problems. She said such local, specific, and individual problem-solving is often more effective than top-down, bureaucratic, one-size-fits-all approaches that governments tend to use. Nice to see that the AVPA fit right in!

At the meeting, we also developed a one-year plan with current, ongoing, and potential future projects. We calculated the funds needed for the current and ongoing projects. This was a very modest $2,200. We would need more information over time to calculate costs for any future projects, but this figure gave us a starting point and a plan. It was a beneficial and fun meeting, and we all felt inspired.

Valerie and Sarah's brilliant suggestion in our October board meeting last year to have small fundraising events had worked out very well. It gave focus and efficiency to our fundraising efforts. We did a number of such events, and they had been successful and added up nicely.

New philosophy: the spaghetti rocked to the max this year!

Fundraising this year, both direct and indirect, was an enormous amount of work but it paid off in several ways. We retired the shipping debt, had a lot of fun, raised our profile, and netted more contacts, volunteers, and participants. You'll be happy to know that there *is* a lot of fun in fundraising. I benefited from the great-hearted kindness of friends, colleagues, and acquaintances, and—as I had in Africa in 1975—from the kindness of strangers.

CHAPTER 4

2010, VOLUNTEERS, AGORAPHOBIA, AND SERENDIPITY

1975

Our trip through West Africa was unusual, to say the least. Of all the riders on that date truck, only Ralph and I headed due south. The others speared to the southeast and down to South Africa, the end point it seemed for most travellers in Africa at the time. Our original plan was to go east to Kenya, but our trip across the Sahara made us realize the continent was a tad big. Kenya was way too far, and we had limited funds. We decided to make our way down to the West Coast and follow it back up towards Morocco.

Africa itself seems a daunting choice in retrospect, but it wasn't at the time. It beckoned because it wasn't the norm or the popular choice. How intrepid, I think now, how adventuresome. But why wasn't I more leery?

It was a very hard trip. But for the kindness of people who took us in, we would never have made it as far as we did. I remember every day that we waited by the side of the road, I was anxious about food. Would we be able to find something to eat that day? (There were few small restaurants or convenience stores at that time that catered to tourists because there were few tourists.) Would we find a place to stay? I never trusted that another nice person would come along and whisk us away to stay at their pleasant abode for a night or two. Someone almost always did though. We used our tent only a few times.

I was never afraid. People were mostly kind and accepting, curious and friendly. It never occurred to me that we might get robbed, beaten up, kid-napped, murdered. I was more scared a year or so later when I visited Saul in Berkley, California. We were walking down a street one evening when a gang of very large teenaged boys snatched the purse off my shoulder and thundered away. *That* was scary.

All this daring and fearlessness is surprising when you consider that at eighteen years old, I had a panic attack so severe that it landed me in the hospital. Over the next several months, this event led to full-blown panic disorder and agoraphobia, and I was suddenly housebound and my life drastically restricted. This condition lasted for several years. Little formal help was available then. Behavioural therapy and cognitive therapy had yet to become mainstream. The idea that fear itself was a learned response that can be unlearned was not well known. A psychiatrist I went to for a while listened politely but was hapless and ineffective. My family doctor wrote in my file that I was suffering from an anxiety disorder. Really? That was the best he would do? *I* could have told him that.

Saul, the friend I visited in London in 2008, was the first of only two people to help me. I told him about my panic disorder and agoraphobia that summer we hung out together so long ago. My worst fear was that I was crazy. He said, "I don't see any signs that you're crazy." I had such respect for him that my fear of madness subsided and as a result my panic and anxiety lessened.

My Mum was the other person who helped. When Ralph and I got married in 1978, I had another bout of panic and had to quit my job. My world again constricted, and I was in despair. Yes, I was crazy! No, I would never have a normal life! I muddled through those darkening days. One night, I had a dream about my Mum. She came to me with something in her hand and held it out to me. She said, "This is the answer." A couple of days later, she and Dad dropped by for a visit. She handed me a book she had found for me in the library. It was called *Stop Running Scared*.

That book saved my life. For the first time, I had specific, practical information on what fear was (a learned response) and what could change that response (behavioural therapy). Written by a psychology professor/therapist and his journalist wife, the book was based on scientific research and filled with explanations, case studies, and exercises on how to deal with and get over fear. Chapter 2 was on agoraphobia. How opportune! For several months, I dedicated myself in desperation to doing every single exercise and technique in that book and devouring every single last page. It was a crash course in mental health. I practiced (without hope) thought-stoppage techniques and found, to my great surprise, that they worked. I could stop my thoughts.

I suddenly realized that thoughts were not reality *and* that I could control them. This was a revelation of gargantuan proportions. My panic went away, much of my negativity lightened, and life became something I could actually live, not wistfully long for. And live I did. Over the years, I have done many things that would have once paralyzed me: took a BA in English an MA in theatre, acted in plays, taught students of all ages, flew in planes big and small, leapt tall buildings in a single bound—that kind of stuff.

That was one of the best things my Mum ever did for me. I guess something eventually would have come along to help me, but how long would I have waited? The information in that book was not common knowledge then as it is now. Today you can google on your phone "panic disorder" and instantly find a thousand times more information than I could back then. I am so grateful for science and the enormous strides in mental health treatments that have been made since then—and grateful for my phone too. I am grateful as well for panic disorder itself.

2010

My January newsletter for this year was full of optimism and plans for the future in Okaseni. Inspired by our successful fundraising last year, we were good to go.

And so the year began. I cannot emphasize enough how humble Dale and I were, how unprepossessing, small, grassroots, and earnest. Every donation, every kind word, every person who helped in any way seemed a kind of miracle. We were noticed! We were supported! We were appreciated!

And we were getting stuff done. Our diminutiveness was a huge advantage. Decisions were speedy, plans easily implemented, and conflicts few. But in 2010, we shifted our usual modus operandi and took some volunteers with us to Tanzania.

Volunteers seemed like a great idea. What better way to get lots accomplished, have moral support, and enjoy friendly companionship? In my various AVPA presentations, workshops, and outreach events, I met several people who expressed an interest in coming to Tanzania to help us. Dale, however, was not thrilled about the idea, preferring to work just the two of us. But I was excited and optimistic about what I hoped would be good-hearted and well-meaning folks helping in Okaseni.

There were five volunteers. Diane was a health science instructor at BCIT. She told me she would do anything needed to help and was interested setting up a dispensary. She also came up with a name for the group: the OK-7. Lara and Wayne were a young, recently married couple and were planning a honeymoon in Tanzania. Susan was in business. Both Lara and Susan had experience teaching, so we hoped they could teach the students, teachers, and/or microcredit women. Susan was also keen to research coffee. Wayne and Dale thought they might map the village and research water purification. Sarah, the daughter of our board member Valerie, also signed up to come.

I held several meetings beforehand with these volunteers, both individually and in a group. There were warning signs. Susan gave me an earful of advice about what I should be doing and was supremely uninterested in anything I actually was doing. I listened politely. I told the volunteers that we would be working together as a team and that I was not going to be the boss. I also said that the AVPA was not a tour company or a travel agency and that we were not responsible for anything that might happen to them on the trip. I knew enough to get waivers and prepared one with the kind help of a Bowen lawyer. Everyone signed the waiver right away except for Susan. This was the first in a long line of difficulties with her. The volunteers also had to make their own travel and other arrangements. I did say, however, that I would book rooms for them at Bristol Cottages, not as it turned out, the smartest move.

On May 17, all of us, including Susan's husband Mike, got together so we could meet one other. We put together a list of possible tasks/projects we could do in Okaseni. Things seemed to be going well. I did let them know that we had hardly any contact with the Okaseni folks since the container was released in November 2008. We had no recent info about the village, the costs for the power or the coffee nursery, the number of school kids who needed their fees paid, or what happened to the sewing machines and bikes. Fortunately, Tumaini had just returned to Tanzania from the Sudan and would have internet access, so hopefully, he would get in touch. We assumed that the village still wanted our help, but the lack of contact was discouraging.

The Africa Village Project Association
Winter Newsletter: January 24, 2010

Happy New Year!

Dale and I would like to wish you a (belated) Happy New Year. May all your dreams for 2010 come true.

We have made several New Year's resolutions about our work in Okaseni. In 2009, we did a lot of fundraising and now, thanks to your generosity, we have almost **$6,000** to help us accomplish these resolutions.

School Costs for Kids

Our first resolution is to pay the school costs for the twenty or so children who need yearly help. If you donated to help pay school costs, thanks! These kids need us.

Francisca Antoine, ten years old, is one of the children whose fees we will pay.

Power to the Office

Our second resolution is to finish the electrical power project. Power to the village primary school was completed in November 2008. Now, thanks to your generous donations, we have the funds to finish the village office. Then the electric sewing machines we sent in 2008 can be set up in a communal sewing centre, and women can make clothing to sell and increase their incomes.

Microcredit Program

Our third resolution is to expand the microcredit program. We set this up in 2008 with Can$1000.

These Okaseni women are in the first group who received microcredit loans.

Ten women were selected and trained, and the funds disbursed to them in January 2009. These women have now paid back their loans, and a second group received loans in June 2009. We want to do more because these loans help transform lives.

We could not even begin to contemplate these new resolutions without you. Thanks so much!

I also relayed what Mariana had told me about helping in developing countries: "If you get 30 percent done of what you want to do, you will be doing very well." I wanted to keep expectations modest and stave off disappointment.

Shortly before we left, I emailed Tumaini about our visit and told him we were thinking of buying goats. He responded! He said that Peter Mchau had gone to Okaseni and that the villagers were very excited about the goats. Tumaini said that Venance, the fellow we met in 2007 who worked in animal welfare, quoted a cost of US$100 for a goat, US$180 for a pregnant one, and US$150 for a shelter. I thought this breathtakingly exorbitant and decided to try to find more realistic prices and perhaps get shelters done by a microcredit borrower. However, it was great to have finally re-established contact with Tumaini. I also phoned Melki, John Mchau, Peter Mchau, and Salma. Melki hung up on me, John was thrilled to hear from us, and Peter said that he would contact Melki and let him know. I couldn't get in touch with Salma because she was at her mum's house awaiting the imminent arrival of her first baby.

Diane and Lara had gathered medical supplies, organized them, and distributed them to all of us to bring on the plane. Well done them! Dale and I packed our share in a big old duffel bag that we could leave in the village. We seemed well prepared overall. I had done my best with the volunteers and though it was the first time I had ever been in charge of such a venture, I was, as always, optimistic.

This year, we continued the massive, ongoing task of putting the "fun" in "fundraising." Last year had been quite good although a lot of work. This year was also fruitful.

Our first fundraiser of 2010 was the second book and bake sale at BCIT. I tried to get a Townsquare room as we did last year, but none were available, so we had to settle for the Great Hall. I booked the sale for mid March from 10 a.m. to 4 p.m. We were charged $115.50 for three chairs and ten tables, which was the non-profit rate.

I posted a notice every two days on the BCIT bulletin board from March 1 until the day of the sale. Each notice was either a plea for books and baked goodies or a simple announcement of the sale. The response for book donations was excellent considering the lead time was so short but probably only about one-third of the books we got last year. It was enough. I didn't need a storage locker because the books fit into my office and house on Bowen. We also got many donated baked goods and were well equipped this time with plastic wrap, tape, and such. Diane brought some rubber gloves.

Despite my misgivings about being in the hall, it turned out to be excellent. The first place the Student Association people gave us didn't work well, so they let us move to the ramp and even helped us lug our stuff over there. We were right at the crossroads point in the hall, the best place possible for traffic.

The board members and Sarah were fabulous as usual. A number of other BCIT people also volunteered, including some who helped last year, which was gratifying to see. Several of my students from last year turned up as well. Sales were brisk. We made $519 on the books and $400 on the baked goodies for a total of $920.

Our next fundraiser was a music and presentation evening at Cates Hill Chapel on Bowen on Friday, May 7, at 7:30 p.m. It was organized in its entirety by our Bowen friend, Brooke. This was a first for me not to be the organizer for an event this size, and I just stood back and watched her go. She wanted the event to focus on getting people to sign up for monthly donations. Many regular ongoing donors, even at small amounts, could alleviate the need to do many small fundraisers, which were a lot of work and didn't necessarily make a lot of money. Needless to say, I was tapdancing for joy about her plan.

Several planning meetings were held, attended by Brooke; James, a local musician and businessperson; Lori, who taught at IDLC; and me. We set a goal of fifty people donating $10 a month. The publicity was fabulous. Brooke arranged for an interview for me with the editor of the *Bowen Island Undercurrent*, the local weekly newspaper, and we got a big spread in their April 30 issue. Brooke also asked a local designer to create posters and tickets pro bono. They were gorgeous. Hemlock Printers did the tix and posters at their non-profit rate of $360 (paid by Dale and me). Tickets were $10 for adults and $5 for students and were sold by all us organizers, Phoenix Books, and Bowen Veterinary Services. The venue, Cates Hill Chapel again, cost $130 (also their non-profit rate and also paid by Dale and me).

James arranged for the musicians and wrote a wonderful song, "Africa," to play at the event. Brooke arranged for the guest speakers: Jeff, the speaker at the Bowen Remembrance Day fundraiser; Bruce, a teacher at a local school; and me. Martin, a local businessperson, was the emcee.

The schedule was as follows:

1. Music by the local musicians (45 minutes)
2. Guest speaker Jeff Torres (1.25 hours)
3. Guest speaker Bruce (15 minutes)
4. Me (15 minutes)

Unfortunately, despite all the planning, care, and creativity that went into the event, it was not a resounding success. We received a lot of feedback and criticisms from people who attended. Some were put off by Jeff's presentation because it was not cohesive and seemed geared to high school students, not adults. (A number of people left.) Others said that Bruce's speech started well with a google video/chart but veered into irrelevance with a long, tenuously related student video. (More people left.) Several people said there were too many messages amongst all the speakers, so the main message was unclear.

Other people said that I should have had more time than the others. When I finally stood up to talk, we were three hours in and three-quarters of the audience had left. Also, Bruce had taken his projector, and it seemed deadly to spend time setting up our own projector so that I could do my presentation. I recognized a lost cause when I saw one, so I stood up in front of the people still there and said time was too short for my presentation. Then, for about three minutes, I talked fast about the work of the AVPA, the benefits of supporting us, and the goal of the event (monthly donors). But by this time, of course, it was far, far too late. No mention had been made of the "fifty people at $10 month" until my speech, so the audience was not primed to donate monthly. There had been no request for immediate donations and no place to leave cheques or cash. No announcement was made about mailing in cheques or donating online, and the mailing address on the donation flyer was hard to read. The whole affair was a good attempt but needed more practicality and organization.

However, it was also not a disaster. We raised about $820 in ticket sales, $160 in donations, and $70 for coffee and baked goodies. One person signed up for monthly donations, we later received a couple of cheques, and another monthly donor signed up by mail. Two attendees offered their houses for a party/fundraiser. All good.

Although these were the only two fundraisers this year, they were profitable. In accordance with our new philosophy: the spaghetti chugged along!

This year, Zack, my wonderful nephew and computer whiz, and I started updating the AVPA website. It was by long distance because over the year, he was in Romania for the Peace Corp, then in South Sudan and Florida for the US military. The website turned out to be a much bigger job than we expected. He spent many hours working on it for which I was extremely grateful.

In March, we received happy news in an email from Tumaini: "I wish to share some news that I have been in a relationship with a girl called Monika of Austria and we have been blessed with a baby boy, Isaac. I met her in 2006 while taking a short course at the European Peace University, which is based in her hometown."

We were thrilled for all of them!

TRAVEL JOURNAL
Saturday, June 5

After several weeks of end-of-year BCIT work and travel preparations, we left Bowen today to catch our 8:30 p.m. flight to Amsterdam. We went directly to Charleen and Robert's house. I had accidently put my fear-of-flying index cards in the wash the day before, and they had gotten lint-ified. I made new ones there, but it was painful trying to remember them all. Only by diligent use of such behavioural therapy techniques had I been finally able to fly somewhat calmly. These little cards of positive thoughts ("Flying is the safest way to travel." "I laugh at turbulence, haha!") helped immensely. I carried them in my pocket and read them throughout the day.

Robert kindly gave us ride to the airport. I was very tired on the flight and managed to sleep for about four hours.

Sunday, June 6

I woke up about two hours out of Amsterdam. The plane touched down at Schiphol Airport at about 4 p.m. local time. My beloved Amsterdam! It was beginning to feel familiar and dear, like a cherished friend that you don't see often but whom you love a lot. We put the duffle bag with our share of the medical supplies Diane and Lara had collected into a locker while we headed to Paris for six days.

We caught the 6:30 train, which was crowded, but both of us slept a lot, being very tired. We went through the infamous Brussels train station where we had gotten separated in 2009 (no mix-ups this time) and arrived in Paris at 9:30 or so. It was still light, thank goodness, since it was almost the solstice, and we got a cab to the flat in Montmartre that I had booked online. I felt a bit sorry the driver. He was probably from Algeria, that unfortunate ex-French colony, doing jobs for trying Parisians and obnoxious foreign tourists.

He dropped us off at the Tim Hotel near the Sacre Coeur Cathedral in Montmartre. We had a terrible time finding the flat until we finally realized it was just across the square from that hotel. The instructions that the owner had emailed us were *not* clear. It was quite dark by then.

The building was four storeys high, at least one hundred years old, with a narrow spiral staircase and a rickety two-person elevator. The walls in the hallways were a deep, dark wood, with lovely carved trimmings and details. It was winsome. Our flat was on the top floor and looked like it had been an attic in a previous incarnation, or rather a tiny corner of an attic. It had sheet-rocked walls painted stark white and hardly any amenities. Everything seemed to have been done on the cheap. One of the keys was missing, the kitchen lights did not work, and there was hardly any storage space. But it did have the basics (a dishwasher, a washer/dryer, and the comfiest bed) and was very clean, sans bugs, mice, or rats, so far.

We phoned the owner as requested to let him know we had arrived, then hit the sack about midnight, completely bagged.

Monday, June 7

The next morning, I woke up first and opened the shades to discover to my delight that our new, petite chez nous was airy and bright, and that the one very large window in the room faced south to let the sunshine in. Before me stretched a delicious hodgepodge of slanted, tiled Parisian rooftops with a mass of eccentric chimneys and quaint dormers, waiting no doubt for my oohs and aahs. So très Paris, so beautiful! The disarrangement of the buildings made the vista even more picturesque and enchanting. Could it be any better? Then I noticed, far off across the city, the Eiffel Tower. I was bedazzled.

We ventured out after breakfast to explore the neighbourhood and find some food. Was café life the only option? Montmartre, like much of Paris, is impossibly charming. It was so good for the soul, sheer joy to walk through the lovely, narrow streets, some paved, many with large stones as a surface. There were few cars. The buildings were also of stone, some with plaster finishes, and stood tall and slender and unperturbed by being squeezed on each side by their fellows. They snuggled up together with no breathing room and opened directly onto the street. We walked past an open doorway, and I could see a corridor leading to a light-filled room at the end. On the door was posted a handwritten announcement of the dinner being offered that night. I guessed it was a kind of mini restaurant, serving a tiny, local clientele delectable meals of high French gastronomy. I was too shy to enquire.

We stopped at a large, non-descript restaurant for lunch and had the veal plat du jour, which unfortunately was expensive and disappointing. We should have chosen a café. But we did take our leftovers away in a chien bag, probably not done in Paris, but aussi mal. The area was irresistible, and we continued to wander about, delighting in its beauty and savoring the ambience.

To my relief, we eventually stumbled upon a tiny grocery store that was well stocked and close to the flat. Food! The flat had a great selection of Paris travel books, so I spent the afternoon leafing through them. I thought about doing the Notre Dame walk tomorrow recommended by Rick Steves and hoped I could persuade Dale to come with me.

It was a very pleasant day and evening.

Tuesday, June 8

The next morning, Dale was resistant. (He is not keen on cities but did come to Paris with me so that he could say, yes, he had indeed been there.) He finally decided to come along. We took the Metro downtown, unnerved by how deep underground it was, but it was very fast. We got off at the Place de Concorde. Mon Dieu, quelle intersection! It was insanely busy. We made it across, admired the Lexar obelisk, bought a couple of galettes, then went into the Tuileries Jardins, where people were guillotined during the French Revolution, according to my travel guidebook. Yipes. No evidence of that now. The garden was okay, very spacious, and open with huge walkways made of crushed limestone, which gave it a kind of unfinished look, actually almost barren. We walked along, and there was the Louvre. I would never have recognized it from when I was there as a kid, but anyhow, voilà!

Off we moseyed to Notre Dame cathedral, such a beautiful work of art. I do like Gothic churches, but not for the religion of course. They are very beautiful, but what I like best about them is their ethereal, otherworldly, reverent feeling, invoking a sense of the mysterious and holy. You don't have to be Christian or religious to appreciate that. I know all about the evils of the church and am appalled at how they use the poor for nefarious ends—for example, in Africa, where birth control is frowned upon because more babies are wanted for the church. But they do know how to think big, and the cathedrals themselves are a wonderful expression of the simple and beautiful core of something even more profound than religion.

Dale wasn't having any of it though and wouldn't walk with me through the building. He sniffed and frowned. But I liked it and even went back in to pay my respects to Jeanne d'Arc, whom I had missed the first time through.

We puttered along the Rive Gauche, rejoicing in all the little book stalls, and arrived at Shakespeare and Co., the bookstore founded in 1919. Quelle disappointment. It was basically a present-day business, although with many very expensive older books. Dale bought a copy of *Howl* by Allen Ginsberg, which I thought a hilarious choice and indicative of the fact that the store itself did not evoke its era or heritage at all.

We got to the walk suggested by Steves down Rue Michel, which was wide and touristy. Dale suggested we venture instead down one of the narrow backstreets. What a treat! It was filled with locals of many different ethnicities and sizzled with energy and noise. Small shops abounded selling basic wares, and many humble eateries offered a myriad of different cuisines from far-off lands. Fabulous! This walk was through the Latin Quarter, and it did retain some of the medieval character it must have once had, albeit in modern dress.

This little foray made me less impressed with Steves' walks. I've never been much for travel guidebooks. There is a lot to be said for just wandering and following one's inclinations. You want to see the biggies of course and find out about important things, but you sort of do anyhow without slavishly following a set walk. I also like to have my own reactions to things and figure them out for myself, not have someone tell me everything.

We headed back to the flat. I was so tired and sore after all that walking that I suggested we stay in Montmartre the next day. Dale was okay with that.

Wednesday, June 9
The next day was low-key and pleasant although raining and gloomy. Our big effort was a visit to Sacre Coeur. We took the funicular up from Abbesses Square, which was fun and fast. We went inside—again, what a beautiful church! Again, I was transported. I wandered around, paid my respects again to Jeanne, and admired the incredible mosaic behind the altar. Again, Dale was having none of it. He stood by the exit and frowned at people trying to sneak in (they scurried away) and even at those leaving the right way. He had fun playing a bouncer for God.

Thursday, June 10
The next morning, I wanted to get an early start to see three museums today. Dale was not interested and opted to stay in the flat and work on the book he was writing. In his earlier years, he had hiked and worked in the North Cascades mountains and sketched numerous charcoal landscapes of the beautiful places he visited. He selected fifty of these drawings and compiled them into a book with a vignette from his life accompanying each one. This book drove him crazy and took him five years to complete. He decided to take this quiet day in Paris to work on it for a while.

I left about 10, much later than I had hoped. It was raining lightly. I hopped onto the Metro and headed along the route that I had mapped out yesterday. My first stop was the Pantheon, where it had started raining hard, and alas, I didn't have a brolly, only my light rain jacket. I was getting wet right through, so it was a relief to get inside. I didn't have any expectations about this building and didn't know very much about it, but even then, it was disappointing. It was an enormously tall, open, uncluttered cathedral-like structure but was not religious. Instead, it seemed to be a celebration of France's history: mostly of Sainte Genevieve (the patron saint of Paris), Jeanne as always, and lots of government men and warrior types. It was imposing, grand, and depressing. Was this all they had to celebrate in their history? There was also a crypt for the "grand hommes" of France. Not one woman at all. Oops, non, Madame Curie was there. The building seemed to me hardly worth the architecture. In fact, it seemed kind of lost, without a function big enough for it. It gets respectful write-ups in travel guidebooks though.

I did marvel, however, at its unused splendor. How could a building amongst so many ravishing and important buildings in Paris be so massively impressive and yet so empty and hollow? Africa has very few buildings of that era (the 1700s) and that gorgeous style. Most buildings there have defined uses. It seemed a sad irony in Paris to have so much and say so little. In Africa, there is very little, but there is much to say.

Outta there. The rain had stopped, and it was getting downright hot. I hoofed it across to my second stop, the Archaeological Crypt Museum under Notre Dame square. Fortunately, it wasn't busy. The crypt was the ruins of the many streets and structures that had been built on the site in Roman times and that were used until the cathedral was built on top in 1168.

It was dark and dank and yes, crypt-like. The first thing I noticed was the smell of pee, an eternal mark of humanity, I guess. Ugh. The layout and information were hard to follow. Perhaps it was my jetlag, but anything somewhat complicated I just could not take in. The crypt was interesting for its age though because the ancients had been a draw for me since childhood. But I didn't want to linger.

It was getting on and I decided to bag Sainte-Chapelle, my third stop. It had been a full day although short. I found it a bit nerve wracking at times trying to negotiate the Metro, but at one point I had to stop and think that for several years as a young person, I had agoraphobia and panic disorder so incapacitating I could hardly walk to the corner store by myself to buy a pack of smokes. Now here I was zooming all over Paris: riding the Metro, tromping here and there through crowded tourist sites, walking up and down busy streets, and all alone. It was a feat to have recovered from that difficult time, one of the big successes of my life. I gave myself a modest pat on the back. Très bien, moi!

When I got back, I was beat. We had dinner chez nous, I took it easy for the evening and then conked out. Dale had a good, very restful day in the flat working on his book. I think he had fun.

Friday, June 11

I realized yesterday that we had only two more days in Paris. We had been so tired and low-key that time had quickly slipped by. Maybe we hadn't seen as much as we could have, but on the other hand, it had been healing. What better place to hang out? Paris is so beautiful and good for the psyche that you don't have to do much to feel utterly rejuvenated.

Today, we went to the one musée that Dale wanted to see: the Orsay, the reconverted railway station that now houses beaucoup de Impressionist art. We got out of the flat about 9:45 and zoomed off. At one point, I wasn't sure we were on the right street, so I asked a guy who was walking toward me, "Orsay?" He answered, "Non, la." I got it! I tried to use French as much as possible, which wasn't very much of course, but still it was wonderful to have people understand me. I was also amazed that I understood others at times: par example, on the Metro, an older man beside me said as we pulled up to a stop, "Pardonez, madame, descendez?" Got that too! I stammered out, "Non, non," and tried to get out of his way. Another time on the Metro, a lady sat down beside us with a petit noir et blanc chat in a carry-on case. We told her we had a little one comme ça chez nous. This one's name was Felicia. Ours was Bess. The lady was very kind about my trying to use a petite de mon français with her. It was très sweet.

People were on the whole quite nice, with one very occasional exception, the young shopgirls. Some were tolerant of my stumbling Français, others not so much. They mistook me for a Parisienne, I thought, and then wondered why I was talking like an idiot. Hey, it was kind of a compliment. My pronunciation was not terrible. It was good to have had that grounding in high school French in Canada. Also, I finally lost my shyness thanks to teaching, so I was less inhibited about talking although I still suffered a lot. But I just tried to tell myself that it wasn't the end of the world if I said something wrong and looked like a total and complete imbecile, and people fell on the ground laughing. As David Sedaris said, "One day I hope to graduate from speaking like an evil baby to speaking like a hillbilly."[1]

The Musée d'Orsay was très cool, with renos along each side of the building to create two levels with individual rooms for paintings. The main part of the gallery, the long area running down the middle of the station, was completely open to the ceiling and filled with statuary. Natural light poured in from massive skylights in this central part, and the openness and spaciousness were exhilarating.

The paintings were phenomenal. The variety of work all under the "Impressionism" umbrella was surprisingly big. I had no idea. Van Gogh's work I have always found a bit distressing. Some of the paintings I was expecting to find were not there, on holiday somewhere I guessed. Many were familiar, like old friends. But the best was the statues. I especially liked *Young Aristotle* by Charles Degeorge. A thin teenage boy sat reading, but his legs were those of a full-grown man, as if his very molecules were changing themselves because of what he was learning. I loved it and could relate, being passionate all my life about reading, although my legs are skinnier. The painting I liked best was Van Gogh's self-portrait, utterly heartbreaking.

For the first time ever, I got going to a museum/art gallery. I guess I had always thought of it like a contest. Which painting is the best? But this time there was so much variety that it was impossible not to appreciate a slew of them. So many were amazing. The artist was trying to do something different or had something worthy to say. I began to appreciate each one individually. At the end of the tour, I felt like I had escaped the normal, everyday (but interesting) world I live in and had seen such beauty, visited exquisite landscapes, beheld unimagined sights that I was forever changed. I realized (little bookworm that I have always been) that painting, sculpture, the visual arts in sum, were truly a profound art form that I had for the first time really seen (you should forgive the pun).

Dale (the artist) was not so impressed. He said that no one and nothing there had taught him anything. I paid him no mind and could only be humbled and grateful to view these treasures that many people in the world would love to see but were unable to for various reasons, such as extreme poverty.

After a fast jaunt to the Eiffel Tower (very big, very packed with tourists), we decided to take the #69 bus, recommended in one of the travel books. The weather had turned hot, and Dale was tired, so a bus ride sounded good.

I checked out the map and realized that if we took the bus almost to the end of its route, we could get the Metro there almost directly back to the flat, a*nd* we would just happen to be at Pere Lachaise cemetery and could go and see Jim Morrison's grave. Too cool!

It was odd being in the cemetery. It was peaceful and not creepy at all, even quite scenic with lots of trees and interesting tombs. Who knew? Morrison's tomb was by far the busiest place in the cemetery. We weren't sure where it was but walked in the general direction and started seeing more and more people, and we found it that way. The tomb itself was quite impressive but a little sad, strewn with cigarette butts, scraggly flowers, and faded and wrinkly pix of Morrison. About ten or twelve people were clustered around the grave, while others waited patiently behind them for someone to leave so they could step forward to pay their respects. Respectful it was too, quiet, with soft murmurs, and gentle and polite comings and goings. I felt that Jim was happy people had come, happy and a bit surprised to be remembered, but still a restless, outré soul.

I was thrilled to have seen his tomb although it wasn't high on my list of places to visit, but Jim was of the era of my brilliant youth, and I remembered him fondly. Dale was very sweet. It was nice of him to accommodate me. We went back to the flat by the Metro and hung out for the evening, pleasantly tuckered out.

Saturday, June 12

Given all my tearing around the last two days, I voted to hang out in Montmartre today. Dale worked on his book. I lazed about in the flat and read a short story by Stephen King. Yipes, my first and last. In the evening, we walked up to Sacre Coeur to watch the light show on the Eiffel Tower. It was pleasant although very busy with masses of tourists. Paris is so marvellous, however, that even the crowds can't diminish it. I delighted in it, so romantique, so bohème. It was smashing!

This was our last full day in Paris . . .

As I wrote this chapter, I was overwhelmed to remember the magnificence of this spectacular city. Even though I was trying to help one of the poorest places in the world and even though I was in seventh heaven to be visiting

Paris again, I don't think I ever quite got what a feat of accomplishment the city is. Centuries and centuries of the accumulation of outstanding architecture, art, culture, and civilization is there for anyone on the planet to visit and celebrate its splendor and beauty. It is surely one of the peaks of human achievement. But you probably gotta have some money or backing to visit. Most people who are deprived of the basics of a good life, such as good health care, good food, peace, safety, and enough earnings to have some disposable income, likely cannot reap the joy of visiting this paragon of cities. It was evidence, I realize now, of yet more injustice in the world.

Sunday June 13
We left today, unwillingly. We had time for one last jaunt into the city before we had to catch the train to Amsterdam.

I was keen to see the bird market that a friend had told us about years ago, which sounded enchanting. Off we zoomed on the Metro to Île de la Cité station. It was very busy because—I finally realized—it was Sunday, and tout le monde was out and about. The bird market was right next to the station, nestled in the huge flower market. We walked through it. Oh dear, it was very sad, not what I expected. It was cage after cage of little birds, some terrified, some hen-pecked by its cage mate, all so little and vulnerable and pretty. It made me ashamed to be human that we would cage and maltreat these little creatures. Dale had the same reaction but mostly about their lack of freedom. We didn't stay long. As we were leaving, Dale said, "Okay, you create a diversion, and I'll run through and open up all their cages and set them free." A tender thought, Dale, thanks.

Disappointed and blue, we crossed over to Île Saint-Louis. We walked the streets (just too cute and picturesque), chomped on patisseries (so-so), listened to a group of street musicians (excellent), and generally did the blissed-out Paris thing. It was warm and sunny but still not too hot. Could heaven itself be any better? Africa was a distant, fuzzy memory. The contrast between the two could not be more acute, but today vague thoughts of the extraordinary unfairness of life barely surfaced.

Alas, it was time to go. We took the Metro back to the flat, gathered up our stuff, and caught a cab to the Gare du Nord (huge, busy). The three-hour train to Amsterdam was agreeable, back to the green and treed countryside. Dale was much happier. In Amsterdam, we took a cab to our hotel and saw Susan and Sarah, who had arrived safely that day. We went out for dinner, then Dale and I scooted back to our room and hit the sack.

Monday, June 14

We got up at 6 a.m. to get to the airport by 8 a.m. so we could get seats together. We found a cab right away, but alas, even so early, we *still* didn't get seats together. I cried. All that time (an eight-hour flight) without Dale? What if the plane crashed and we were not together? But I started to feel marginally better eventually.

The rest of the gang turned up, and we all trundled onto the plane. When Dale had to leave me to go sit by himself, he looked choked up, which made me feel a bit better. The plane left at 11 a.m. local time, and the trip was long and tedious. I was socked in the exact middle of the plane between two guys. I tried to watch a movie but could not get the function to work, dozed and slept a lot, watched an episode of *Frasier* and two of *Sex and the City*, and admired how well done both shows were. The time passed, slowly.

We arrived at Kilimanjaro Airport at 8:15 p.m. local time. I had booked the Bristol Cottages' van to pick us all up, but alas, it was not there, so we bundled into two taxis and left for Moshi. Again, with that romantic drive through the African night, but this time, there was more electricity everywhere. Things seemed slightly more prosperous, some new buildings had appeared, and the older ones looked somewhat tarted up. I was happy to see that but a bit sad about all the lights.

We arrived at Bristol Cottages, which was pretty and even nicer than usual because it was still the rainy season, and everything was green. We got settled in and then we all met for a beer in the dining room and listened to complaints, mostly from Susan, about the cost of the cabs and the lack of a group discount from Bristol Cottages. It was unsettling.

Then the missing van pulled in. I went to check with the driver about what had happened with our pick-up. Suddenly Susan appeared beside me and started berating the guy for not getting us and costing us $100 for the taxis. I was outraged. How dare she treat a service person like that? I stayed only a little longer, said my goodnights, and tripped off to bed to follow Dale, who had left earlier. I had a hard time getting to sleep I was so annoyed at them all. Oy, so not a good start.

Tuesday, June 15

The next morning, our first day in Moshi, started slowly. It was noon before everyone was up. We had lunch together and then had an orientation meeting in the dining room. I made the following speech:

> Great to be here with all of you! Glad you could come. Looking forward to our visit to you. We are now officially the OK-7!!
>
> I think this meeting today is a good idea to discuss what we want to do and to get organized for doing stuff in the village. I do want to reiterate things that we talked about back home in Canada which are important to remember.
>
> Dale and I and the AVPA are not a tour company or travel agents. All of us are here now in the relationship of friends. The AVPA is very small and fairly new, and we do not have the capability to officially take volunteers. You are responsible for yourselves and your own well-being on this trip.
>
> Things will go wrong. This is Africa. We need to expect that things might be difficult. So let's be pleasantly surprised when things go well (they will!). And if they do not, let's remember the 30 percent rule: only about 30 percent of projects done in Africa are successful. For example, something obviously went wrong with the Bristol Cottages van last night. But there is no point in getting outraged about it.
>
> Let's also remember that back in Canada, we decided not to complain about things. It is just too demoralizing and unproductive. Things can screw up, we would be better trying to solve the problems and not complaining.

For example, if you are unhappy with Bristol Cottages, you certainly don't have to stay here. There are other hotels and places that might suit you better. Also, please remember that I did the booking here as a favour. I probably shouldn't have since you are responsible for you own travel arrangements. So let's not get all bent out of shape that we did not get a group rate—it is just not worth it.

This brings me to the final point: money. I know people have different comfort levels with spending money. Some don't mind spending; others don't like it much. But one rule of thumb I have about spending money in Africa is to compare the prices here with those back home. Most things are cheaper, so I usually just pay.

Also, I keep in mind how poor Tanzania is, one of the poorest countries in the world. The average income is US$1 per day if you have a job. The population is about thirty-nine million, a little more than Canada (2010). Unemployment is estimated at about 50 percent. The disparity between Canada and Tanzania is huge, so I'm usually happy to just pay the asking price and to tip generously.

I also try to remember why we are here: to help an African village achieve self-sufficiency and improve its standard of living. Just by being here and spending our tourist dollars, we are helping the country. That is my ultimate goal: to help Okaseni and Tanzania, not to get the cheapest rates or the best deals for everything.

I hoped they got the message.

After all that, the first order of the day was to get some money. Sarah and I went to one of the small exchange places and cashed some traveller's cheques. We walked back to the hotel to meet Dale et al., but everyone had left. Hmm . . . we ventured back out and saw them all were walking back to the hotel—with Melki! It was great to see him, although I thought he looked a bit funny, sort of guilty? Shy? Intimidated? He looked uneasy, not as confident and vigorous as I remembered.

We went back to the hotel and had a beer and chatted to Melki about all the things that we hoped to do. He was very amenable, of course. What's not to say no? He asked Lara if she would teach a math class at the high school. There were a lot of things we could do. Sarah and I made a list, and I realized we could easily spend all the money we had, and more.

Late in the afternoon, Melki headed back to Okaseni and the rest of us headed out for dinner at a restaurant that Susan had noticed. It was awful. Dale and I had the chicken, which was as tough as the proverbial nails. I could not finish mine. Back at the hotel, we hung out on the patio, and Sarah set up the OK-7 blog and did the first entry. I was so tired that I headed for our room early and conked out. Dale too.

Wednesday, June 16

Today was a great day. Melki arrived at about 10 a.m. He had arranged for a dala dala, a van or minibus that you could hire for yourself or hop on one that went along a set route. This was an excellent choice for us and a good price. We scrambled in and left for Okaseni. It took about half an hour to drive the 10 km there. I had forgotten how bumpy the road was. We went first to the primary school where we were greeted by Justin, the head teacher, and another teacher, Felix Kimbi, who taught math. He and Melki talked to Lara about teaching the math class. Felix was a very kind and earnest guy and later told me the school needed Class 6 textbooks. The government had changed the syllabus but hadn't sent them any money for the textbooks, so they didn't have a single copy. He gave us a list of what they needed, and I told him we would buy some.

We marvelled at the lights in the teachers' room, where we were sitting. Wilhelm had finished the installation, and the whole school sparkled with brightness. Dale said it looked very clean and that Wilhelm had done a good job. I was delighted! Then I asked Justin if he could show me the books that we had sent in the shipping container, expecting to see an adorable wee library filled with those thousand books. Justin took us down a hallway to a small cupboard hanging on the wall. He opened it with a key, and inside we saw about twenty little books propped up haphazardly on the shelves.

I was stunned and speechless. It took me awhile to realize that the rest had disappeared.

We went to the village office where we picked up a dozen tree seedlings for a coffee transplanting ceremony on a nearby farm. We bundled into the dala dala, each carrying a couple of pots of seedlings, and drove to the farm. On the way, we passed many coffee shrubs on the properties of the villagers grown from the seeds we had bought in 2007. How gratifying! We had indeed accomplished something worthwhile. When we got to the farm, each of us transplanted a seedling, helped by two younger guys who dug the holes, added fertilizer, etc. They were really sweet, very nice.

We visited with the person who owned the farm. He was an older, retired man who wanted to start a dispensary on his property. He had a small building good to go, but no supplies, so he asked Diane if she could get him a microscope. I admired his ambition although the chances of success seemed practically nil. But perhaps we could do something as Diane had already mentioned setting up a dispensary in Okaseni.

Next, we went to the village office to see the sewing machines that we sent in the shipping container. Three machines had been set up and three girls were sitting at them sewing. A woman was standing there too. A fourth girl was sitting by the window at another long, narrow machine. I was thrilled and looked around at them all with delight. It dawned on me that the woman might be Happy. "No," she said, and pointed to the girl by the window. I realized she was at the knitting machine that the AVPA had leased to her. I was beaming for joy this point. Then I realized that the woman was Justine, whom we had met in 2007, and that this small room was a sewing school, the girls were the students, and she was the teacher. Wow!

Dale and I tried to figure out which sewing machine might have been my grandmother's, the one Charleen and I had donated to the project. We took many pix to show Charleen. Justine offered me a kenga and wrapped me up in it. Much laughter! Pix were taken of her and me, and she hugged and kissed me. Aww! I was over the moon about this successful sewing centre. How sensational it was that Justine was now teaching the young ones.

After all this excitement, we headed back to Bristol Cottages, where I conked out. Everyone else rested too.

This young person is learning a skill that will serve her well.
Her machine might have been my grandmother's.

When I woke up, I stayed abed and unfortunately had the chance to mull over a couple of run-ins I had had with Melki. The first was at the planning meeting on Tuesday. He and Susan seemed quite taken with one another, and he agreed to accompany her as she researched the local coffee industry for the AVPA. They talked about checking out some of the coffee farms in the village.

He asked her, "Are you okay to walk?"

"Yes, I am," she said. "No problem."

"Sheena can't walk," he said and started laughing and laughing, just chuckles, not howls of laugher or guffaws, but he would not stop.

I said, "Yes, I wasn't able to walk much last time because of the kidney stone."

Still, he kept laughing and laughing.

Exasperated, I snarled at him, "Ha. Ha. Ha." This did shut him up. Finally.

The second run-in was today as we were walking back from the coffee farm. Dale and I were a little ahead of Melki and Susan, who were talking about a safari that Susan and her husband were planning to take when he joined her in Moshi the next week.

Melki started laughing and said, "Sheena didn't go see the lions." I guessed he was implying that I was too scared and timid to go see them. That was it. I kind of snapped.

I turned to him and said, "Please stop that, Melki. Just cut it out. I don't like it. It's not nice."

Would he shut up? No. So I kept repeating it while he kept yapping and yapping.

"Well, I was just saying that you haven't seen the wild animals."

"Yes, we have," I said. "We went on a safari on our first visit here." That slowed him down a bit. I kept repeating myself until finally he apologized—and stopped.

Always slow on the uptake, I couldn't believe that he thought such behaviour was okay. Perhaps chumming around with Susan had emboldened him, thinking he might have an ally. His hostility brought back many bad memories about how he and Tumaini acted on our first visit. In this last year or so, I had lost patience with the world. Self-effacing, humble, accommodating, I was always ready to give people a break despite their unacceptable behaviour. This behaviour was not egregious, just common meanness and put-downs. I had always been shy and that prevented me from calling people out on their snide comments and spitefulness. But something in me had changed. I was done putting up with this bad behaviour and was now more than ready to tell Melki to stop it. Dale said later that Melki was quite subdued after I did. Good.

Anyhow, back to the day. I phoned Salma to invite her for dinner tonight. It was grand to see her, and she could hardly stop hugging me! We trundled off to the Indo-Italian restaurant where we discussed the microcredit program, went over the paperwork, pondered the future, and even kicked around ideas to help the young men. It was brilliant.

It was a pretty good day overall, despite a certain someone.

Thursday, June 17

Our big goal of the day was to get money. We walked down to Chase where the kind person we had been dealing with since 2007 told us that, alas, we could not get cash advances on our Visas anymore. I guess the 2008 financial global meltdown had put the kibosh on those transactions forever. I was prepared for this, however, and had a Plan B: ask Charleen to wire money to us through Western Union.

Melki turned up, and Dale and I had a quick meeting with him to discuss funding the school fees and electricity for now. I also told him about an idea I was keen about: getting chickens for the villagers, one for every household. Melki said no. The climate did not suit chickens. They were vulnerable to viruses and needed vaccinations to protect them, which were expensive, as were the doctors' fees for that service. The chickens also needed to be kept warm, so they would require a heating system and an airtight coop. It was disappointing but did explain why I never saw chickens in the village. Then Melki said that it was possible to raise broiler chickens for eating. Oh dear. They would be raised from baby chicks. That was a viable business. Gulp. I said thanks, I would think about it.

Melki left to jaunt around with Susan finding out about coffee. Diane, Lara, and Wayne went to the Christian Bookstore to get some textbooks (their personal donation to the AVPA) and then left to volunteer at a local orphanage.

Dale and I enjoyed some quiet time by ourselves and had lunch at the hotel. We discussed what else we could fund on this trip and had a brain wave that a computer might be useful. It would be easier to stay in touch with Melki and helpful to him and the villagers as well. We could get two perhaps, one for the village office and one for the primary school. Printers too would be good. This sounded like a plan.

Susan and Melki turned back up. They had gone out for lunch and had a great time exploring Moshi. Melki really liked Susan. She was his kind of woman (strapping).

Nuria arrived at the hotel. We were so happy to see each other that we cried. She said she had had malaria and did look a bit frail and thin. We chatted for a bit and then I asked her about buying goats. She told us there was a market near Moshi where you could get them for US$25 each. This was excellent news and much better than the $100 and $180 goats that Tumaini had been talking about. Melki and Susan joined us. We told Melki we wanted to get cheaper goats from the local market. He looked as if we had hit him in the stomach, just awful, as if he were going to cry. We continued yakking about getting a truck, securing the goats for transport, preparing the village. He still looked awful and was glaring at me with hate and anger, like he wanted to kill me.

I had no idea what was going on. Nuria noticed it as well and thought she had done something wrong. Dale didn't notice anything. I thought perhaps I had done something, always a possibility with Melki.

I asked him, "Is this okay? Can you handle this? Are you okay?"

"No, it is fine," he said. "I'm just worried about the truck."

"No worries," I said. "We'll pay."

"Well," he said. "I am still worried about the truck."

Yeah, right. Dale said afterwards that Melki had probably made a deal with someone and was going to get a kickback. That would explain his reaction.

Nuria left soon after, still upset about Melki's behaviour. Melki left too. I phoned Charleen about sending more money. The others returned from the orphanage, where they had a wonderful time, and told us sweet stories about the kids. Susan mentioned to me out of the blue that Melki had told her tipping wasn't appropriate. Seriously? She was so cheap. I told her that I was still going to tip, generously too, given how much money we had compared to Africans. She feigned not to hear me.

Another fun day with not fun people.

Nuria and I are best friends forever.

Friday, June 18

The first chore for the day was to get the money that we hoped Charleen had sent. Melki arrived to take Susan to a coffee board meeting in Moshi. Late as usual. He still didn't look happy but at least not like he wanted to kill me.

Dale and I went off to get the loot. It had arrived. We left most of it in the hotel safe. At 11 p.m. Melki and Susan arrived back from their meeting, and we all left for the high school near Okaseni where Lara was to teach the math class. George, John's older brother, kindly ferried us around for the day. At the school, we signed the guest book and met the academic mistress. Lara and the math teacher talked for about half an hour about what she should teach. We scheduled an English class for next Thursday, to which Susan objected. Of course. She said we should try and do it today (no, too short notice), and that we were leaving Thursday (yes, but in the evening). She also commented that we were getting very booked up. (Yes, and that was a good thing.) She did not seem keen on doing much except swan around with Melki.

With all this going on, Dale became quite upset and told me this was all a complete waste of time. I said that we could leave if he wanted. Lara seemed fine about the teaching, and the others went with her to watch her class. Dale and I weren't needed for anything else, so we slipped away and asked George to take us back to Moshi.

Back at Bristol Cottages, Dale felt better. We allotted funds to the various projects, got some envelopes for this money, asked the infinitely kind Mr. Aggarwal for the use of his van, and sallied forth to buy the computers for the office and school. After much back and forth between two stores, and a quick trip back to the hotel for more money, we bought two laptop computers and two printer/photocopiers. We had now spent nearly all the money Charleen sent us, except for a bit still with Mr. Aggarwal.

The gang arrived back at the hotel. They said Lara's class was fantastic. The students loved her and her prizes and jokes. Lara told us that their regular teacher made some critical mistakes for teaching, such as standing in front of the board, mumbling, and such. (I wonder now as I write this if she ever realized why.) After the class, they did a tour of the Okaseni coffee farms and nearby plantations, which they all enjoyed.

Melki took Dale for lunch at the local Police Mess Hall. Dale said it was gross. The cook was using a meat cleaver to chop up chickens to cook, and bits of bone and flesh were flying everywhere, splattering the tables, dishes, and customers. The cook then used the cleaver to move the food around on the grill. Dale could hardly stomach it. He told me later that he felt Melki wanted to ask him something or get something from him but didn't. He chickened out maybe? (You should excuse the pun.)

I gave Diane and Lara US$500 for school materials and went with them to help buy the textbooks, exercise books, and chalk. Diane and I got the exercise books from a general goods store and took them back to the hotel. Dale arrived back from lunch, washed the flecks of meat and bone off himself, and then he and I went down to the bookstore to help Lara with the texts. Oh dear, what a muddle. Lara had made a mistake in the purchasing and was trying to return several books about 30 minutes after closing time. It finally all got straightened out.

Diane told me later that she had passed a boy about six years old lying unconscious by the side of the main road. She checked his pulse. He had one, but his breathing was fast and shallow. She surmised he had been hit by a car and that someone had pushed him off the road onto the shoulder. There was a medical clinic a block away, so she picked him up and carried him there. It was a sorry excuse of a clinic in a rundown building with hardly any equipment or staff. The receptionist told Diane to put the boy over in a corner and someone would look at him later. Diane left him there and came back to the hotel quite shaken. So was I on hearing the story.

Everyone went out for dinner except for Dale and me. We ate at the hotel, and then staggered exhausted to our room where we stayed quietly till morning.

Saturday, June 19

I got ten hours solid sleep but still felt beat in the morning. We were to be picked up at 9:30 a.m. for the 10 a.m. meeting of the village council. I wrote my speech for the meeting, asked Sarah to help me with flyers for the council about the goats, got the computer presents organized, and packaged up gifts for the council (Canadian flag pins that Susan had gotten from the government).

Fortunately, the van arrived late, at 11. Melki's undermining me again? Off we went to Okaseni. The meeting began. Melki welcomed us all, got us to introduce ourselves, and gave us presents: kengas and shawls for the women and shirts for the guys. He then reviewed the projects that the AVPA had done and the ones we hoped to do. The translator was a very nice older guy who did a great job. He didn't have an agenda or include a running commentary, just did an excellent word-for-word translation that was very clear.

I stood up and gave my speech. I said how happy we were to be back and to see them, and that we thought of them as friends. I thanked Melki and Salma for their sterling help and then introduced the volunteers. I reminded the crowd that the AVPA was very small and didn't have much money, and that we did not get paid for our work and paid all the expenses, but that we wanted to still fund the power installations, the school fees, and the water system upgrades.

Then I asked them about the goats. We suggested the meat goats at US$25 per adult goat but left it up to them to decide which kind they wanted. They opted for milking (pregnant) goats at US$180 each. I was very disappointed because that meant far fewer goats to go around. But our modus operandi was to do what the villagers wanted, so I could not say no. By this point, I knew that "villagers" meant the "village council," and that the village council would get the goats. When we sent the bikes in the container in 2008, I expected they would have a lottery to give everyone a chance, as they did for the school kids and their fees. I had asked Melki a few days ago who got the bikes we sent. "The council," he answered blithely, with absolutely no shame. I knew without a doubt that the same sense of entitlement would apply to the goats too. I did not have the wherewithal then to suggest a lottery, and that I regret to this day.

The meeting continued. We gave them the computers and printer/copiers. They applauded like crazy. It was uplifting to see familiar faces and a couple of new ones, and I was touched looking at them. They seemed more hopeful and trusting than before, like they believed we *would* do what we said we would. But I got the feeling that life had not changed much in the day-to-day for them and that it was still very difficult.

Melki and the council members who
got some of the fourteen bikes we sent
to Okaseni in the shipping container.

The speech did go well. Afterwards, even Melki said it was good. (Go figure!) Wayne mumbled "Good job," but no one else said much. Oh, well. I realized later that I had hardly been nervous. Who'd have thought I used to be a shy, panic-stricken wee thing? I felt I should quietly congratulate myself, suffering as I had from shyness so acute that I rarely said anything in a group of more than one person, as well as from panic disorder. This speech and my roaming around Paris by myself were evidence I had conquered them. Now I cannot be shut up.

We were then dismissed by Melki so the council could continue their regular meeting. Back to Moshi we went where we had a rest break and then decided to go check out the goat market even though those goats were a no-go for the council.

The market was not too far from town, out in the country past the verdant slopes of Mount Kilimanjaro. It was on a large, dry, rolling plain with a few hills off here and there in the distance. The market itself was a huge, sparsely treed area of brown, dusty dirt surrounded by a low stone wall. By this time (mid-afternoon), the sales were over, and it was quiet. Even so, you could get a sense of what it must have been like earlier in the day: bedlam.

Near the entrance was a huge cattle pen filled with massive, horned cows that didn't look very happy. They were beef cattle apparently, poor things. There were also some scraggly looking goats and a few Masai here and there. In the distance was a small crowd of more Masai and more livestock. We didn't venture closer. George, our driver, told us the Masai were very rich and that they did most of the selling at this market. They got good prices, I guessed. They also didn't want their pictures taken unless they got money, and it wasn't cheap: US$20 per pic. They are not my favourite group, given their tradition of female mutilation, and I would never try to help them, not that they need help actually. They have done well materially on this great, complicated continent.

They do make a striking picture, however, and evoke a romanticized image of Africa. The market itself seemed like the essence of Africa, exotic in a rustic kind of way. To my surprise, I noticed across the road a huge truck like the one Ralph and I rode on across the Sahara. I walked over to take a look. It was not a MAN truck but a Scania. Close enough! A wave of gratitude flooded me for having survived that difficult journey.

We left about 3 p.m. and drove back to Moshi and through the central marketplace. It was a-humming! Filled to the max with people milling around, it was colourful, lively, and filled with energy and power. That was so good to see and très Africa.

We walked en masse to the Indo-Italian restaurant for dinner, passing the usual disabled people and lepers on their blankets with pens, baubles, and such to sell. A couple of our volunteers stopped to take pictures of them. NO, I wanted to shout. DO NOT TAKE PIX. These people are not here as novelties to make your trip interesting. They have lives you obviously cannot even begin to imagine. You could at the least drop some money into their collection tins, for goodness sake. But I gulped back my words.

Anyhow, on to the restaurant. The dinner was good, but out of the seven orders, the waiter, whose name was God, got only two right. It was funny and none of us, including Susan for a change, got perturbed about it. We moseyed back to Bristol Cottages by twos and threes and then hung out in the dining room for the evening. I chatted with Sarah about her parents, whom I have known since high school, regaling her with tales of their past. It was fun for both of us. Dale left for our room to work on his book. I went to the patio to help Diane and Lara work on their materials for the school classes on Monday. Susan joined us and read us her blog (tonight) and Wayne and Lara's (last night). Susan said something in her blog that really offended me, and I kind of snapped at her. Oh, dear. I *instantly* regretted it. Everyone else was still there, and I looked like an idiot. Susan was really pissed off. I took her aside and apologized profusely. She was not appeased.

I went back to our room, complained to Dale, and went to bed. As I was falling asleep, I had a vision of a large pair of feet, all with broken toes. Weird. Susan had broken a toe a couple of days ago, and that's what it looked like, times ten.

Sunday, June 20

Sheesh, what a day!

It started at breakfast. Susan joined Dale and me. Still annoyed about last night and out for revenge, she began complaining about her room at Bristol Cottages, and how she had gotten stuck in a room by herself, and how I had forced her to do this, and how Diane also felt like she hadn't had a choice about the rooms either. I blew up and said that I should *never* have arranged the rooms for them, that I had only done it as a favour, and that they were supposed to be responsible for themselves. I stomped off to check with Diane. Still Susan would not shut up. She continued complaining to Dale, and *he* blew up and said she was a big ball and chain, and that the AVPA was 90 percent my project (he being the other 10 percent), and that she was trying to hog it. Whoa, he was pissed! Susan started crying and left. Hmm . . . she could dish it out but couldn't take it.

Diane looked a little sick when I talked to her, so I felt she probably had sided with Susan on her complaints. But she was fairly nice and did not add any complaints of her own. I was so angry though that I didn't want anything to do with the lot of them. Fortuitously, Dale and I were booked for the night at the Parkview, a nearby hotel, because our room at Bristol Cottages had an earlier booking for this night. Dale and I marched off to the Parkview, registered, and then zoomed back to grab our stuff and scram.

Also fortuitously, nothing had been planned for today, so Dale and I mostly rested at the Parkview in our large, sunny room or by the pool in the courtyard. It was very nice and very quiet. Nuria had invited us all to her place for dinner that evening, and I wasn't sure what to do. Dale said not to worry. At about 4 p.m., Diane and Lara turned up, very apologetic and afraid we would write the lot of them off. Lara said Susan was difficult.

I appreciated them coming over to make amends and said that we should all got to Nuria's as planned for dinner, despite the fracas.

So off we went. Happily, it was a lovely evening. Nuria's house was on the outskirts of Moshi. It was smallish by Western standards, with two bedrooms, a front room/dining room, and kitchen, all very tiny. It also had indoor plumbing. Nuria took us outside to see the chicken house that money we sent her had bought. It was a sturdy cinder-and-block construction behind the main house and large enough to store a dump truck. She was nearly in tears and hugged and hugged me with gratitude. She now had a business and was making money.

She showed us the rest of her property. The lot was long and narrow with a few shrubs here and there. Behind the chicken house was a very small shed made of twigs and mud which, we found out later, she rented out. The word "hovel" came to mind, and it was hard to think that a person could actually live in there. Then she told me about her family, especially her beloved mother, who had built the house in which they were living. Nuria had inherited it, and it was in her name only. She was a very smart and resourceful person.

Back inside, we chatted and socialized. Diane tried on the beautiful dress that Anisa, the older daughter, had been wearing, and then Anisa gave it to her. Fatima, the younger daughter, started crying because her mum said she might not be there for ever. I got very scared for Nuria and worried. She did look frail. But it was gratifying to be with her, and her hospitality was touching. I think everyone else enjoyed it too, and all seemed well, which was a big relief after the day.

Monday, June 21

We got up at 6:30 this morning because today was the big day, filled with planned teaching, gift-giving, coffee tours, and a meeting with the micro-credit women in Okaseni. John Mchau came with us; we were so pleased to have his company.

But what a mess. We had a careful schedule planned, which got completely mixed up. First, George, our driver was over half-an-hour late. Then, Melki had gotten the times wrong for the teaching, the gift-giving ceremony, and the microcredit meeting. Three out of three. (This happened frequently as you might have noticed, but ever the innocent, I only realized years later that he had likely done this on purpose with malevolent intent to screw things up for me.)

However, each event by itself was very good. At the Okaseni primary school, Lara taught a math class, and Diane taught an English class. Both were superb! It's always interesting watching other people teach: one of the best ways to improve one's own skills. Then all the students, teachers, and the OK-7 gathered outside the school for the gift giving. We gave the books, textbooks, paper, and other supplies to Melki and Felix, the teacher who had requested the texts. The students lined up, and we doled out pens, notebooks, and pins. They seemed a bit usure about this bounty and clutched their goodies close.

Dale, Susan, and I left for the village office, where we were late (thanks, Melki) to meet the microcredit women for a workshop that Susan was going to teach. Salma was there and introduced us to the women, who seemed subdued and unfriendly (shy perhaps?). I was so pleased to finally meet them in person. Susan started her class. It turned out she could teach. She told me later that the lesson was a crap shoot because she didn't know how much the women knew, so she talked about basic planning and evaluating the plan periodically. Salma was very pleased. She said that was exactly what the women needed and that she and the trainers had focused on handling the money and paying the loans back, not on running the actual businesses. While Susan was teaching, I watched the faces of the women and could see they were getting lot out of it.

Afterwards, Salma and I talked about improving the income/donations for Okaseni. Her idea was to open up Okaseni to volunteers and visitors who were already in Tanzania to volunteer, climb Kilimanjaro, and/or do a safari. They could come to the village to see what the AVPA had done and what a difference it has made. It sounded good. I also told her about the possible poultry project that Melki had mentioned. She was positive about this as well.

The rest of the crew turned up in George's van and then left with Susan for Peter Mchau's place to see some coffee processing and go on a coffee tour. Salma drove Dale and me back to Moshi and over lunch at the Parkview, we talked about John how we could help him. He was having trouble furthering his education. She said that many Tanzanian colleges often didn't want students to do well because they wanted to keep the standards low. Oh dear. My teacher's heart was wounded. I wondered if Dale and I might be able to help him.

Salma mentioned offhand that she needed a laptop. Dale and I both thought—yes! She could stay in touch with us easily, keep the microcredit records efficiently, and document results and progress (or lack of it). It would also be a way to partially pay her back for her pro bono administration of the program. We all zipped over to the computer store and bought her one. She was pleased; we were pleased. Win, win, win!

Dale and I went back to the Parkview where he lolled about and I went for a swim. The pool was unheated and getting in was a shock, but then it wasn't bad. I did laps for about 25 invigorating minutes. My body sang the swim electric. (Sorry, Walt.) In the evening, I wrote in my journal, and Dale watched TV. It had been a satisfactory day despite the scheduling mishaps.

Tuesday, June 22

The big item on today's agenda was to get the second wire transfer from Charleen. It eventually arrived. Diane and I had talked to Melki about setting up a dispensary in Okaseni, and he had arranged for a room in a private house near the village office, so I gave funds to Sarah and Diane to get medical supplies and a cabinet. They went in the van with George. Dale, Melki, and John went to Tanesco, Tanzania's power authority to pay for the power hook-up, which took them about two hours. I gave Lara and Wayne funds to get more school supplies. It was good to get all that money wisely spent.

The guys came back about 2 p.m. and we had lunch. Then we went to the bank in Moshi so Melki could deposit the remaining funds into the Okaseni bank account. This money was for the water system upgrades, goats, and school fees.

Melki was to do the dispersing, let us know the final costs, and snail-mail us the receipts. It was kind of creepy though. He was okay to me until the money was deposited, and then he was a jerk again. Oh well. I felt kind of detached about it at this point, but still it wasn't fun. Alas, the worst was yet to come.

146

The Africa Village Project Association
Fall Newsletter: September 6, 2010

Autumn Greetings!

Happy fall! The AVPA has been busy, but I have good news to tell you about.

June Trip to Okaseni Village

Our third trip to Tanzania this June was successful, but very different from our earlier trips in that we were accompanied by three women, the husband of one of these women, and Sarah, the daughter of Valerie, our AVPA board member. With them, we accomplished much more than Dale and I could have by ourselves.

Medical Dispensary

One of our companions, Diane, has a medical background. She noticed that many of the village kids have deep scars on their faces, arms, and legs, a result of cuts getting infected because they had not been treated with antiseptic. She suggested setting up a small dispensary in the village. We were delighted with her idea, and Melki, the village chair, found space for the dispensary in a house near the office.

Diane with Sarah and the village ladies in the new mini dispensary.

With $800.00 of AVPA donations, Diane and Sarah bought supplies and storage cabinets, and then set up the dispensary and stocked the cabinets. Diane trained several Okaseni ladies on using the supplies to help keep the villagers healthy.

Diane shows the ladies and Melki supplies in the dispensary cabinet.

Thanks so much, Diane and Sarah, for your wonderful work! Thanks to our donors too. You have helped fund this mini dispensary, much appreciated!

We went back to Bristol Cottages where we found everyone and heard about their successful day shopping. We had dinner and then all trooped back to the Parkview. Lara, Wayne, and Susan went for a swim and the rest of us watched but declined to join them (too cold). It was a pleasant evening and a worthwhile day, despite Melki (yet again).

Wednesday, June 23

Today was also eventful and even fun! Dale and I walked down from the Parkview to meet the gang at Bristol Cottages. Diane and Sarah had gone on a safari today and Susan had an early morning coffee-research appointment. Unfortunately, she had taken the key to the room, so we could not get the supplies for the dispensary. Melki and George arrived in his van. Dale, Wayne, Lara, and John wanted to do more mapping, so off they all went to Okaseni.

I had a 3 p.m. appointment with Salma and waited for her in the hotel dining room, writing in my journal. Unfortunately, Susan appeared, back from her meeting. Salma arrived soon after in a cab to pick me up. What could I do—just leave without Susan? It was tempting, but I could not be so rude. So off we all went to Salma's mother's house.

We saw Salma's new baby—so tiny, so cute! He was only two months old. I'd forgotten how tiny little babies are at that age. Susan talked a lot as usual. We met Salma's brother, Aman, who had helped train the microcredit women. We discussed the microcredit program and concluded that yes, it was going well. It was an excellent meeting, and Salma as usual was fantastic. Goodness knows what Susan thought about the whole thing, probably how to get out of paying for *anything ever*!

We left at about 5 p.m. in the same cab that had brought us. Everyone else was back at Bristol Cottages. They had a great time mapping and GPS-ing and had even bushwhacked their way through an area that they later found out sometimes harboured mambas (great, big, bad snakes). They seemed content to just sit there and yak, so I slipped back to the Parkview, rested, went for a swim, and had dinner in peaceful solitude. Greatly refreshed, I walked back to Bristol Cottages where there was now a big OK-7 party going on. We ate more food, chatted, drank libations, toasted everyone and everything. Diane was an absolute hoot, practically doing a stand-up comedy routine. We laughed and laughed. Melki was getting a bit looped and started talking about lions ruling and other local myths. I suddenly got a strong impression of him as deeply steeped in religious explanations of the world. It made me realize why it is sometimes hard dealing with him and why he is so put off by me. It also made me have even more respect for science, which not only explains the world but also makes our living conditions infinitely better.

Thursday, June 24, Wednesday, 25, and Thursday, 26

Our flight left this evening at 9:40 and after the usual stop in Dar for refuelling and a new crew, we made it to Amsterdam on Wednesday at 7:40 a.m. local time. We spent the night at the Mercure, an elegant, all-hours hotel inside the airport building where you could rent quiet, minimalist rooms for any length of time. On Thursday at 5:30 p.m., we caught our flight for Vancouver. It arrived at 6:10 p.m. local time, 40 minutes later. No, just kidding!

We zoomed to Bowen, very, very happy to be home.

HOME

At our next board meeting, I gave the following report:

> In retrospect and despite all the annoyances and difficult people, I deemed this year's Okaseni visit a great success. It was good to find many of the former projects going well. The coffee nursery had one more iteration to go and then would be done. The water system upgrades had improved access to water although the storage point needed upgrading. Power had been installed in both the village office and the school. The electric sewing machines and the medical supplies sent in the shipping container were in storage at the office. The microcredit program was going well. The first group of borrowers was finished, and the second group had staggered end dates. Salma suggested we start a third group. We were pleased to see the positive results of our work and use of our funds.

We also did a lot on this trip. We set up a small dispensary near the village office, thanks to Diane's suggestion and know-how, and paid for medical supplies and storage cabinets. Diane and Sarah purchased these supplies and organized the dispensary itself. The medical supplies that all of us had brought, thanks to Diane and Lara, were also set up in the new dispensary. Diane trained several Okaseni women in providing first aid and using the supplies.

We bought school supplies, including the desperately needed Level 6 textbooks, a map, pencils, erasers, as well as paint and brushes for the blackboards in the school itself. We paid the final fees to get power run to the village office and the wages for the coffee gardener. Dale and Wayne started getting GPS points for the map but found it was a huge job. About one-third of the village was done.

Sarah managed the transportation money, set up the blog, photocopied materials, created the goat flyer, set up the computers for the school and office, and was a great help to everyone, especially me.

There were a few difficulties, including getting the funds from Canada and dealing with the recalcitrant volunteer and Melki. Dale's GPS disappeared, never to be seen again. We did not get a report from Susan on her coffee research/findings, which was a big disappointment.

But we had accomplished much more than Dale and I would have done by ourselves. I felt that I had done a fairly good job of managing the volunteers. I got them organized, gave them the chance to be constructive and useful, welcomed their ideas and suggestions, and greatly appreciated their participation. It was a first for me but not too different than teaching. They made it a sociable trip: friendly and enjoyable, especially the evenings of chatting, drinking beer, and taking turns writing the daily blog. Despite the trials and difficulties, I was pleased. It had been good fun and had worked out well.

The Africa Village Project Association
Fall Newsletter: October 25, 2010

(Belated) Happy Thanksgiving!

Dale and I hope you had a great Thanksgiving. We are always thankful that we are able to help in Africa, even on such a small scale. We are also very grateful for your support, without which we could not do it.

Microcredit Program

On our third trip to Tanzania in June, we saw that the microcredit program we set up in 2008 was doing well. In January 2009, ten Okaseni ladies received loans of $75 to $100 to start small agricultural businesses. The loan cycle was a year. Most of the women paid back their loans completely with interest or still owed only a small portion.

In June 2009, halfway through the first loan cycle, we had enough funds in repayments to start a second group. Five women got loans and started businesses such as preparing and selling meals at local construction sites and making banana beer.

One of the ladies in the first group, Happiness Mushi, asked for a loan to buy cloth to sell. Her long-term plan was to purchase a knitting machine to make school uniform sweaters for students. Salma, our wonderful

manager, suggested that we buy the machine outright and lease it to her with the option to buy. Happiness lived up to her name when she got the news—she was ecstatic!

Happy Mushi sits at the knitting machine she leases from our microcredit program.

I love this picture. It's an African Vermeer—a beautiful young woman in the natural light of an open window working on a domestic task. We were delighted to help make her dream come true.

One of our volunteers taught a class to the ladies about setting business goals and objectives and how to evaluate them. This was the first time the ladies had heard these ideas and found them very helpful.

Your donations have funded the Okaseni microcredit program. Thank you so much!

I was pleased to be able give the board members such a positive report of our trip with the volunteers. Ironically, I knew I could thank the panic disorder I suffered way back in my unseasoned youth in part for the successes of this year. Conquering that harsh, emotional challenge had brought me unforeseen, valuable gifts and helped me in many ways. It was a kind of blessed serendipity. I learned how to cope well with the bumps, trials, and difficulties of life, such as divorce and physical health problems. That success also gave me a kind of fearlessness. It was not that I never again felt fear. Instead, I was not *afraid* of fear and knew I could manage it. I was never reckless or dumb, but I was unafraid to be unconventional, follow my own path, and do what I wanted.

Vanquishing panic disorder even gave me the courage to tackle the problem of world poverty and adopt a needy village in Africa.

CHAPTER 5

2011, AFRICA NIGHT

1975

Ralph and I made our way south from Niamey, the end point of the journey on the date truck, down through Nigeria towards the coast of West Africa. We had left the Arab countries of the Mediterranean behind and were now in Sub-Saharan Africa. Gone were the tight, close towns of the north, with their narrow streets, mosques, and cramped medinas. Gone also was the Sahara Desert. Niamey is in the Sahel, a stretch of territory across the continent that separates the Sahara from the southern regions.

The Sahel is a semi-arid expanse of savannas and grasslands. The towns that we went through were open and spread out, and they sometimes seemed almost empty. Streets were wide, and people moved slowly. South of the Sahel are the West Africa Forests and Savanna. They run along the coast to about Dakar in Senegal and are lusher and more verdant than the Sahel. When we got to Nigeria, we were in this region.

Sub-Saharan Africa was a surprise. Unlike the north, men didn't wear long robes and swaddled clothing. Women didn't wear burkas or cover their heads but instead doffed brightly coloured and patterned kengas. They were out and about in the world and not stuck in some room somewhere. People were friendly, chatty, and welcoming. The area had just come off a seven-year drought, and everywhere people seemed optimistic and cheerful. It was very pleasant.

We hadn't expected that. In fact, we had no idea what to expect, given that we had made a thoughtful but only slightly informed decision to head there. We had done no research before we decided. We hadn't googled West African cities and towns, hadn't checked Expedia for places to stay, hadn't looked up maps on our phones for best routes or modes of transport. No, just kidding. This was the pre-internet/smartphone era for sure.

My grand plan, however, was to do something adventurous, venture into untouristed places, and experience the unexpected and unfamiliar. Happily, our vague and fuzzy plan worked out very well.

2011

I am happy tell you that I got a lot better at planning as life went on. In January 2011, I took early retirement from BCIT. It was a difficult decision because I absolutely loved my job. It was the best one I ever had. The salary was more than I had ever made in my semi-impoverished adult life, and I was grateful every single payday. I loved what I taught. The people I worked with were collegial and kind. The students were lively and hardworking, and I liked them a lot. So why leave?

The biggest motivator was the AVPA. I had plans. It was impossible during a regular school year to do much on the AVPA given my heavy workload, and the thought of having scads of time to devote to it was thrilling. I would do more fundraisers and get more money! I would network with businesses and other organizations and make more contacts! I would expand our work in Okaseni and encourage more small businesses! Oh, and did I mention get more money? Sad though I was to leave BCIT, the thought of a new career as the full-time manager of the AVPA flooded me with enthusiasm and energy. I could hardly wait. My plans were exuberant and raring to go!

You may remember that quote from a Robbie Burns poem, "The best laid plans of mice and persons gang oft agley" (often go wrong).

Early in the year, Brooke, my Bowen friend who had already done so much for the AVAP, suggested doing a large fundraiser on the island. She brought with her a ready-made planning committee that had recently put together a hugely successful fundraiser and was eager to do another. They were Britt, Lexie, Cathy, and Kelly. Brooke invited Dale and me to dinner on January 28 to meet them and discuss possibilities. They were enthusiastic and decided the fundraiser was a go. I was delighted. My plan to plunge into the AVPA full time was starting off well.

My last official day at BCIT was March 16. I went to my office, got rid of files, checked emails, and then handed in my keys and ID card. I was choked about leaving. It had been the best, but I reminded myself of the occasional sense of futility and was glad to be leaving on a high note.

Brooke scheduled a meeting in March with some the gang at a restaurant on Bowen. Most of them were late. As usual, as befitting of the manager of an NGO and a now ex-instructor, I had an agenda. It was ignored. The discussion ranged far and wide with lots of great ideas and detail. There was much talk about the venue and how to make it spectacular, and but not much focus, organization, or decision-making. Herding urban cats came to mind. However, I appreciated their enthusiasm and doggedly moved ahead with the agenda and took notes. Here are my minutes.

AVPA FUNDRAISER MEETING: MINUTES

Date: Friday, March 11, 2011
Time: 12 p.m.
Place: Artisan Eats, Bowen Island

Present: Brooke, Lexi, Britt, Dale, Sheena

1. Welcome: The meeting started about 12:30.

2. The venue
   - We decided on the Bowen Island Community School (BICS) because it is available, has a kitchen, and is big enough for the event. We also won't have to worry about the weather.
   - The gym can accommodate 150 for a sit-down dinner.
   - The costs are:
     - gym: $32/hr (adult cost but non-profit rate might be lower)
     - kitchen: $11.20/hr
     - custodian: $25/hr, and twice for overtime
   - We need to get a plan to Sarah, the BICS info person, immediately. Sheena will do this.

3. The date and time
   - We decided on June 4 (BCIS is available and people will still be around before the summer holidays). It will be from 7 to 10 p.m. with 3 hours set-up and 2 hours tear-down (total of 8 hours).

4. The event
   - Dale suggested the name "Kilifest"—great one!
   - We discussed
     - an adult only event. We could charge more and serve liquor, which could be quite lucrative. We could possibly charge $40/head.
     - a family event (an Africa family party). Getting kids aware and involved is great, but the adult event would be more lucrative. If the primary purpose is fundraising, the adult event might be better.

5. The food
   - Brooke suggested Gojo, an Ethiopian restaurant in Vancouver. Their price is $13/a head.
   - Another option is Qi Cafe on Bowen. The owners were thrilled to be asked and will let us know a price.
   - We decided that some kind of food is a good idea but were not sure if it should be a full sit-down dinner, finger food, concession/cafeteria style, samples, or . . . ??
   - We discussed selling tix for both the dinner and show and tix for just the show.

6. The liquor
   - If we want to serve liquor, which would be lucrative, we cannot have kids or teens there.
   - We will need a liquor licence.
   - Servers will need a Serving It Right certificate. As the manager, Sheena will too.

7. AVPA presentation
   - Sheena will do a presentation on the AVPA (another reason BICS is the best choice).

8. The entertainment
   - There are several options for entertainment:
     - The Jackie Esembe dance and drummers group. The cost is about $200 each plus travel expenses. We watched a video clip of them—they were great!
     - a DJ for dancing
     - a singer trio called Navarno suggested by Chaz, an old friend of Dale's on Bowen. Chaz was a local musician and knew someone in the band. They were a modern African trio, and their style of music was currently popular in Africa.

9. The raffle
   - Brooke said a recent Island Pacific School raffle went very well—it is worth doing.
   - We will need a gaming licence.
   - We could get kids to help sell the tix.
   - African art could be a prize, also fair-trade items.

10. The financials
    - We discussed the price for tix. It depends on whether it will be a family event or adults only. We can charge more for adults only and also serve alcohol, possibly $40/head.
    - We need a budget. Sheena will do one.

11. Next steps
    - Sheena will compile all the info and get in touch with everyone separately about the tasks.

12. Next meeting
    - The next meeting is scheduled for 12:30 p.m., Friday, April 1, at Artisan Eats.

I got to work on booking BICS as the venue. The school district required an application and a plan. I submitted this letter to Sarah, the community coordinator at the school.

PLAN FOR AFRICA VILLAGE PROJECT FUNDRAISER
JUNE 4, 2011

March 28, 2011

Sarah Haxby
Bowen Island Community School
Bowen Island, BC V0N 1G0

Dear Sarah:

It was great talking to you this morning. Thanks for keeping the booking for the Africa Village Project Association (AVPA) fundraiser at BICS in June. We are pleased to confirm it. As you requested, I am submitting this plan.

We would like to book the BICS gym and kitchen:
  Date: Saturday, June 4, 2011
  Time of event: 7 p.m. to 10 p.m.
  Total booking time: 4 p.m. to 11 p.m.

We are planning a dinner and entertainment, including
  • a raffle for various prizes
  • an African-themed dinner of one or two main dishes and several side ones
  • a PowerPoint presentation on the AVPA
  • musicians and/or dancers.

We will be serving wine and beer and will get a liquor licence and comply with the regulation to limit attendance to adults only. We will also get a gaming licence for the raffle.
  • Tickets will be sold for the event as follows:
  • 100 tix for the dinner and entertainment @ $25.00 each

- 50 plus tix for the entertainment only at $15.00 each. Please note that the total number depends on the capacity of the gym.

Could you please let us know how many people we are allowed to have. We will also need a stage for the entertainment and presentation, as well as any sound equipment that you have.

Thanks very much, Sarah.

Sincerely,
Sheena Ashdown
Project Director
Africa Village Project Assocation
Official Registered Canadian Charity # 84551 5154 RR0001

In late March, I talked to Brooke and Chaz about the music. Brooke had heard of another group called Kokoma, a traditional African band with huge drums and a stunning singer/dancer called Maobong Oku. Brooke raved about them. Chaz raved about Navarno. They were quite different, and I checked them out online. I made a tentative booking with Kokoma.

Through all this, Dale was busy too. He was building a small zendo on the property of Brooke and her husband as a thank-you for all their help on the fundraiser. He spent hours on the design.

On April 1, I turned up for a meeting at 1 p.m. with the some of the Kilifest folks at a local restaurant. It went well. I had an agenda, and yup, it was ignored. There was a lot of discussion on the same points in the first agenda, but nothing much was decided on. Brooke suggested that we call the event an Africa Dance/Party Night. All agreed. Dale's suggestion of Kilifest was no more. We decided to book Navarno, the duo suggested by Chaz, at $500. Brooke and I said we would create a schedule of events. Britt offered to design the posters, tix, and flyers. Cam agreed to do the sound and DJing. There was also much discussion about decorating the venue. We were still waiting for approval from BICS.

So, as we decided in this meeting, I cancelled the tentative booking with Kokoma and booked Navarno. A couple of days later, several people in the group told me they did not want Navarno. They insisted I book Kokoma and cancel Navarno, which they deemed not good enough. Kokoma was high-end, they said, more African and sophisticated, and not embarrassing. If I didn't do this, they told me they would stop working on Africa Night.

Hmm . . . perhaps I should have taken them up on that "offer." Instead, I caved. I cancelled Navarno and booked Kokoma. The cost for Navarno was $500, and the cost for Kokoma was $1,680 with tax. This seemed exorbitant for our little NGO, but when I voiced my concerns, they replied that I should just take it out of the gate. I told them that CRA's guidelines were not to spend more than 10 percent of the money brought in on fundraising. It did not register. They blithely went ahead.

Our next meeting was on April 15. In my daybook that evening, I wrote "Meeting today, nine people, went very well. Wow! They are all wonderful, too good!" Several new people turned up, including Dharma, a local chef who said he would be able to do the food. He had some excellent suggestions about serving (staggering the tables, seating ten people per table, and feeding the volunteers first). I reported that I had cancelled Navarno and rebooked Maobong Oku, bowing to the committee's argument that Kokoma was traditionally African and more appealing. The name, Africa Dance/Party Night, remained the same. We were still waiting for approval from BICS.

This meeting was fun and somewhat valuable, but again, it was a free-for-all. Again, the main topic was the venue. Decisions about it that I thought had been made last time were re-discussed, rejected, changed, and/or new suggestions introduced. I realized this would be an ongoing thing, and I could not afford the time to be involved. I told them they should form a decorating sub-committee for the venue and go ahead without me.

The drama about the music continued after this meeting. When Chaz heard that Navarno got cancelled, he phoned me in a rage and demanded that I book Navarno and not Kokoma. He ranted and berated me and was practically hysterical. I tried to explain the decision, but he wasn't having any of it. He would not stop.

I finally said, "Chaz, this is unacceptable. I'm not listening anymore. I am hanging up now." Click. I was shaken and scared that he might turn up at our house in person to continue his harangue. I called Dale, who was working at the zendo, and told him. He was angry that Chaz had frightened me.

A couple of days later, Chaz turned up at the zendo while Dale was working there.

Chaz muttered a greeting and then didn't say much.

"Chaz," said Dale, "You have to apologize to Sheena for what you did. It doesn't have to be in person. You can just leave a message on the answering machine. But you have to apologize to her."

Chaz didn't say anything. Then he started to cry.

Dale said, "It's not the end of the world, Chaz. You don't have to get upset. All you have to do is make it right."

Chaz cried some more. Then he left.

Dale told me later that Chaz probably thought Dale was attacking him. He never did apologize. Fortunately, I didn't hear from him again.

On April 19, we were approved for BICS but had to wait for the custodian to be confirmed. Our plan to serve alcohol needed separate approval and was okayed on May 3. On May 4, I signed the contract with BICS. We had a venue! I had a drink that evening. It might have been two. Dharma called me to say he was unable to do the food for us, which was disappointing. I think he realized when he attended the meeting that the event could be challenging, to say the least. I had been given the number of Yvonne, a person on Bowen who had catered many local fundraisers. I called her, and she said yes. She had many good suggestions.

Our next meeting was Friday, May 6. The core group turned up. I reported that we were booked for the BICS gym for Saturday, June 4, for 100 to 200 people (including volunteers) for a dinner and dancing event with alcohol. We decided on $35 each for tix. I told them about my talk with Yvonne. A revised schedule was presented. There was another report on the decorations. The name was changed to Africa Dance Party.

On May 9, I went to the Bowen RCMP office to find out about serving alcohol. Getting approved involved some paperwork but seemed manageable. The clerk told us we needed a Special Occasion Licence (SOL) from the BC Liquor Control Board (LCB) for public events like ours. To get an SOL, I first had to fill out an application form. Then I had to submit the application form and a proposal to the RCMP for their endorsement. If it was okayed, I had to submit the application with the RCMP endorsement/approval to the LCB for the SOL. (Whew!)

Here is the SOL proposal I submitted to the RCMP:

SPECIAL OCCASION LICENCE PROPOSAL

The Event

Africa Night is a fundraiser for the Africa Village Project Association (AVPA). It will be held on Saturday, June 4. The purpose is to raise funds to buy malaria nets for Okaseni village in Tanzania, Africa.

The organizers are Sheena Ashdown and Dale Hamilton, directors of the Africa Village Project Association. The guests are friends and supporters of the AVPA and other Bowen Island residents. A maximum of 200 guests is expected. The event will run from 6:30 p.m. until 10:30 p.m.

Location

The event will be held in the gymnasium at Bowen Island Community School on Bowen Island. The AVPA has received permission from the West Vancouver School Board to have this event and has complied with all BICS requirements. Municipal bylaw concerns will not be addressed as this event will take place indoors, and there will be no open fires, etc.

BC Liquor Control and Licensing

No minors will be present at this event (adults only). The guests will be able to buy beer and wine. They will first purchase a drink ticket from a table on the west wall of the gym. They will then get the drink itself from a table on the south wall of the gym. The drinks table will be supervised by Katherine, a Bowen Island resident, who will be assisted by two or three volunteers. Katherine has her Serving It Right certificate. Servers are aware that they are not to consume or be under the influence of liquor while serving.
Site Treatment

Several volunteers are responsible for making sure that only adult guests with tickets (no minors) are allowed in. All the liquor and food servers will monitor alcohol consumption. A free bus ride home will be provided. BICS's fire prevention and exit requirements will be observed. All decorations, catering materials and refuse will be cleaned up by the caterers, servers, and other volunteers at the end of the evening.

Then we waited.

There was much activity over the next few days. I had to get a Serving It Right certificate, a government requirement for anyone serving liquor at events, bars, restaurants, and events like ours. You took the online course about the laws and responsibilities of servers and then did the test online. All good, I passed, and my certificate was emailed to me. I had a quick phone call with Yvonne confirming the food for the event. All was fine. On May 11, I sent out a save-the-date email. A couple of days later, Britt emailed me the poster she had designed. It was fabulous.

Amidst all this sound and fury over Africa Night, my nephew Zack and I continued working this year on the AVPA website. It was a huge job, but he was a joy to work with. Our task was a gentle counterpoint to and welcome reprieve from the Bowen drama.

We held another committee meeting on May 16. My daybook note said, "Excellent!" I reported that I talked with Yvonne and that she had agreed to do the catering. She was unable to donate her time. Britt showed us her fantastic poster. I mentioned (again) that I could not take the expenses out of the gate because of CRA guidelines about spending limits, so Dale and I would be covering the costs and would need invoices for everything. The name was changed to Africa Night. This one stuck.

The revised schedule presented at this meeting. This one stuck as well.

6:30: doors open

7:00: dinner

7:30: presentation (Sheena)

8:00: first set of music (Komoko)

8:30: break and last call for drinks

8:50: second set of music (Komoko)

8:50/9:00: bar closes
9:20: DJ and dancing (Cam)
11:00: evening ends (hopefully)

The day after this meeting, Brooke, Lexi, and I checked out BICS and toured the gym and kitchen. It looked good. The school was well set up for handling big events, which was encouraging.

A retirement party was held for me in mid-May. It was very congenial with many of my wonderful BCIT colleagues in attendance. They gave me a silver-coloured fountain pen engraved with my name. I made a little speech about how much I loved and appreciated BCIT, which they seemed to like and said I was sad to be leaving. It was hard to say goodbye.

I trekked into Vancouver to see Brad, our long-time agent, to get the special event insurance. He also told me I also needed special event liability supplemental insurance because we would be serving alcohol. Yipes. (Dale and I happily paid for this too.)

A local bus driver for the late-night transportation. He was to arrive at BICS at 10:30. The charge was $52 per hour. He said he could probably be done in an hour if the crowd wasn't too large.

I sent the following public announcement to the *Undercurrent* inviting the island to attend:

Come to Africa Night on June 4!

You're invited to Africa Night on Saturday, June 4, at BICS on Bowen. Come enjoy an evening of fun, food, and fabulous music!

You'll feast on a traditional African dinner and be entertained by the amazing Kokoma African Heritage Ensemble featuring Maobong Oku, voted one of Vancouver's favourite performers by the People's Choice of BC. There will be a raffle and dancing with DJ Cam. Doors open at 6:30 p.m. and a ride home will be provided. It's a chance to get together with your friends, have a rocking night out, and support a great cause.

Africa Night is a fundraiser for the Africa Village Project Association. We need your help to raise enough money to buy malaria nets for everyone in Okaseni, Tanzania. Malaria kills about three million people every year, most of them children in the developing world. But the most effective way to prevent malaria is to use a simple, insecticide-treated malaria net. It can cut the rate of malaria to about zero. We'd like to buy nets for all 4,000 residents of Okaseni.

Tix are $35.00 (adults only) and are limited, so get yours right away. They are available at Phoenix Photo or by calling Sheena.

Hope to see you there! For more info on the Africa Village Project Association, visit the website at www.africavillage-project.org.

The next few days were a whirl. I phoned Kokoma to confirm the time-line and the invoice. Lexi did a fabulous spreadsheet of available cutlery and dishes. On May 24, we all bustled over to Brooke's place to make malaria net cards to sell at the event. Some very kind people were there to help and chat and drink wine. It was a sociable evening and time well spent.

Things were chugging along. Then suddenly, all our careful planning went agley. On Saturday, May 28, one week before Africa Night, we made the unhappy decision to cancel it because the BC Canucks hockey team was playing a game in the finals on June 4. Excitement was high all round, but Africa Night was a no-go. Too bad!

This was my submission to the *Undercurrent* on May 31:

AFRICA NIGHT POSTPONED UNTIL OCTOBER

The Canucks have made the finals—yay! We will all be cheering them on.

Because the second game of the series falls on June 4, we have decided to postpone the Africa Night fundraiser for the Africa Village Project. There is no point in trying to compete with this big event.

We are rescheduling Africa Night for October 1 and will let you know as soon as the bookings are confirmed.

If you already have tix for the event (thanks!), you can get a refund or donate the ticket amount to the Africa Village Project and get an official tax receipt. Please call Sheena to arrange this.

Hope to see you in October. In the meantime, go Canucks, go!

At 6:30 on June 4, I waited outside BICS in case anyone turned up for Africa Night. No one did. It was a beautifully sunny, very quiet evening. Was everyone watching the game? No matter, it was sweet to be outside. My thoughts turned to our new date of October 1.

By the way, the Canucks lost the seventh and last game of the playoffs 0 to 4 on Wednesday, June 15. Before the game had even ended, people started rioting in downtown Vancouver. By the end of the night, there was $5 million in property damage. Nine police officers suffered injuries as did about 140 people, and over 100 were arrested. Over 300 suspects were eventually charged with various offenses, and most of them pled guilty.[1] It was a sad, sorry ending to the season.

June turned out to be a quiet month, except for the riot. Zack and I continued to work on the website. It was a much bigger job than either of us expected, and I appreciated his dedication so much.

I received an excellent proposal this month from Salma about starting a broiler poultry project as I had discussed with her and Melki last year. It was pages long and listed in detail the costs for heating systems, vaccinations, and doctor visits. It also included several timelines for raising broilers from chicks to dinners. I was persuaded and very pleased, so I sent them funds to get started. This money was a loan under the microcredit umbrella.

For the first couple of weeks of June, I did a lot of ticket refunds and had to write out and mail many cheques. Quelle pain. I let Kelli, Kokoma's agent, know about the cancellation and received an invoice from her for a 50 percent cancellation fee of $756. On June 16, I met her in Vancouver to give her the cheque. She was a very nice, efficient person, and I enjoyed doing business with her. Meanwhile, Dale continued to work on the zendo.

In early July, I got a call from a former colleague at BCIT about a short-term teaching job in September in Kamloops, a town in the interior of BC. It sounded good. An appointment for an interview was set up for July 11 which went well, and I got the job. I was glad but would not realize until later how fortuitous this job actually was. I picked up the textbook a couple of days later and prepped for the class on and off during July and August.

Meanwhile, back at planning committee headquarters, we began again on Africa Night. I met with Brooke and Cathy in the Cove to touch base, and my heart sank at the urban-cats vibe again.

I rebooked the gym.

It was dawning on me that I needed help with the bookkeeping for the AVPA, especially because Africa Night involved so much money. I phoned Ellen, a bookkeeper on Bowen, and asked her for a crash course in basic Excel. She said yes. I met with her on two mornings for half an hour each to learn the basics. It cost me $30 per session and was worth twice the price. Ellen saved me hours of time over the next five years, and I was very grateful.

At 12:10 on July 22, I arrived at Artisan Square on Bowen for a 12:15 meeting with a planning committee member (who was 40 mins late) and a Bowen musician (who was 30 minutes late). The meeting was not a success. There was bad temper and impatience. I left utterly disheartened and suddenly very glad that I would be away for two weeks in September and would get a break from all this meanness and spite.

The planning committee met on August 8 to discuss Africa Night redux. My daybook notation said, "Pretty good. Cathy a pain though." As usual, I did minutes.

AVPA AFRICA NIGHT MEETING
MINUTES

Date: Monday, August 8, 2011
Time: 11:30 p.m.
Place: Artisan Eats, Bowen Island

Attendees: Brooke, Cathy, Dale, Sheena, Cameron, Kelly

1. Welcome and thanks!

2. The event

- It's Africa Night redux!

3. The venue
   - We are booked for the BICS gym for Saturday, October 1.

4. The decorating
   - Brooke and Cathy will organize a meeting for the decorating committee.

5. The food
   - Brooke suggested a restaurant on Commercial Drive in Vancouver called Harambe. Brooke, Cathy, and Sheena will check it out.

6. The entertainment
   - Maobong Oku/Kokoma are confirmed.

7. The alcohol
   - Lexi and Sheena will handle this.
   - Sheena will apply for the non-profit exemption.

8. Article for *Undercurrent*
   - Cathy and Sheena will work on this.

9. Next meeting: TBA.

In August, I met Brooke and Cathy (still a pain) at Harambe restaurant about serving their Ethiopian food at the event. We had an enjoyable time for a change. The food looked appetizing and was delicious, and the owners were available on October 1 to do the catering. It was a go.

I continued prepping for my Kamloops teaching gig in September, reading a text called *Grammar on the Go*. I love grammar! It is my idea of a fun read.

Lexi got the lowdown about raffles. They were strictly regulated in BC by provincial gaming laws, and one of the requirements was that the money raised in a raffle for a charity endeavour had to be spent in British Columbia. So that put the kibosh on an Africa Night raffle.

Also this month, I wrote a card to Milton Wong to tell him how he had inspired me to adopt a village in Africa and to thank him. I sent out an email to everyone debunking a rumour that I was going to make the volunteers pay for stuff for Africa Night. (Sigh).

We had another meeting in early September. My daybook note was, "Good!" Things were progressing somewhat, but the meeting itself was repetitious of many previous ones.

On September 5, I went to Kamloops for the short-term teaching gig. It did not go too well although I received some amazing and touching commendations from several students. I got back two weeks later, hugely relieved it was over. I still had marking and the end-of-term submissions to do, and then I put that baby to bed. For my troubles, I got a very chunky paycheque.

At noon on September 20, the planning committee held a meeting, for which I did not do an agenda or minutes. Again, it was more of the same. But I noted in my daybook: "Good!"

On September 22, I received the final approval from the LCB for the SOL. The RCMP had approved our event and endorsed the application. We were good to go, although with stipulations. We had to purchase the alcohol from a government liquor store, prices could not exceed the LCB designated guidelines, and the licence had to be posted in plain view at the event. Okay, we could do that! I immediately zipped into town to the nearest liquor store. They issued me the SOL that allowed me to buy the alcohol. The RCMP requested a report after the event.

The next day, I worked on a script for Cam at the event and began work on the final schedules for the event. I decided to do two: one for the event itself and one for the tasks. That afternoon, Brooke phoned. She was upset, argumentative, and aggressive about bamboo plants for the gym. I kept telling her she needed to talk to Dale as he had promised to help her. (I did not want to get involved with venue stuff at this late date.)

Lexi phoned me the next day. I think she must have heard about Brooke's rant because she was kind and sympathetic, which I appreciated. I finished the schedules. I sent an announcement to the *Undercurrent* almost identical to the one I had sent in May.

On Sept. 25, I sent this email to Brooke, Cathy, and Kelly about a schedule I was working on for the committee, hoping to make sure that all would go well on the big day.

Thanks again for your amazing work for Africa Night. Dale and I are very grateful.

Attached is the schedule for the event itself, which I hope will be helpful. I know you've all worked on many fundraisers and have a lot of experience with them, and you may feel this schedule is unnecessary. However, this fundraiser is the biggest one Dale and I have ever done, and it has become bigger, more complicated, and much more expensive that we ever imagined.

If anything goes wrong, it's our butts on the line and it's the reputation of the AVPA that will be affected. It's also our personal financial loss. Already the expenses are over $6,000 and counting. Even if we sell out, the gate is only $7,000. Liquor profits will probably be about $1,000. The number and amount of donations is unknown.

But we have been willing to take this risk. The potential benefits are the publicity, the monthly donations, and the goodwill in the community. We also want to do our best to make sure the event runs as smoothly as possible. Thus the schedule. Let me know if you have any changes, corrections, or additions. Thanks again!

September 26 was a busy day. Lexi and a friend stood outside the Bowen General Store and handed out flyers for the event. People seemed interested. About midday, an email arrived from someone who saw two men tearing down our posters in the Cove. That was weird. Another email arrived from a member of the decorating committee about changing the set-up in the gym. She suggested moving the drinks and donations tables to different spots and putting another table near the door. (Sigh. After eight months of work, this layout was still not finalized.) I was beginning to get back spasms.

That evening, the planning committee met at Britt's house. We started going over the schedules I had prepared for them. Lexie suddenly started berating me. She waved the schedules about and said, "These aren't going to work. Where is the connectivity between these two? These aren't good enough." Then Brooke leapt in, and they both went after me. The other person there did and said nothing but looked extremely uncomfortable. Moments before, Dale had gone outside with Britt to give her some supplies from our car. I knew the yelling and attacking would *never* have happened if he had been there. He and Britt came back inside. The harassment ended immediately. I sat there stunned for a couple of minutes. Then I gathered up my papers and walked out, very, very angry. I had not been that angry in years. Dale followed me out and we drove home.

Cathy phoned later to see if I was okay. I told her what had happened. She was very kind about it, which was nice, considering how unpleasant *she* had been lately. Go figure.

On September 28, I met the gang at BICS to check out the venue. This time, Britt was mad at me, and Cathy too. A kind of numbness started settling over me, and I was beyond caring at this point. Brooke, however, was much nicer. Sigh.

The next morning, I got a call from Katherine, the person who had volunteered to staff the bar. She must have known what I had been going through with the group because she was very supportive and kind. I so appreciated it although I could not shake off the numbness. Britt emailed everyone about a new schedule she was working on, having been told no doubt by Lexie and Brooke that my schedules just would *not* do. By October 1, there were five schedules and lists of things to do floating around. My back pain was getting worse. I finished the script for Cam and delivered it to him. I practiced my PowerPoint presentation. That I felt good about. Brooke emailed me the last details for the dinner from the Harambe guys.

By September 30, I was having major back pain. Various people phoned that day about last minute things. Dale picked up twenty pots of eight-feet high bamboo plants in the truck. They looked sort of jungle-like. There was a big demand for tix. I dropped off two tix to a person who said, "Oh good, now I can be part of the in-crowd!" Lexie phoned and sort of apologized. At this point, all was forgotten. I didn't have a second to think about her anymore.

October 1 had finally arrived, the Big Day!! The gym looked fabulous, romantic, and exotic. All that work had paid off big time.

The evening went well. Maobong and the band were spectacular and kept everyone spellbound with their drumming and dancing. The food was delicious, and the serving volunteers did a great job. My presentation was acceptable although I felt shellshocked and subdued. (My back was okay for the event itself but very painful before and after.) After the band left, Cam continued to play great dance music into the night. That I enjoyed to the max. It was so liberating to dance freely with friends after all that strain and turmoil.

However, there was a lot of hostility from the group towards me during the evening. I could not fathom it. The meanness and pettiness reached a peak that night, but I was so emotionally shut down that it hardly affected me. Several of the husbands were mad too and ignored me. (Weeks later, I ran into one of them in a shop on Bowen. He discreetly flipped me the bird.)

The next day I was exhausted. My back pain was intense. I took a two-hour nap. I worked on a thank-you article for the *Undercurrent*. By afternoon, I felt okay and decided to go to the funeral for a popular elderly gent on Bowen called Jan Furst. He had been supportive of the AVPA and interested in working with us. He was quite the character and apparently had a lot of girlfriends. The funeral was packed, lively, funny, and the best time I had had in a very long while.

Over the next few days, I did post-Africa Night chores. I received an invoice from BICS for $662. The bus driver told us there was no charge for the bus because he hadn't taken anyone. Six people signed up for monthly donations from $10 to $25 per month, which was heartening and much appreciated. I sent a thank-you letter to the *Undercurrent* and submitted the report requested by the RCMP.

We received some very kind messages before and after the event.

> Jambo Sheena! We are looking forward to your evening and celebrating Africa and your village and the wonderful work you and your husband are doing.

> What a wonderful event Africa Night was—fun, the band was awesome and the community spirit so fantastic! You spoke so well and even though you said you were nervous, it didn't show one bit. You did a fantastic job of speaking from your heart— which always works.

What a GREAT night for sure! The energy in that room was so uplifting. I think when people hear now about the AVPA, they will think, oh yeah, Africa Night. Everyone will now know who they are talking about and will have good feelings it.

What an amazing night! Thank you to all the folks that worked so hard to put this wonderful event together. I am listening to Maobong's CD as I type this!

We also heard other enthusiastic compliments:
- The gym looked good. I was really impressed.
- It was a fantastic event.
- Thanks, it was a wonderful event. I was happy to be part of it.

My gratitude for these messages was boundless. The *Undercurrent* also gave us a fantastic spread of amazing pictures of the event called "From our Village to Yours."[2] I was thrilled and very grateful.

I later presented this summary of Africa Night to the AVPA board.

Africa Night finally happened, after having to be rescheduled to October because of a Canucks hockey game in June.

Putting on this event was an immense amount of work that took months to plan and organize. The six people on the planning committee were incredible and put their hearts and souls into it. They were responsible for its success. They were a very good-hearted and earnest group. They had a lot of ideas and were hardworking and enthusiastic. But they were quite scattered and unfocussed at times and didn't like to follow agendas or be systematic.

I found them extremely frustrating to work with. They sort of ignored me and charged on without much consultation or agreement from me. Some of them were also quite rude, condescending, and patronizing. Whenever I brought up the costs and expenses, they said, "Just take it out of the gate." They nonchalantly disregarded the CRA requirement that only 10 percent of donations should go towards fundraising.

The total receipts, including the gate, donations, and alcohol sales, were $10,333. The expenses included the band, food, venue, alcohol, insurance, and materials, and totaled $6054, about 66 percent of the receipts. The net take was $4279.

It was impossible to pay for the event from the receipts. CRA would have been horrified. Our average yearly donations are about $6,000 to $8,000. We simply could not pay for the event out of the donations. Fortunately, I got a good short-term job in September and was able to pay for some of the costs. The remainder Dale and I paid for from our savings.

So, was it worth it? It's hard to say. We did sell out and it certainly raised our profile on Bowen. However, there are many worthy causes on the island already, especially the schools, and Africa is not a top priority. Only five people signed up to donate monthly, and we have not received other donations since the event.

Having a similar event every two years might be a possibility, but Dale and I cannot pay for it again. If I had not gotten that job, it would have been very difficult. For next time, we might want to consider the following:

- streamlining and simplifying the event so that it is less expensive and does not require so much labour
- ensuring that everyone understands what is feasible and what isn't and that, as a registered Canadian charity, the Africa Village Project is bound by Canada Revenue rules and public expectations
- selling more things at the event (art, cards, etc.)

Ever the glutton for punishment, I did two more fundraisers this year, both on Bowen. In December, we got a booth at the Christmas Fair at BICS and a booth at the Christmas Fair at Collins Hall. We sold our home-made malaria net cards, Africa cards, and baked goods. These two fundraisers didn't bring in much money, but they were painless and hardly any work. The total amount of money we raised this year was about $12,000.

For someone who had taken early retirement in January, I had a very busy year. It was non-stop emails, phone calls, meetings, banking, account updating, account reconciliation, Excel, letters, emails, postings, articles, spreadsheets, reports, cards, website design, fundraisers, public relations, volunteers, committees, posters, tickets, refunds, receipts, budgets, and thank-yous of all kinds. Oh, and did I mention fundraisers? By the end of the year, I was so completely done. I realized that I did not want to spend my days working full-time on these clerical, administrative, and organizational tasks. I did not want to spend all my time doing what was entailed, unfortunately, in running the AVPA.

When I looked back on the year though, I saw that Africa Night was indeed hugely successful. The net proceeds, including our personal donation of $6,000, were $10,333, much more than we had ever raised in one year. People loved the event. It got rave reviews and many hosannahs. We got fantastic coverage in the *Undercurrent* with spectacular colour pictures of Maobong, the band, and folks rocking the dance floor. The paper called it "a fundraising event the likes of which Bowen has never seen before."[2] But this success came at a great personal cost. I had never had such a difficult time with a group of people and began to seriously doubt myself. This uncertainty was reinforced by others, including someone who asked me what I had done to antagonize all those people.

However, redemption awaited. While I was writing this book, a friend who was reading my first draft sent me these comments on chapter 5: Africa Night.

> I was really drawn into [this chapter] because of my experiences being on a committee much like yours. A lot of what went on for you was what I experienced too. My chairperson was basically unaware of finances, and I soon was the

treasurer. By the time I left the group, we had $60K (US) in our bank account. I just heard recently that they had gone through the $60K and [the major annual event] may be in its last year(s).

So all of this is to say that I loved chapter 5. I can totally relate to all the frustrations. So don't feel like you had an overly difficult group. From my perspective, you did a great job of pulling it together. It worked! You made money and it helped your endeavour. Good for you.[3]

Thank you, Karen. You made me feel so much better even after all those years. Very much appreciated!

But unfortunately, the difficulties and unpleasantness of Africa Night destroyed something in my soul, and I was never able again to get back my intense passion and joy for the project. This year saw the high point of the AVPA, and it began a slow, steady path downward. My best laid plan for retirement and the AVPA had indeed gone dramatically agley.

CHAPTER 6

2012, MICROCREDIT, EDUCATION, AND DAVOS

1975

Ralph and I enjoyed Sub-Saharan Africa for the openness of the people and their good nature and friendliness. It was a pleasant change but much poorer than the north. I had never seen such poverty. It wasn't so much about what they did have—humble houses, wild-west transportation vehicles, many small businesses, a few paved roads and sidewalks—but what they did *not* have. There were few cars, no large stores, limited food choices, few amenities, no luxuries, and also no industries, manufacturing, or big businesses that we could see. When Ralph and I arrived in Montreal at the end of our journey, I was sickened by the excess and over-abundance of just about everything. My culture shock returning to Canada was far greater than my culture shock arriving in Africa.

The above list doesn't even begin to factor in the lack of medical care, the poor quality of education, the limited opportunities. Young men would come up to us on the street and ask us where we were from. When we told them, they pleaded, "Canada? Please could you take me home with you? Can you help me get to Canada?" It was discomfiting to have to say that we couldn't. It made me ashamed of my good fortune. What on earth had I done to deserve the incredibly good luck of being born in a rich, peaceful, and healthy country? Nothing, of course. It was the luck of the draw, and I had drawn the queen of spades.

2012

On January 30 of this year, I saw on the local news a series about teenage foster kids who wanted to be adopted. I would love to do that, I thought, never imagining the impact that ordinary news item would have on my life . . .

This year, Dale and I made our fourth trip to Okaseni and visited Switzerland on the way back. Dale had never been there before, but it had beckoned and beguiled him since high school, loving mountains as he does. He was quietly elated to finally get there. We also saw in Okaseni the results of the work we had done, some very good, some not so much.

This year was low-key for fundraising, but we were in good shape financially because of the success of Africa Night. We received donations from our website, several monthly donors and other random generous souls. The big push over the last two years was to raise money for malaria nets. A month or so before our trip, the US president announced funds to buy nets for everyone in Tanzania. In May, we received an email from Peter Mchau that said malaria nets had been distributed to households throughout the country. Mission accomplished! We now had **$13,000** to spend on other things.

In May and September, I did presentations for the Bowen Island Rotary Club, with hopes of getting funding from Rotary International. I eventually joined the club and attended meetings, which I enjoyed, but the process of getting funds from Rotary seemed Byzantine, tedious, and far beyond my capabilities as a one-person show.

A big success at home this year was our updated website. My nephew, Zack, and I had toiled for ages, and we finally got it finished in the spring. I was ecstatic and so grateful for his amazing work. The website was terrific. The postings looked more professional and less down-home than my newsletters. New postings would be sent emailed directly to people who signed up for them. Only about fifty people signed up, so I sent out an email to folks on our original mailing list to encourage them to join, which garnered some success.

I had big plans this year to do a workshop for the Okaseni primary school teachers. In 2010, when we returned home from our trip with the volunteers (who had taught classes), Charleen suggested that we forgo classes for the kids and instead focus on the teachers. She said that students will come and go, but that the teachers will be there for the long-term. If we did workshops and classes, it might help improve their teaching skills and their English. This seemed an excellent idea. With a generous donation from Valerie, our board member extraordinaire, we bought $1,000 worth of various teaching supplies and materials and stuffed them all into a huge, green suitcase given to us by two kind Bowen neighbours. Good to go!

Africa Village Project Association
Mid-Summer Newsletter: June 1, 2012

Malaria Nets and the Best Laid Plans

If you have been getting our recent updates, you know that the AVPA has been raising funds to purchase malaria nets for Okaseni. We put on the wildly successful Africa Night in October and sold cards at the 2010 and 2011 Christmas Craft Fairs on Bowen. About $13,000 was raised, enough to buy nets for everyone in the village.

Dale and I are leaving for Africa soon and planned on this trip to buy these nets. But we recently heard that the government of Tanzania had purchased and distributed nets to the country. This endeavour was funded by the Gates Foundation and the Global Fund.

So our plans for the purchase and the slogging away by many wonderful people on various fundraisers were for naught. No, just kidding! This is of course fabulous news! We are so grateful that these organizations donated malaria nets.

The villagers will now be protected from malaria, which is a devastating disease especially for kids and pregnant women, who are particularly susceptible. Malaria nets can dramatically reduce the rate of infection and help keep everyone safe and healthy.

Happily, the AVPA can now focus on other things. New ventures might include starting a communal vegetable garden, purchasing and raising broiler chickens to improve nutrition and increase income, running workshops for the teachers to improve skills, and purchasing goats for milk and offspring.

With the funds raised for malaria nets, we can now purchase other things for Okaseni, such as goats—like this one, who seems to have just gotten his hair done.

So the best laid plans do sometimes get derailed—but not always in a bad way. Sometimes we just get rerouted to a shiny new track for an exciting zoom to a new adventure. Wish us luck! Will keep you posted about our trip.

TRAVEL JOURNAL
Tuesday, June 5

We left Vancouver today at 4 p.m. on the KLM flight to Amsterdam. The flight was okay. I watched *Iron Lady* with Meryl Streep as Margaret Thatcher. It was appalling. Streep was fantastic and deserved the Oscar for her brilliant portrayal, but Thatcher, ugh. I didn't know much about her, having too many struggles back then to be up on politics or current events, except to know I would never have voted for her. In the movie, she was awful, with harsh economic policies and no sense of social responsibility, a Reaganite to the core. They have a lot to answer for, those two, and are why we are in the mess we are today, with the one-percent sucking everything up. The movie made helping in Africa seem even more important.

Wednesday, June 6

We arrived in Amsterdam at 11 a.m. and immediately headed to the Mercure. We settled in and conked out about 2 p.m. local time. Those rooms were made for sleeping, and that's just what we did.

Thursday, June 7

I woke up about 3 a.m. and went down to buy a sandwich in the terminal. It was a-humming. Despite the hour, a lot of people were hanging around waiting for flights, chatting, and wide awake. It was very cool. It reminded me of my early travelling days: odd hours and the excited anticipation of far-flung places. Nostalgia and appreciation of my wondrous youth swept over me.

We caught the morning flight to Kilimanjaro, which was comfy because the side rows had two seats instead of three, so I wasn't squashed in the middle for a change. Dale watched *Twilight: Breaking Dawn*, which he said was pathetic. I watched *Albert Nobbs*. It seemed like it might be too sad and tragic to bear, but I decided to watch it anyway.

It turned out to be totally worth it. Albert was a waiter at a hotel in Dublin in the late 1800s, a shy, quiet, middle-aged man who was excellent at his job: thoughtful, discreet, very observant, and kind. He made good tips and was obsessively saving to buy a little shop. It was a hard life. He had no home and slept in a tiny attic room in the hotel. The British class system was in full swing, and the inequity between the rich (a few people) and the poor (almost everyone else) was beyond sickening. Unemployment was common. Albert had done well for himself, given the limited opportunities and low expectations most people would have had for their lives. But he had dreams and hope. There was one small catch: he was a woman.

By sheer coincidence, he meets Page, another woman in the same circumstance working as a painter. But this woman is much stronger, more sure of herself, angrier, and living with and married to another woman. This is a revelation to Albert. He thinks to have the same and tries to woo Helen, a young maid at the hotel. It is hopeless, of course. She is young and pretty and in love with Joe, a no-good young guy who is a drunk, con-man, and bully. She gets preggers. Joe is planning to abandon her and leave for America. Albert tries to save her. Joe slams him into a wall. Albert dies.

It is very sad. Albert did have a restricted life for sure and a heart of unfulfilled dreams. But on the other hand, he was part of an extraordinary sub-set of women (one that had only faintly come across my radar), who lived and worked as men in earlier times. So brave, these women were, and so smart. Why put up with the degrading choices available to women then— governess, maid, prostitute—when you could have the independence and better income of the men? (It was not that the choices for poor men were fabulous, but they were at least marginally better than for women.) They were so admirable, these women, tough, and free in a way. I could only salute and admire them with all my heart.

But poor Albert. His dream of love and a happy home were unfulfilled, at least by himself. At the end of the movie, Page comes to the hotel for a painting job, called by the hotel owner, a conniving, greedy person called Mrs. Slade, who had discovered the money that Albert had stashed away. She is putting it into upgrading her hotel, ironically a smart business move by another smart woman.

Page, now alone (his wife died of typhoid), is staying in Albert's old room. He discovers there an empty wooden box of Albert's and realizes that Mrs. Slade has taken Albert's money. Page also finds a picture of Albert's mother, seemingly wafted by a breeze that also calls him to the window. Down below in the garden is Helen, the young maid, with her new baby. Page goes down to talk to her. She is in dire straits: soon to be turfed from the hotel and have little Albert Joseph taken from her. Page says, "Well, we can't have that now, can we?" The two are drawn to each other: the lonely, bereft man/woman and the vulnerable, broken-hearted girl with her baby. You know that Albert's dream is coming true, that he brought them together so that they can live his dream for him, and for each other.

By the time we arrived at Kilimanjaro Airport in the early evening, I had stopped crying. It was a poignant movie but uplifting to see women negotiating the unfair world, as do the village women in Africa even today. What had seemed like a small, tragic tale was actually a triumph of power, fortitude, and love. Women around the world live these triumphs everyday.

Salma picked us up. So good to see her! Dale and I were quite groggy, so she took us straight to Moshi and Bristol Cottages. During the hour-long drive, we chattered non-stop about the AVPA, excited and eager to get things done. She dropped us off, and we made plans to meet for dinner the next night.

Friday, June 8

On this first morning in Moshi, it was delicious to wake up at Bristol Cottages. The weather was refreshing, cloudy, and cool for a change. We chowed down breks in the dining room and admired the garden, which was quite lush as it was the end of the rainy season. The plants and bushes were noticeably bigger. This beguiling place seemed like a dream, so beautiful and pleasant, a mini garden of Eden.

After getting organized, we went to the bank around the corner and picked up one of the Western Union batches we had sent to ourselves before we left home. This was the best option at the time, as we were no longer able to get cash advances on our Visa cards. Although pricey, Western Union was at least reliable. We had sent the US$4,000 in Dale's name.

Moshi looked better, with new shops and older places now painted and spruced up. Many people were actually working at things such as street construction, maintenance, and gardening, which was stupendous to see! We explored the refurbished park across from the hotel. It was nicely redone, a mini-Tuileries with gravel walkways, grassy areas, hedges, trees, and flowers here and there. I enjoyed it a lot more than the original. Little food shops had also popped up, and we had lunch at one of them. It was all very heartening.

Melki arrived at the hotel about mid-afternoon. It was nice-ish to see him, despite everything. We chatted for a while, catching up and planning this visit. We had decided earlier to give him a "salary" and so presented him with an envelope of several hundred dollars for his help. He looked choked and surprisingly even said a few nice things: that we had made a difference to Okaseni and that the villagers appreciated it. He did too perhaps?

Salma arrived at about 6 p.m. and off we all went to the Indo-Italian restaurant, still there, still amazing food. We talked about current and future AVPA projects. Salma had some grandiose ideas (or so it seemed), such as buying land in Okaseni that would belong to the AVPA. We could put the AVPA poultry site there, she said, and possibly a dispensary, a coffee shop for tourists, a cultural display centre about the AVPA and Okaseni, or a shop for manufacturing building blocks. Perhaps the poultry venture could include slaughtering and packing. (This was probably a good idea but a distressing thought.) The land could be used in perpetuity for AVPA. If there were ever a changing of the guard and Melki was voted out of office, we could lose the coffee nursery and the chicken shelter currently on village land by the office. There would be no protection, and all our work and investment could vanish. With our own land, we could prevent that.

It seemed a good idea. A piece of land was available in Okaseni near Tumaini's mother's place. It was a one-acre field and might be good for a mini-industrial park, African village style. Apparently, the cost was about US$15,000.

This we could do in the long run. It would entail a lot of fundraising for sure. But the focus would be *not* on aid (for a change), but on jobs, businesses, sustainability, self-sufficiency. I thought this would appeal to donors. It would make us rare amongst organizations that depend on fundraising because we would eventually be putting ourselves out of a job and stopping our pleas for donations.

It was exciting chatting to them both, the dinner was delish, and the wine dizzying. Dale and I were finally too beat to continue the fun, so Salma drove us back to Bristol Cottages. A great day!

Saturday, June 9

I slept very well last night and then chowed down the fabulous traditional English breakfast that Bristol Cottages did so superbly, appreciating the coolness of this lovely day at the end of the rainy season.

Salma picked us up at 10 a.m. to meet with Melki in Okaseni at 11. We made a quick stop at a huge (for Moshi) spanking new supermarket that might sell our chickens if we packaged them correctly and then peeked into a small, trendy coffeeshop. Moshi was hopping. Salma said the economy had picked up mostly because of increased tourism. It was encouraging.

We zoomed off to Okaseni, impressed by all the upgrading and paving being done on the road to Moshi by very large trucks and rollers. We discovered later than such projects were being done all over Africa and the world by China as part of their One Belt One Road Initiative. Salma dropped us off at the village office and left. Melki showed us the very small poultry house beside the office. It was too sad to see the little chicks in there, so crowded together and stressed and pecked. Most of them had lost at least some feathers. I was appalled. Dale and I talked about this later, and he said that they should have an area in which to fun free, and that all that was needed was a roof and netting for walls. That sounded much better. I thought there would probably have to be some provision against theft, but it did seem workable. Otherwise, this project was going well. We later talked to Melki about getting a second project set up that would be run by a group of youths headed by a young guy called Valarian. We gave Melki funds in cash to do this.

We went to the new water station/storage house that holds runoff from the mountain streams and then pipes it into the village distribution system. It looked solid and well constructed, and Melki looked like he had won the lottery, practically hugging it. We met a couple of the microcredit ladies and chatted with them for a few moments. We also saw a lot of splendid coffee shrubs on many of the properties: one, two, three, and four years old. How gratifying! We walked to the primary school where I checked out the new murals on the outside walls. They were nicely done and educational, including maps, and paintings of flowers, the night sky, and other scientific things.

We phoned Matthias, the cabbie, who picked us up and took us to see the land that we could buy. It was a massive corn field, very open and flat, with gobs of potential. I liked it.

Matthias took Melki back to the village office and us to Bristol Cottages. I was beat. But after some food and a rest, I perked up. Salma arrived about 6 p.m. We chatted about the land, scholarships, and teaching the teachers. It was exciting and stimulating although Salma seemed a bit competitive, so it was less of an exchange of ideas and more of a contest to see who could do the most talking. She won that one for sure. At about 8 p.m., we called it a day, and Salma left with plans to pick us up tomorrow to take us to a church procession that Melki had invited us to.

Sunday, June 10

Salma took us this morning to the Okaseni church for the Life of Christ procession. As usual, Melki had given us the wrong time, so we waited outside until the mass was over. A young boy came up to talk to me. His name was Calvin. He was fifteen years old although he looked about ten.

"I am studying at a special high school," he told me. "I want to go into aeronautic engineering. I went to the Okaseni primary school. I remember you. You taught the math class I was in." (Actually, it was Lara who taught that class in 2010, the year of the volunteers, but I was hugely complimented that he thought it was me!)

"Good for you to be in school, well done!" I said. "I used to teach at a technical institute in Canada, and I know how important education is. Dale and I might try to get scholarships for the primary and high school students in Okaseni."

"That's a nice idea. But education is not important for the villagers. Money is. They would always prefer money over education."

"Oh, tell me more," I said, intrigued.

"What villagers really need are jobs. They need development. It is only if they move to the city that they realize education is important. But in the village, if they get a job and make money, that *is* development."

Wow, talk about your message from the universe! This was exactly what we were trying to do, among other things. It was one of the best conversations of the trip. Thanks, Calvin!

The procession finally started and turned out to be pretty cool. The masses (you should excuse the pun) of people in the church became an immensely long line that plodded out to the street and off into the distance. It was cheerful and pretty, this throng of people in their Sunday finest. Surprisingly, I rather enjoyed it.

After everyone had left the church, Matthias whisked us back to Bristol Cottages. Salma and Melki met us there at 3 p.m. I got them to fill out work reports for their pay and showed them all the materials and supplies we had brought for the teaching workshop. They were duly impressed although stingy on the thanks.

It was a very good day. No AVPA roller coaster to be seen.

Monday, June 11

Salma took us to Okaseni to meet with the council and villagers this morning. The meeting was good. Salma, bless her heart, raved about it afterward, and even Melki was fairly positive. I gave a quick speech, saying that we were happy to work with Okaseni and to have done so many aid projects, such as the water, electricity, fees for school kids. However, we wanted to help them be independent and able to support themselves, so we hoped to expand the microcredit program and possibly fund and/or help set up small businesses that would employ others.

Salma did a great job of translating, and Melki did not undermine me for a change. At the end, I asked for their feedback, and did they ever give me some. The first thing was that the loans to the microcredit ladies were too small to make much of a difference. They requested instead a loan for a truck. They said that their avocado and banana crops fetched a nice price in Dar, but they were paid only a pittance for them and the Dar merchants took most of the profits. They wanted to have their own truck, eliminate the middle person, and take the profits themselves.

I thought this an excellent idea. I was especially pleased that they asked for a loan and not a truck. It seemed respectful of our limited capabilities and was practical and cooperative. We asked for a proposal ASAP.

They also wanted help with the coffee industry: fertilizer, pesticides, and such. I find coffee quite iffy, given the difficulties of the international marketplace. But coffee used to be the main work of the men, and it occurred to me that they desperately needed to have work. For that reason alone, I was happy to fund it. We asked for a proposal for this too. (We never did receive either proposal.)

They also asked for a dispensary. They had been kicked out of the house in which the dispensary had been set up in 2010. The owner wanted the villagers to pay her for their visits, which was outrageous. The dispensary was now housed in the village office, but they wanted a bigger, dedicated space that couldn't be taken away from them. We said we would try.

We were all pleased with the meeting. The villagers wanted whatever help we could give them. Dale and I were happy to do whatever they wanted. Melki wanted to keep his constituents happy. Salma wanted what is best for them. Win-win-win-win.

As we were leaving, I was followed by Dominican, the sweet guy who had done the enthusiastic translating at our very first village meeting in 2007. He was very kind at the meeting today, saying that we had done a lot for the village and that they really appreciated it. He took me up the road a bit and showed me a piece of property that the owner was trying to sell. It was about half an acre with a fairly large but dilapidated building and a smaller out-building behind it. The inside of the house needed a lot of work, and the whole place looked utterly abandoned. But I liked it. It seemed solid and had potential. The owner wanted about Can$9,000, which was more than I expected but market-appropriate apparently.

This building was for sale in Okaseni, and we thought it
might work as a dispensary if renovated.

The building was probably used to house animals in its latter days.

I took Dale and Salma to see it. They both liked it too. Salma said that we should ask Melki to tell the council that we might want to buy it. We scurried off to let Melki know and then headed out.

Back at Bristol Cottages, Salma and I started going over the microcredit files. They were very confused. She had a hard time with the names and the terminology for the three loan cycles/groups, which led to endless confusion until I finally got her to tell me the specifics of each group separately. That worked. The financial records were also a mess, and she had to go through each person's individual record to figure it all out. Then Dale appeared and asked Salma to help him get a card for his new phone, so they went off while I continued to toil away.

I discovered from the records that two of the ladies had stopped paying their loans back two or three years ago, including Wilfrieda, the albino woman we met on our first visit, who had opened a small store. Another lady had paid back the loan itself but had not the interest. I was quite perturbed. When Dale and Salma came back, I told them these loans had to be cleared up before we would loan any more money to anyone. They were both a bit dubious, but this could not be a precedent. We could not let it go.

We treated Salma to dinner, and she told us about how she and Daudi had broken up and gotten divorced two years ago. It was an hour-long, depressing story, and I really felt for her.

She left about 7 p.m. I was so exhausted my eyes refused to stay open. But they cooperated while I read for a bit to stay on Tanzania time, and then I went to bed where they were much happier.

Tuesday, June 12

I slept for about nine and a half hours last night and felt much better this morning, hallelujah!

Salma and Melki picked us up about 9 a.m. Our plan was to research the poultry industry in the area, so we drove to Kilacha, a chicken production facility that the Catholic church ran outside of Moshi. It was interesting but showed us nothing we didn't already know. Still, it was fun to get out and see something new. I was curious about the church's motivation though.

On our way back to Moshi, we stopped at two teachers' colleges to find out about education for teachers. One seemed promising and told us that they could send a teacher to the village for a week to teach the teachers. (This never did materialize.) In Moshi, we stopped at a small take-out place to order boxed lunches for the teachers' workshop tomorrow. We got back to Bristol Cottages in the late afternoon with plans for Salma to pick me up in the morning for the workshop.

In the evening, we took it easy. Dale read an East African newspaper with an interesting article about the local rise of the middle class and the subsequent rise in coffee drinking as we Westerners know it. It was all chichi and familiar and seemed rather wholesome.

I did a lesson plan for the workshop and organized all the materials and supplies, which was to my liking. I was looking forward to teaching again. We went to bed early as usual, and Dale conked out right away. I read a bit and fretted about Salma, who had been quite rude at times. I was forever slow, always assuming as a rule of the universe that people are nice, always surprised and dismayed to find out that they might not be, always slow to realize that they *had not* been. Sometimes, years later, I have recalled something someone said to me and suddenly got that it was a put-down/cutting remark/snide comment. I was always a bit naive.

I decided to call Salma out on her behaviour and eventually fell asleep.

Wednesday, June 13

Got up, hair, make-up, nice clothes, good to go! Salma arrived at 9 a.m. We picked up the boxed lunches and headed to Okaseni. Dale waited at Bristol

Cottages for Melki. They were going to shop for water pipes and supplies for the dispensary and then join us at the school.

The workshop started at 10 a.m. in one of the classrooms of the primary school. Ten teachers attended as well as Eutropia, the principal. I gave them some basic stuff to start with: notebooks, pens, nametags. We then talked about teaching in general. I told them stories about how important teachers are, and how dictators and psychopaths killed teachers to help maintain their power. Teachers had to go because they are a serious threat to fascism and tyranny. They might encourage their students to think, ask questions, and challenge the status quo—every despot's nightmare.

Then we worked with some teachers' aids, such as foam and plastic replicas of the planet Earth, the human eye, the heart, a plant and such. I gave each teacher one of these aids and had them prepare and do mini presentations for the class using them. Some of the aids were easy and obvious to use while others were quite difficult but hopefully challenging in a good way. (Justin, the head teacher, explained a foam-ball globe, and as he did, I realized one of the teachers had no idea what a continent was.) Then I got them to read to each other some of the simple kids' books that we had brought and ask each other questions about them. The books themselves were not the best for this exercise because most of them were not stories, just rhymes and songs about counting. But the teachers seemed to enjoy it and perhaps discovered how to get more out of reading something.

We took a break at noon for lunch and gave them the boxed lunches (chicken burgers and other goodies). These were a hit. Of all the things that I did in that workshop that day, the teachers liked the lunch the best by far. It was probably better than the normal fare they would have had in a day.

In the afternoon, I had them do another presentation on one of the new educational murals on the outside walls of the school. Then I showed them the other goodies that Dale and I had brought them from halfway around the world, including more aids, books, and several picture dictionaries. These were another big hit. So well done, so bright and cheerful, with masses of useful vocabulary, these dictionaries are great for anybody learning a new language, no matter how old the person is. All the teachers wanted one, but alas, we had only brought three.

The last session of the workshop was a short mental health briefing. I gave them a list of things they could do to be happier and effective in life and work, such as writing down three things a day to be grateful for. But it seemed a kind of first-world technique, and I felt embarrassed, wondering how appropriate it was given how difficult life is in Africa.

Salma was helpful at first as I was teaching but unfortunately became her usual bossy, know-it-all self and began telling me what to do and taking over explaining things. I finally said, "Salma, please. I am the teacher. I will explain things. I know what I am doing." That stopped her.

Dale and Melki arrived near the end of the class, and we gave Melki the honour of handing out the certificates of completion. The participants applauded, thanked me, and said the workshop was excellent. I was chuffed to bits!

Afterwards, I spoke to Melki about the outstanding microcredit loans I discovered yesterday. We had talked to him about buying the land near the office the day of the council meeting. However, I was so ticked off about the non-management of the loans that I now told Melki that we were not going to buy the land unless the loans were cleared up.

He looked absolutely crushed. He *really* wanted that land! Then Salma leapt in and demanded that we work out a plan for the women and give them a month to pay back their loans. These were women who had gotten loans in 2009. I said absolutely not. They had until Monday to get the loans resolved. Monday! Panic and consternation! I said calmly that if the loans were not paid back by Monday, we would stop all aid to Okaseni and never help them again. More consternation and panic—and shock! They seemed not to believe me. But I kept repeating myself, and it slowly sank in that I did indeed mean it.

As Salma drove us back to Moshi, I said I felt the village as a whole ought to step up to solve this problem and that they could be helping one another. Some of the council members (mostly men) seemed to be doing okay. Maybe some of them could help. She seemed befuddled. (Melki also did when I told him this earlier.)

Dale and I rested back at the hotel, and I girded my loins for the next big AVPA rollercoaster moment that was surely on its way. Sigh.

Salma arrived in the evening bringing her friend Afrique, a lawyer, about buying land in Okaseni. He was fabulous and kindly gave us the scoop pro bono.

"Thanks so much for coming to talk to us, Afrique," I said. "We want to buy some land in Okaseni that we can use for projects for our charity, the Africa Village Project Association. Would it be hard to do this?"

The Africa Village Project Association
Summer Newsletter: July 16, 2012

School Days

You might be pleased to know that we spent some of the money we raised over the last two years for malaria nets on education. Funding from the United States for nets meant that we now had money for other worthwhile projects in Okaseni.

Okaseni Primary School was built in the 1950s when Tanzania was still a British colony. The inscription on the building reads "Knowledge is Progress."

We are keen on improving education in Okaseni, and Charleen, our AVPA board member, suggested teaching the primary school teachers. Help for them would benefit not only them, but their students too. Great idea!

A workshop for the teachers sounded good. Charleen and I purchased over $1,000 of teaching supplies and materials, thanks to a donation from our board member, Valerie. Dale and

I managed to get it all into one huge suitcase and safely across all three continents without too much trouble.

We held the workshop at the Okaseni Primary School from 10 a.m. till 3 p.m. during a school break. Ten teachers attended, including Eutropia, the principal, and Justin, the head teacher. Each teacher was given a notebook, pens, pencils, markers, blackboard chalk, and a nametag.

I review a list of teaching aids that the teachers had brainstormed.

The purposes of the workshop were to discuss the profession of teaching and practice using teaching aids. We first talked about the vital importance of teachers to all societies. Some of the teachers looked surprised to hear this.

We then discussed specific teaching aids and how to use them. Each teacher created a five-minute lesson using one of the foam replicas we had brought that represented the globe, a plant, or parts of the body (the eye, the heart), and such. Some of the teachers presented their mini-lessons, and then as a group, we analyzed the strengths of each presentation and how it could have been improved.

Joseph Mushi, one of the teachers, presents his mini lesson using a foam replica of the globe to review the continents of the world.

The teachers then checked out the maps, books, and English picture dictionaries we brought. In pairs, they practiced how to use them in class, and one pair demonstrated their techniques to the class.

The final activity was a discussion on how to maintain a positive outlook in this demanding job. We then gave them the remaining supplies and materials, and each teacher also received a certificate of completion.

There was a standing ovation at the end, a thank-you speech, and many compliments. Several teachers wanted more workshops as they were useful and motivating. We were very pleased that the day went well, and that the workshop seemed appreciated.

Justin Mushi (the head teacher), Mary Shayo, and I talk about using a world map in the classroom. All the teachers received copies of this map. Tanzanian schools are not well funded and have few such resources, so the teachers were thrilled.

The highlight of the day was the box lunch that we purchased for them. The villagers do not always have high-quality food, and they loved it! The most popular item we brought was the picture dictionary. I could have done the whole workshop on that book alone.

This workshop was a good start on our goal of improving the quality of education in the village. We were happy it went well and hope for many more in the future!

"Land is very simple to buy in Tanzania," Afrique said. "But only citizens can buy land in this country. A piece of land in Okaseni could be owned by the villagers, but it is not recommended. It can be misused and there can be many disputes."

"Oh dear," I said. "That doesn't sound good. Could we buy it through the AVPA instead of just us?"

"Yes," he said. "It could be purchased in the AVPA name. The AVPA would own the land and you would share it with the villagers. You would need to write a document that says why the land is being purchased and what it would be used for, emphasizing that it would be in the interest of the community. The document would have to be reviewed and verified by a lawyer. It must be clear, and it must not be done in the village. It is a formal contract and needs to be signed and witnessed. It cannot be signed by any villagers that are related to one another. As well, the sales contract itself would have to be reviewed by a lawyer."

"Hmm, okay, I guess we could do that. I didn't know it could be difficult with the villagers."

"Yes, that is something to remember. But here is another idea. You could start an organization in Tanzania that is related to the AVPA. You could call it the Africa Village Project Tanzania. It would have to be registered with the government here. To start such an organization, a constitution is needed. You must also have representatives called trustees. Tumaini and Salma could be trustees, and you and Dale could be as well. Then you would register the constitution and pay a fee at the Kilimanjaro Community Development Office in Moshi. This does not take a long time. That new organization can purchase the land."

"Okay, that sounds good," I said.

"What about the title search for the land before we buy it?" Dale asked.

"Tanzania does not have title searches. Instead, you have to get witnesses from the neighbours. They will walk around and show you the edges of the property."

I gulped. Seriously? This procedure sounded like a recipe for fraud and contention. But Afrique seemed earnest and didn't mention any problems with it. I held my tongue. (Years later, I took a university course called Greek Civilization. We learned that the ancient Greeks followed this same procedure when buying and selling land and properties. I was floored. Drat! The Greeks have always done everything first, long before us. But it was disconcerting that a little African village in the twenty-first century had not yet updated a two-thousand-year-old procedure.)

Afrique continued, "The villagers will put rocks around the edges of the land, and later the government will come in and put stakes along the border. After the sale, you will get the title (deed) from the Land Registry office. Then the land is yours."

We were so pleased to get all this information from Afrique and thanked him heartily. It was very kind of him to take time from his busy law practice to come and talk to us. Dale and I decided later that we would ask Salma and Melki to do a constitution for us.

Thursday, June 14

I wrote a letter this morning to the Okaseni village council, the villagers, Melki, and Salma, telling them that we would stop the AVPA if the microcredit loans weren't paid. I made photocopies at the stationary shop across the street. Salma arrived around 1 p.m. to take us to Okaseni for a pre-scheduled meeting at 2 p.m. with some of the microcredit ladies.

By 2:20 p.m. or so, three of the ladies had turned up. We chatted with them a bit and interviewed one of them separately about a loan. She seemed like a good bet, but I told her there was a problem with the microcredit program. Until the outstanding loans were paid, we could not lend any more money. She got all teary-eyed and said that made her sad. Me too. But we were doing nothing until the loan situation was resolved.

Several more women arrived. Some of them had been great with the loans, all paid, all on time. Others not so much. One of them was the person who had paid the loan but not the interest. That was not a mistake. Another person had changed her plan mid-stream and bought a piggie, which seemed a good idea although she should have checked with Salma and Melki first.

Our meeting began. Salma started by berating the woman who still owed the interest on her loan. They got into a big argument about the day the woman was supposed to pay. She said she had gone to the office five times to pay but Melki was never there. Then Salma turned on the woman who bought the pig and berated and argued with her for doing that.

I got fed up listening to all this. I stood up and asked to speak to Salma alone.

"There are unpaid loans," I told her. "Until these are paid, we will not help Okaseni. We have done a lot here. We have enjoyed helping and we want to continue helping. But until the loans were paid, we will not help anymore."

I said goodbye to them all and left.

I walked down to where Dale and Melki were measuring the land and the house. I told them about the meeting and gave Melki the letters for him and the council. He said there already had been some action. The council members were meeting later to talk about the situation, and apparently someone was willing to take on the loans. Hallelujah! Melki said he hadn't slept the whole night, sick with worry that the land thing was going to fall apart. Good, revenge for how he has treated me.

Melki said that Marietha, a woman who owned a little shop across the street from the land we wanted to buy and who wanted a loan, had invited us over for coffee. Her house was pretty and very clean. It was soothing and relaxing to be there after the meeting with the microcredit ladies under the village office tree getting chewed on by mosquitos. We said we could probably give her a loan. She was mildly pleased. Her face was intelligent and thoughtful, but it was difficult chatting as she had hardly any English, ditto us for Swahili.

At about 5 p.m., we gently excused ourselves, and Salma drove us back to the hotel. That evening, Dale and I chatted in the dining hall with a friendly person called Vivien, who was helping a tiny orphanage near the tech institute. She was from Cultus Lake, a small town about 100 km from Vancouver. Quelle coincidence! She was a retired social worker and quite the go-getter. In an eight-month period, she had raised Can$9,000, which impressed me no end. We enjoyed hearing about her project, an uplifting way to end the day.

Friday June 15

Our plan today was to give a loan to Renatus, the owner and creative genius of the foundry business. Salma picked us up, then Melki in Okaseni, and we zipped off to Renatus' place.

I was astonished to see how his business had grown. There was now an assembly line with people polishing and cutting metal and Renatus doing the pouring. They were creating small religious symbols, figurines, decorations for doors, windows, and such. To see this busy, constructive, unusual little business in an impoverished village in Africa made me feel both honoured and humbled.

We sat down with Renatus to talk about the loan. I asked about the staff, assets, debts and loans (none), and the purpose of the money we would be loaning him. Salma was her (now usual) scornful self, especially when I was writing down the names of the employees. It was a lot of information, and I was a bit slow. She was impatient and bad-tempered, and I was ready to poke her.

We asked Melki to give Renatus the money in a little ceremony, took pix all round, and enjoyed a cup of coffee served by his sweet wife. Renatus then asked me to do a tour of the shop rooms so that I could give suggestions on how to improve them. I did my best. We left feeling very good about the loan. Renatus was thrilled.

We dropped Melki off at home and continued to Kikilora, the local credit union, to check our account. All was well, with over US$3,500 and all the deposits noted. As I was reviewing the account, Salma tried to explain the odd Kikilora structure, again with the impatience and aggression. I said, "Salma, please don't patronize me." That shut her up, and she instantly become much more polite and less impatient. But what a pain.

She took us back to Bristol Cottages. That evening, Melki arrived with Peter Mchau, who had just arrived from Dar for a couple of days. We were well pleased to finally meet him. We yakked away about Tanzania and the fact that something needed to be done about corruption in the government. No kidding.

We told him about the microcredit situation, and Peter said that Melki needed to put pressure on the women to pay. I suggested (again) that the village come together to try to help for the greater good. That idea (again) went nowhere. Peter berated Melki, badmouthed the women, and slammed the villagers in general, saying that they were hopeless and hardly worth helping. He also dismissed the idea of buying a truck for them because they would fight about it constantly and let it fall apart. I had been naïvely (as usual) hoping that he might cough up the loot to cover the loans. No way. The conversation was utterly dismaying. The two of them left at about 8 p.m.

It took me awhile to fall asleep because I was fretting about not getting the loan payments and then having to shut down the AVPA. That would be a nightmare. I finally did fall asleep, sans nightmares thank goodness.

Saturday, June 16

We talked to Vivien this morning at breakfast, asking her about the little orphanage she was helping. It had been started by two young men who took in homeless kids, mostly off the street, and housed them, clothed them, and kept them in school. Vivien was helping to pay school fees, furnish the house, and provide food and clothing. It was very touching, and she and I bonded forever about the trials and triumphs of running a tiny NGO in Africa.

We had arranged to get together this afternoon with Salma, but after yesterday, I was not keen. She texted at about 1 p.m. that she was on her way, just as I was going to text her not to come. Drat. She arrived.

Sheesh, what a meeting. First, we worked out the loan contract for Renatus and talked about the loan payments for the poultry project. She was helpful, and more polite and subdued than usual. She seemed very worried about the microcredit program ending. After the business discussion, she pulled out all the stops to persuade us to continue. Her arguments were reasonable at first.

"Why," she said, "should a few difficult women and a few hundred dollars end all the good that could be done for so many other people and the village in general?"

Well, I thought, that was a good point. But it was the principle of the thing. Also on the "no" side were the hard work and aggravation of running the AVPA, not to mention fundraising and dealing with recalcitrant people at home and here in Tanzania too, I might have added.

But then, she started to criticize us irrationally.

"You should have told everyone that it was just you and Dale, and that you didn't have a lot of funding, from BCIT for example."

Hmm . . . I thought. What a great idea. I could have sworn I had done that ad nauseum.

"Also, you are very disorganized," she continued. "You need to have a plan. You bought dinners for me and Melki one evening. You need to become better known to the villagers and should plan to do this for the future. Also, Sheena, you should talk to the villagers and try to keep your temper and not get angry. You should do your best to stay calm."

These last comments took my breath away with their inappropriateness. How could she have thought that this was acceptable?

Some of her ideas seemed okay, except for the ones after the fact and the completely crazy ones (I think she was getting desperate), but the way she said them was very off-putting. She was aggressive, critical, and lecturing. I tried to defend ourselves as best I could and even get a word in edgewise, always a challenge with Salma. I did manage to say that we had done a lot for the village and that the villagers did know us. But the "keeping my temper" comment was just over the top. At that point, I had had enough.

"Okay, this conversation is finished," I said. I got up, said goodbye, and left.

Needless to say, I was upset, especially about the "temper" comment. It seemed almost abusive (in fact, a lot of her behaviour on this trip was), and I just wanted to get rid of her.

I wasn't sure what to do. But after all the trouble with the microcredit program, the council members' dissatisfaction with it, the unpaid loans, the seeming inability of the village to get a grip and resolve the situation, and now all this unpleasantness with Salma, I decided to shut the microcredit program down. The still active loans to Renatus, Happy, and the poultry groups I would convert into business grants.

Dale concurred. I sent Salma a brief text from Dale's phone to that effect (which she never got) and felt such relief I can't tell you. I had been completely dedicated to the AVPA and found it very satisfying. But after I took early retirement in 2011 and was thrilled to be able to work on it full-time, I discovered that it was masses of wearying, tedious drudgery (financial records and endless paperwork). Then came Africa Night. Twice. That experience completely sucked the joy out of the AVPA for me. Then came this trip with the usual disappointments and annoyances, and now this aggressive young person whose discourteousness was breathtaking—it was the death blow. I could not keep devoting my heart and soul irrevocably to the AVPA anymore.

I felt a twinge of sadness about it but also felt the proverbial weight fall off me. Could I actually have a life of pleasantness and enjoyment?! I could hardly imagine it. Happy, fulfilling days doing fun stuff I enjoyed with Dale and other people I liked, was that possible?! I wondered what things I might do instead. Hmm, I couldn't think of anything. I decided to just let it evolve. The first thing to do was make it through and recover from this trip. I would then just rest, recuperate, and see what came up.

I went to our hotel room to freshen up for a visit from Nuria, Anisa, and Fatema mid-afternoon. I choked up with joy to see them. Anisa was now twenty years old and quite the going concern: bright, articulate, thoughtful, and bossy. She was always telling her mum what to do. She was applying to Moshi University to study business and finance, and for that they need help. Fatema was fourteen and overshadowed by her talkative, outgoing sister. She didn't seem to have a voice or know what she wanted to do, but she was still very young and once she got into a sister-less school situation would probably blossom.

We gave Nuria funds for Fatema's next term at high school, with the promise that we would help with her second term and with Anisa's first year at university. She and Nuria were going to Dar the next day to begin the application process, which was very time-consuming apparently. We hoped she would get in.

Arif, the girls' father, turned up and he and Dale had a nice chat about cars, and such. At about 5 p.m., they had to go, which was rather doleful. They were such sweethearts. As they left, Anisa took both our hands and thanked us so much, saying she would not be where she was today if it weren't for us. It was so sweet of her and consoling to think we had done some good, especially for such dear people, unlike others who came to mind. It was a heartwarming visit. Nuria seemed calmer and less frantic about the safety and future of her kids, and perhaps even hopeful, which was *very* good to see.

Oy vey, what a day.

Sunday, June 17

This morning, we received a text from Melki saying he was coming at 4 p.m. to see us. We wondered with what news.

It was a quiet day. I rested a lot. Then I organized all the paperwork for Melki. We also did a funds assessment and planned what to do with the money on hand. I also did some packing for our departure tomorrow. Not soon enough.

Melki arrived looking tired and subdued. He told us that the village had managed to cover all the loans. Good. He said that the council and the villagers met last night and this morning and that it was beyond drama. There were arguments and anger and tears. Wilfrieda cried a lot. Her grandfather paid some of her loan. The council paid some as well and also took over the rest of the loans, so the women will pay them directly. The woman who refused to pay her interest finally did. It sounded quite the scene, and I was sorry I hadn't been there. Dale wasn't. Whatever, the loans got paid.

We then told Melki that we were cancelling the microcredit program and doing business grants instead. This program would be much easier to operate and probably more effective. We forgave the loans to Renatus (the foundry), the poultry people (a group of women that had taken over the office site and Valerian with the youths), and Happy (who was leasing the knitting machine), so they could focus on their businesses, debt free. We also gave small grants to two reliable and competent businesswomen, Mama Marietha who owned the small store, and Mama Augustine, one of the first microcredit ladies. We told Melki to use the repaid loans and the remaining funds in the Kikilora account as the down payment on the land. We also asked him to deliver to Salma the money we promised her for her help and expenses during our visit. (I sent her a text about this.) I also got Melki to sign a slew of receipts for everything.

Melki didn't hang around as he had a workshop to go to tomorrow on the rights of the child, given by a Danish NGO. In the evening, I sent Salma a text from Dale's phone saying we were disbanding the microcredit program. And so to bed.

Monday, June 18

Departure day! Not a moment too soon. We had some running around to do for the final tidying up of everything AVPA, as well as the packing and organizing.

We were having lunch when who should appear but Salma. She joined us and told us she had received our text about the money and gotten it from Melki. Then she started talking. I kept quiet, wanting to hear what she had to say. But Dale interrupted her and launched into an explantion of why we were shutting down the microcredit program. She was quite bewildered because apparently, she hadn't received our text about shutting it down. I showed her that text on Dale's phone, and she gasped. Then she started to explain why she had come.

"I feel like something has been wrong with you since Wednesday, Sheena," she said.

That was the day I told her and Melki that the outstanding loans had to be paid back by today. I didn't think I had come across as angry or deranged or whatever she meant by "wrong," but I had been firm and unmoved. It was odd that she would have misinterpreted that, especially since I was quite apologetic to Melki about having to do it. Then I remembered that was also the day she interfered in my teaching workshop, and I asked her to stop. Oh dear.

She continued, "I cannot take your money because obviously things are not right between us."

Dale leapt in again. "The money is yours. It is what we promised you for your expenses, translating, assisting us, travelling around with us, and giving us rides. You have certainly earned it for all your help."

"I feel like something has gone wrong," she repeated.

Dale continued, "Sheena has put a lot into the AVPA: time, energy, work, even her own money. She spends a lot of time working on it. At times, it is too much, and I would like her to do less."

I, in the meantime, had maintained a stony silence and stared off into the distance. But when everyone had said their piece, attention turned to me.

I said (in calm and measured tones, Dale told me afterwards), "Some of your behaviour has been very inappropriate. At Kikilora, you were patronizing and laughed at us."

She became a bit defensive, a bit apologetic, and a *lot* uncomprehending.

"I hadn't been aware I acted like that," she said.

"It was not the way someone should treat people who are essentially your bosses," I said.

"I was doing the project for friendship and love and perhaps I should have thought of you more as bosses."

"No, we think of you as a friend too," I replied. "But a person shouldn't treat a friend like that."

"I wasn't aware of it," she repeated.

"If that is so, you might want to look at your behaviour. In Canada, you could get fired for acting like that."

In truth, she had just gotten fired. Dale kept saying no, she wasn't fired. But her department had just been abolished, which is a way in the business world of firing someone.

I did respect her for coming to talk to us and told her I appreciated it. She did not exactly apologize, however, but I was a lot less angry at this point anyway. Something told me to keep my distance, but I also said maybe she could be my long-distance assistant so that I could have someone to keep in touch with. We might be able to pay a small stipend. She left, seeming still unsure and bewildered.

We left after dinner for Kilimanjaro Airport in the Bristol Cottages van. It was the usual crazy check-in, the usual long wait. Then we walked out over the tarmac to the enormous KLM airplane and climbed up the clunky mobile staircase. This huge hunk of metal and people and equipment glided elegantly along what passed for a runway and gently lifted itself off the ground and into the sky. The ebony African night enveloped us.

Tuesday, June 19

Schiphol! Ah, heaven! We debarked the plane and caught the train to Utrecht to begin our trek to Lauterbrunnen, Switzerland. Even though I had not gotten much sleep, I was amazed at how good I felt. It was not Africa! No need to worry about the water, food, mosquitos, taking our malaria pills, Salma, the AVPA, Melki, the funds, the loans, the donors, having to tote around large quantities of cash! No long list of things to do, no schedule, no DEET, no deadline. It was glorious.

The Africa Village Project Association
Summer Newsletter: July 6, 2012

African Returns

Dale and I arrived in Tanzania in June, for the fourth time since we started the AVPA to help Okaseni in 2007. On this trip, we noticed some dramatic changes.

You might remember that we did a lot of fundraising over the last two years. Our goal was to buy malaria nets for the village. But we discovered just before we left on this trip that the Gates Foundation and the Global Fund had paid for nets for the entire country. Such a positive initiative was breathtaking for us. We have never seen evidence of large-scale projects in Tanzania, only the work of small organizations and dedicated individuals. We rejoiced at this watershed project!

More changes unfolded before us in Moshi, the large town near Okaseni where we stay during our visits. The number of young men hanging around shops and street corners was fewer, and we were able to make our way along the streets with fewer touts accosting us. Had they found jobs? More people did seem to be working, tending stores and clipping hedges.

The park across from our hotel, barren and uninviting before, was now a pleasant garden with walkways, flowers, shrubs, and a food court serving yummy local meals. Another surprise was the road work. The main road north from Moshi, previously pitted and bumpy, was being graded and paved. We could hardly believe our eyes.

These huge machines were grading the road we take from Moshi to Okaseni, which will make our trips there much easier.

We still saw many lepers and other beggars by the roadsides, but the changes we saw were signs that money was being spent ethically and responsibly. Even the money itself had been upgraded. New Tsh 10,000 notes had been printed and the old grimy ones were gone. How good was that? It was indeed a new day and our return to Tanzania was joyous.

At Utrecht, I was walking at Africa speed through the train station and saw this Middle Eastern guy standing amid the rushing river of humanity pounding through to catch trains. He was trying to sell an alternative newspaper and looked so desperate and pleading. Everyone ignored him. I was too dozy to take it all in and walked past him although with sympathy. Later, I realized how stupid I had been. I should have stopped and bought a newspaper from him. That much I could have done in solidarity and support of poor people everywhere in the world trying to survive. I felt terrible and kicked myself for months over this.

We caught the train to Frankfurt, transferred to the Interlaken train in Switzerland, and caught the local to Lauterbrunnen. It was a very long day, over nine hours on trains, and late when we arrived. Lauterbrunnen was dramatic and gorgeously breathtaking, but mostly I was just relieved to be there. We traipsed along the main drag to the Hotel Jungfrau at the other end of this very small town. Jungfrau was a misnomer because the hotel was quite old, but the staff were very pleasant and fed us even though we were so late. Our room was small and humble but very clean, and the beds were covered by those puffy white eiderdowns so common in the Netherlands. O joy!

Wednesday, June 20

Our first full day in Lauterbrunnen was splendid. The village was in a narrow valley between two massive cliffs that sported numerous waterfalls, including the famous Staubach Falls, a thin, high waterfall just outside of town. It is so high that the water sometimes becomes just spray on the way down. We walked here and there and oohed and aahed. Many of the houses were old-school Swiss chalets, and the hotels and stores that lined the main road were modest and unprepossessing. Green meadows sloped up to the base of the cliffs and were dotted with cows and sheep placidly partaking of grass. The village was not modern or urban or glitzy but rather quaint and fetching. My kinda town. (Sorry, Frank.)

In the afternoon, we went to the Lauterbrunnen Valley Museum, which was just a small house by the river. Although tiny and modest, it was nicely done, with super displays and lots of information. It was touching to see how the village Swiss used to live even as recently as the 1920s, with lace making being a main source of income. It was much like Africa, with very hard lives and unending work but in places of great beauty, and with probably a lot of satisfaction. Well, maybe the last doesn't apply to Africa. Anyhow, the museum was an unexpected treat.

We also climbed up to the base of Staubach Falls, the dramatic waterfall close by. The path started at the village church and wended its way upwards through a field or two. We passed some sheep grazing on the grass, each with its own little neck-bell tinkling away. Nearby were several cows with their large bells clanging in harmony. Just then the church bells starting ringing, on and on, calling us to prayer I guessed. It was utterly lovely: the tinkling, the clanging, the fat and woolly ones earnestly trying to get their fill on a steep slope of green. Dale got a video of it that delighted me every time I watched it. It was my kind of prayer.

Back at the Hotel Jungfrau, we watched from our balcony a team of maintenance workers repave one of the lanes of the small main road through town. They worked swiftly and easily doing their various tasks. One of them poured out the hot tar onto the road from a small dump truck. Two others raked and smoothed the tar across the lane, followed by another person driving a street roller to flatten and compact the tar. They looked healthy and strong, focussed, and efficient. It was a pleasure to watch them, working as they were on a worthwhile and beneficial task for the good of the community.

I was struck by the difference with Africa. Things were so minimal there, notwithstanding the huge road-grading machines we saw in Moshi this year courtesy of China. Paved roads in general, not so much. Useful machinery, rare. People who had a good standard of living and all the benefits of a developed country, such as education, health care, opportunities, reasonable wages, were a minority. Gratitude for my own good fortune flooded through me, as did the desire to keep helping Okaseni as best we could, despite my many doubts. It was a surprise to feel that way.

In the evening, Dale fell asleep early, and I went down to the lounge to watch the news and write in my journal. The lounge was homey and old-fashioned with red leather couches and a tray of little glasses and a carafe of sherry on a small bureau. The room faced east towards the Jungfrau and the Monch, her protector from the evil Eiger. I wrote away madly in this comfortable and friendly place, trying to catch up since Saturday, the last time I wrote anything. It was scrumptious to write. The simple act of writing is enough to make me happy and helps me to live and understand my life. It's also an excellent record, just in case I ever wanted to write a book.

Thursday, June 21

The longest day of the year! It didn't seem like it though—it was good fun.

I need to mention the food. The food! We could not eat well in Moshi as the food was not the best. For expediency's sake, we ate most of our meals at Bristol Cottages: always the full English breakfasts (very good) and then butter chicken for dinner (okay, but not great), but with no variety. On the KLM flight to Amsterdam, we were served a dinner of fish and potatoes. Okay, it was just airline food, but it was so superior to anything we had eaten in two weeks that my body went berserk with joy. I could feel all my molecules leaping and dancing, busy, busy, absorbing all the luscious nutritiousness as fast as they could. Every succeeding meal was like that: the breks on the flight, the sandwiches at the Utrecht train station, the wiener schnitzel at the Lauterbrunnen hotel. Joy! Delight! That just-won-the-lottery feeling! That first morning at the hotel, I had yogurt and granola, the first time since home. I chowed down bowls and bowls of it. I could not stop eating, it was so fabulous. Yes, the food!

Today we went to a bank to cash some traveller's cheques. They wanted to charge us 9 SF each (Can$13)! We declined. The Swiss bankers also keep old (limited) banking hours, probably to count all their loot.

I was exhausted today. I felt like I had been hit by a bus, truck, train, car, bike, motorcycle, donkey, all at once. The drama and trials in Okaseni and the running on adrenalin instead of good food had knocked me flat. Despite that, I was keen to do our plan today to take the train to Wengen. These little trains, bright and shiny like a row of polished buttons, climb up the high, high mountains by electric power and little steel cogs that they latch themselves onto. It is scarcely believable that such a simple and elementary system can zip people up, down and around a multitude of mountains, some very high and very steep. Anyhow, it does.

Our train was stalwart and quite the thrill, chugging its little way up the slopes, over sturdy bridges, through old stone tunnels, around curves and obstacles bestowing on us a revolving scene of spectacular mountain vistas. We arrived in Wengen, which was directly above Lauterbrunnen with a great view of the village and valley. It was a cute town but quite touristy. We walked around a bit and checked out a small cemetery where a lot of tombstones mentioned death by mountain misadventure. After a couple of hours, we hopped on the button train again. It was as fun as an amusement park ride.

I began to feel better at about 4 p.m. For dinner, we had rosti at the hotel, a typical Swiss dish with minced potato, cheese, and ham, too good. It had been a very nice day.

Friday, June 22
I felt better today, thank goodness. We decided to do a walk.

We headed south down the river. It was a gorgeously sunny day but fortunately not hot, and a brisk breeze kept us from getting overheated. The river was unnerving, sporting a major spring run-off, so you would not want to fall in. It was a bonny stroll through pastoral Switzerland, with classic views of sloping green meadows, sturdy chalets, the accoutrements of farming, the sheep, and cows. Honestly, Switzerland is just too cute for its own good. You just want to smack it. It's always mentioned how practical the Swiss are, and you can see it everywhere: in the trains, the "uber-development" as Dale calls it (no stone left unimproved), the abounding tourist industry. As well as all that charm and pragmatism, they also have the mountains: the universe's majesty before their eyes every day. The country seems a kind of peak of human achievement (you should excuse the pun). It's nice of them to share it with the rest of us.

Back at the hotel, I rested and read. Dale tromped off to the south end of the valley to check out Trümmelbach Falls. He had to pay to get in, so he said no way. He was very distressed when he got back because he heard gun shots near the pathway just outside town as he walked past. Our waitress told us that it was from a local shooting range. The Swiss like their guns apparently. Dale was not impressed. We chowed down our wiener schnitzel and omelets and then lumbered off to bed.

Saturday, June 23

Our plan for the day was to go to Kleine Scheidegg. We got some sandwiches at a tiny internet café near the station and caught the 10:30 train.

Again, I marvelled at the steadfast and adorable little train, chugging us first up to Wengen, then on to Kleine Scheidegg. As we neared it, we got some dramatic views of the Jungfrau: it is a *very* big mountain. The Monch was shrouded in cloud, but just before Kleine Scheidegg, we got a good view of the north wall of the Eiger. It was utterly concave and looked extremely dangerous to anyone crazy enough to be thinking of climbing it. I was surprised how thrilled I was to see the mountain in person, as it were, I guess because of how famous it is and also having recently watched *The Eiger Sanction*, starring everyone's favourite psychopath, Clint Eastwood.

We arrived at Kleine Scheidegg, the summit of a mountain pass, where there was a hotel, tourist building/souvenir shop, a few bars and restaurants, the train station, and not much else. It is however at the base of the Eiger, a decided claim to fame, with the Monch and Jungfrau lolling about behind it. Spectacular! More oohing and aahing. Dale told me that he wanted to walk the Eiger Trail, a path that ran along the base of the mountain. It would take two to three hours and was as close to the mountain itself as most people would ever want to get. I did not even want to get that close, but I had not known of Dale's plan and so had brought nothing to read. I bought a (very expensive) copy of *The Eiger Sanction* from the souvenir shop to read while Dale did the walk, and I waited for the Monch to make an appearance.

Off Dale went. He had a great time, huffing and puffing his way along the trail and scampering through an area of falling rocks, which he managed to avoid. Unfortunately, clouds had moved in over the Eiger, so he wasn't able to get any good pix although he waited about an hour. But he was very pleased. That evening, he told Brigitte, the lovely owner of the hotel, that he had wanted to see these mountains for years. He said that it was surreal being here, having read and thought about Switzerland since high school. It was even better than he imagined. I was glad to hear that. He also told me later that he found Switzerland very developed with no wilderness, unlike home. True. But that was partly its charm, and we would soon be on our way back.

While he did the hike, I sat on some bleachers that were the town's meeting place for tourists and visitors. They afforded me a good view of the Monch, and I settled down with the book. I didn't know what to expect, but it turned out to be way better than I thought it would be. It was well written, with great sentence structure and word choice although a bit over the top with the erudite vocabulary. It was funny, clever, suspenseful, well constructed, and utterly spellbinding. It was also a heartless book, cold, devoid of any gentle or kind human emotion, cynical, bitter, contemptuous of every last soul on Earth, just like its protagonist. It was also violent. Ugh. Even so, I could not put it down.

Dale turned up a couple of hours later, pleased with himself and the mountain. Back at the hotel after dinner, I read the book. There were no journal entries that night. I read and read. Dale eventually conked out, and I continued to read till about 11 p.m. I was two-thirds the way through the book by the time I finally put it down and closed my eyes to sleep.

Sunday, June 24

We decided to walk on the east side of town on the path to Wengen. Being Sunday, everything was closed except for the internet cafe, where we bought a quiche and a sandwich. We then began our walk. I felt a lot better today, still tired but functioning.

The walk was capital. The path went first south by the river, then up into woods, past streams and over bridges, then beside meadows where farmers were working like crazy to get hay in before the rain, which was on its way. We saw placid cows, heard birds chirping in old Swiss, saw a horse by itself in a field, and got pix of the train going up to Wengen. Again with the utter cuteness of Switzerland. It got hot. Dale took more pix. We sat on a stone wall and ate lunch.

We got back to the hotel mid-afternoon. I was beat, hot, and dehydrated, so I passed out on the bed. When I woke up an hour or so later, Dale—and my book—were gone. I could see him from the balcony on the outdoor patio down below, having a beer and deep into the book. I stayed upstairs and rested some more. Later, we went for dinner, I wrote in my journal, and he read my book. We went up to the room, and I packed, and he read my book. We went back down for a drink, I wrote in my journal, and he . . . yup!

We paid the bill and told Brigitte, our sweet hostess, how much we had enjoyed our visit and appreciated her kind hospitality. Back up in the room, I tried to get to sleep early as we were leaving the next day. I had enjoyed it here so much despite being so tired. It was hard to imagine a more beautiful, interesting, healthy, and restful place for some rest and recuperation, especially after the many trials of Africa. I was grateful that I was fortunate enough to come here. Like Dale and his mountains, it had been much better than I expected.

Monday, June 25

We were up at 6:30 a.m., and caught the 7:00 train to Interlaken, then on to Frankfurt and Amsterdam. At Frankfurt, we got off at Amsterdam Central, which was too soon. Utrecht would have been better. Maybe I would have found that newspaper guy and bought a paper from him. Anyhow, it was insanely busy. I tried to stay calm. We finally got the right train and were off to Schiphol.

We arrived about 10 p.m. and went straight to the Mercure. Dale crashed and I went down to watch the sunset, so late so far north. It was a treat. I found a book in the airport bookstore called *23 Things They Don't Tell You about Capitalism.* It was worth the price. My favourite was "Thing 13: Making rich people richer doesn't make the rest of us richer." Hah, I thought as much. Books like this on economics were just what I needed, not the theoretical kind but economics as it relates to the world we actually live in. It talked about global inequities and inspired me somewhat to keep on trucking in Okaseni.

Tuesday, June 26

I was so excited to be going home today. Our cat was very happy to see us, but not as happy as I was to be back at home and with her.

HOME

This year, I joined the Bowen Island Rotary Club, which turned out to be unexpectedly enjoyable. I loved the guest-speaker evenings that were held twice a month. The variety of speakers and the breadth of topics were astounding. I made a new friend, Eva, who impressed me with her energy and engagement with life. In November, I went to a Rotary Leadership weekend workshop, ever hopeful we might be able to get some funds. The workshop was good, but I re-discovered that Rotary was very bureaucratic and overly organized. My hopes of getting funding were totally dashed this time.

When we got back home, I emailed Tumaini about buying land in Okaseni. He was working for the UN in South Sudan. In August, we received this email from him:

> Sorry for the long delay. The trip to South Sudan was difficult this time compared to past experiences. I got malaria and could not do anything for about a week. Since I am doing everything myself, I had to wait to recover to do the remainder of the work. I am planning to travel back to Austria on Thursday this week. Monika and Isaac are doing fine. Isaac talks a lot these days and has started kindergarten. He speaks German with Monika and learns my poor English and a bit of Swahili.
>
> About the decision to buy land, please do not drop this idea. It is the best way to make the project sustainable for years to come, and in fact this is what will make it easy for the project to solicit funding here in Tanzania. The AVPA has already done so many things and stands high chances of getting funding from sources within the country.
>
> Now what has to be done is registering an NGO here in Tanzania that would own the land. The laws in Tanzania allow registration of entities in which the members of the governing board are foreigners provided that the team involves locals. I am willing to prepare the paperwork for this, and the best way in my experience is to register a "trust." The members of the board of trustees could be you as chair, Dale, Salma, me, Melki, and Peter Mchau or any other person of your choice (the minimum number is two). Then the land would be registered in the name of the trust.

The constitution would provide for the manner in which the trust property could be disposed of in the event of a dissolution. There is a lot of freedom in writing the constitution of trusts, so it is possible to prepare them in such a way that they satisfy your vision. Being a non-profit, there is no annual fee for running a trust. What they need is an annual record of return of trustees to indicate those continuing and those who have ceased to be trustees.

That is all for now. I appreciate your willingness to continue supporting Okaseni.

In October, I got in touch with Melki and Salma about writing a constitution. Nothing had been done. I let Tumaini know, and fortunately, he returned to Tanzania later that month and began working on the trust. The constitution he prepared seemed to be based on a standard template probably provided by the government. It was detailed and very long, and it contained eventualities far beyond anything our little organization was capable of, such as creating governance positions: secretary for the board, office of the treasurer, and management and implementation committees. There was also a mention of having an office in Okaseni for the AVPT. Sigh. Always the wet blanket, I told them that such exigencies were impossible for us to even contemplate.

Tumaini continued work to set up the trust. The trustees were him, Salma, Melki, Dale, and me. Dale and I would eventually have to be accepted for the positions. The registration documents were executed and submitted. We now just had to wait for approval.

All in all, it had been a good year for the AVPA. Nonetheless, throughout this year, my gentle turning away from the AVPA continued. My realization in 2011 that I did not want to spend my days doing the masses of administrative work the project required allowed to me to lift my head up and look for other possibilities. Seeing the news item in January of this year about foster-care teenagers wanting to be adopted made me want to help. Maybe we could adopt one! I asked Dale. He said, "NO!" Okay, but maybe I could still help. Perhaps I could try to help a kid who was ageing out of the system. (When foster kids turned nineteen, they lost all government support and had to fend for themselves, often with disastrous results.) Perhaps I could let a kid live in a tiny studio condo I owned in the suburbs. I could help them, encourage them to get an education, shower them with affection and kindness, bring them into my family, and get them off to a better start in life than otherwise.

So I decided to try to find a kid. Here is what I wrote in my journal:

> I did a lot of phoning around and finally got in touch with two social workers from an adoptive-families organization. I met with them for lunch in February. They were very nice but quite discouraging, saying that I should probably find a kid first and establish a relationship with them before setting them up in a condo. They said it would take time and that finding the kid was the issue. They said they would try to find one for me. It was disappointing, but I will keep trying.
>
> Some people have been wonderfully supportive about this idea, even thrilled, while others have been dubious and hostile. Sheesh. But I am used to this. Some of the things people have said to me about the AVPA are awful to remember. When I first had the idea to find a kid, I could not believe the joy that I felt and the love for these forsaken ones. It was thrilling, and this venture seemed the perfect vessel for my compassion and energy, and for my desire to do something good in the world.
>
> Over the next months, I went to an adoption workshop that the social workers recommended. I phoned and kept in touch, and talked to even more social workers, including one who was outright hostile about my idea. Nothing happened. They never found me a kid and eventually refused to take my phone calls. I finally gave up in October, realizing it was a lost cause. I contacted Youth Center Resources, an organization that tried to find property owners willing to rent out cheap to foster kids. They were thrilled to rent my condo, I was thrilled to rent it out to them, and the foster kid was over the moon—success all round. The kid was moved in by mid-November.

It worked out very well. I rented the condo to that organization for the next nine years. Although I had to give up finding one kid to help personally, I was happy to provide a place to live for a few of them.

It was quite the year, and looking back over it, I remembered one incident in particular. It was in Lauterbrunnen when Dale and I watched the road crew from our hotel balcony paving the town's main drag. We had just flown from one of the poorest countries in the world to one of the richest, and it was unreal and slightly disorienting, as we watched the road crew, to see and recognize the oceanic differences between the two. Switzerland is home to Davos, a popular town for alpine sports and the place where the World Economic Forum (WEF) holds its annual meeting. Rich businesspeople from around the world come together to discuss the global economy and how to improve the world. But for whom? Only themselves? A lot of interesting ideas are floated, but these ideas seem mostly concerned with first-world problems. The attendees pay scant attention to the developing world, and they also refuse to pay taxes in their own countries. Worsening inequality in the world seems not to faze them, and they perhaps can't imagine a future in which the poor might turn up on their doorsteps with pitchforks and torches. As Martin Luther King said, "We all too often have socialism for the rich and rugged free market capitalism for the poor."[1]

Rutger Bregman, a Dutch author who was a guest speaker at the WEF in 2019, suggested to the billionaires in attendance that they pay taxes. He said, "I hear people [at this conference] talking the language of participation, justice, equality, and transparency, but almost no one raises the real issue of tax avoidance, right? And of the rich not paying their fair share. . . . Taxes, taxes, taxes," he said. "All the rest is bullshit."[2] He was met with a stony silence. He did not receive an invitation back the next year.[3]

On the other hand, Mackenzie Scott, former wife of Jeff Bozo, er, Bezos, the founder of Amazon, is on an extraordinary mission of philanthropy that puts her husband and every other billionaire on the planet to shame. Committed to giving away 50 percent of the US$37 billion she received in her 2019 divorce settlement, she decries the accumulation of wealth in the hands of a few and is trying to readdress this inequity.[4] She donates to small colleges, grassroots organizations, social service organizations, Big Brothers Big Sisters, Habitat for Humanity, with no restrictions on how the money is used, and no reporting or auditing required.[5] She and Bridgespan Group, the consulting firm she works with, carry out diligent searches for recipients, evaluating effectiveness, successful outcomes, and conscientious management.[6] In a posting on her website, Medium, she said that they started with 6,490 possibles, then after more research whittled the list down to 822, and finally donated to 384 organizations.[7] She seems to have inspired Melinda Gates to do something similar[8] and yes, even her ex-husband, who in 2022 donated $100,000,000 to Dolly Parton.[9] I'm sure she really needs it. (Just kidding. Actually, it was for Parton to fund other charities, including her own.) In four years (to 2022), Scott donated US$14.4 billion to worthy causes.[10]

She truly is an admirable and amazing person. However, what about all the rejected colleges and the social service organizations that did not make the cut, such as the inner-city schools that struggle to keep teachers, have crumbling school buildings, can't afford books, and have no lunch programs? They undoubtably need more help than the organizations that Scott helps, but poverty and social conditions have likely caused flaws that make these organizations unacceptable for Scott's particular largess.

What Scott is doing is so commendable that one hesitates to softly breathe even one tiny little suggestion. How about paying taxes, Mackenzie? Just a thought. Despite their bad rap, taxes are good. They allow governments to do what they do well: provide universal programs and initiatives that help *everyone*, not just the selected, incomplete groups that Scott is helping, humble and worthy though they all may be. "It is justice, not charity, that is wanted in this world," said Mary Wollstonecraft in 1792. Still true today, Mary.

Taxes can provide justice. They can not only fund national programs but also foreign aid programs. Canada's own Lester Pearson help set a goal in 1969 that developed countries spend .7 percent of their annual GDP to fund international development. Canada has yet to honour that commitment. More systematic help overseas would be a godsend to countries like Tanzania. The malaria nets that George Bush got credited with sending were a huge boon. With the generous help of carefully managed and widespread government programs, there would be little need for small organizations like the AVPA, which are able to help painstakingly and minimally only at the micro level.

I repeat: taxes are good. If you have ever used a public library, driven on a highway, or had medical treatment in a Canadian hospital, you have benefited from the taxes that you and others paid. Taxes help give us the bountiful lives we have today. The tax bill that Canadians pay hasn't risen appreciably since the 1960s,[11] and we have more goodies, leisure, opportunities, improved health care, and a higher standard of living than people did then. Don't even mention what billionaires enjoy these days. It is beyond aggravating to see the sense of entitlement of the rich, to watch the Elon Musks of this world being fawned over and applauded even as Musk sneers at criticism that he might be a tad greedy.[12] It is heartbreaking to then remember a small group of worthy people halfway around the globe struggling mightily every day to stay alive.

Surely we privileged people in developed countries owe some thought and care for the poor and disadvantaged, at home and abroad. May all countries one day feel that they too have drawn the queen (or king) of spades.

CHAPTER 7

2013, CONSTITUTION, LAND, AND GRANTS

1975

Ralph and I had been warned about Lagos, Nigeria's capital, as a dangerous, densely populated, crime-ridden city, so we skirted it and headed directly east.

The last place we stayed in Nigeria was Ibadan, a university town close to the border with Dahomey (now Benin). An older British professor picked us up and invited us to stay with him for a few nights. He was very kind, and lonely I think now, but probably a solitary guy by nature. His house was spacious and beautiful, with walls of a rich, dark wood, lots of windows for light, and rustling shade trees outside to block the direct sun. He had a library where I found a copy of *Tess of the d'Urbervilles*. I subscribe to the adage of Logan Pearsall Smith: "People say life is the thing, but I prefer reading." I'm down with life too though. I devoured the book over the next few days and cried at the end, so sad for poor Tess.

The professor invited us one evening to a movie at the university. It was held outside in a small parking lot but sans any cars. Folding chairs were set up auditorium style, a big projector was propped up at one end of the lot, and a large movie screen was suspended at the other end, allowing for excellent sight lines. No trees blocked the view of the horizon. The sun sank quickly, the sky gently darkened, and the movie began.

It was a 1973 film called *Pat Garrett and Billy the Kid,* directed by Sam Peckinpah and starring James Coburn, Kris Kristofferson, and Bob Dylan. It was a guys' flick for sure: violent, harsh, bloody, with some kind of wild-west male code of honour, I guess. Ugh. The only thing I remember is Dylan. I had been a huge fan of him in my teens (although later got very disenchanted) so was interested to see him acting. I later mentioned this to our host. He had heard the name, and I explained who Dylan was. Our host said, "Hmm, the man with the intelligent eyes."

It had been surreal to watch that movie during an exquisite dusk and ebony evening, to see swaggering American male actors act like thugs, to enjoy the kindness of a quiet, congenial chap, and then to remember suddenly that we were in Africa, this massive and mysterious continent, and that North America was very far away indeed.

2013

In my first newsletter of the year, I wanted to update our supporters about the shutdown of the microcredit program and the switch to grants. It was news worth sharing.

This year started out with very good news from Okaseni. In January, Tumaini emailed us a copy of an official document saying that our sister organization, the Africa Village Project Tanzania, was officially a registered charity in Tanzania. We were very pleased. Our trust had been approved by the Tanzanian government and the Certificate of Incorporation issued on December 27, 2012. The next step was to get us added as trustees. We sent copies of our drivers' licences, our resumes, and photos to Tanzania. We then waited . . .

In February, we received some very bad news. We were copied on an email of condolences from Robert, John Mchau's brother, to Tumaini about Monika's death. She had died of brain cancer in late December.

In March, we received the following email from Tumaini.

> Dear all,
>
> I wish to thank you for the kind calls and messages relating to the passing away of Monika. My apologies for the delay, but as you can imagine we (me, Isaac, and Monika's relatives) are going through a very difficult period. People say death is death no matter how it happens, but Monika's was very sudden.

The Africa Village Project Association
Mid-Winter Newsletter: January 2, 2013

New Year, New Beginning . . .

Happy New Year! A new year is always a great time to make a new beginning. In Okaseni last June, we experienced a new beginning as well. We regretfully said goodbye to one venture but welcomed, with hope, a new one.

Dale watches as the villagers carry plastic piping for the water system upgrades. This infrastructure project was one of the many aid projects we completed in the village.

But first, the back story. When we set up the AVPA in 2007, our goals were to improve the standard of living and help the village become self-sufficient.

Improving the standard of living was fairly easy—it involved aid projects. We funded infrastructure projects (the water system, electrical power, a coffee nursery), started a health dispensary, and supported education.

These projects did improve the living conditions in the village.

But aid projects were not a long-term solution, so to help the village become self-sufficient, we focused on business development, specifically, microcredit. Our microcredit program started in 2008, and loans were given to three groups of women over a three-year period.

However, the program did not do as well as we had hoped. The women found it hard to make a living, and some had difficulty paying back their loans. Others did not seem to take seriously the opportunity that microcredit provided. It was not possible to run the program from here in Canada, so we reluctantly disbanded the program. It was very disappointing.

One of the last microcredit loans we gave to Renatus Minja, the villager who has a small foundry. His business was successful, and he wanted funds to upgrade his equipment to increase production. He employed a staff of about fifteen full- and part-time people—many young men who would otherwise have absolutely no prospects for employment in the village.

We had a brainwave! Why not change the loan to a grant? Renatus seemed like a sure bet. Giving him a grant would benefit him, his business, and the village at large.

Renatus Minja shows off an iron that he created in his foundry in Okaseni. The stand holds hot coals to heat the iron.

His workshop is small and crowded with several assistants but very constructive.

Renatus and his assistants maneuver around this space carefully but gracefully. He wants to renovate it to make it safer.

We were also glad to give Mama Marietha Mushi a grant. She has a small store in Okaseni across from the village office, selling food, dry goods and drinks. With her grant, she can sell meat—an excellent choice for her business and the villagers. She would also like to sell fodder for the cows that the villagers own.

Mama Marietha shows me the many goods she stocks in her store. It is the only store in the village and sells many useful products for the villagers.

Mama Marietha also plans to hire villagers for a catering business for local parties and events. We were thrilled to hear this. Like Renatus, she will be creating valuable jobs for others, exactly what we were hoping for with grants.

We were sad to end the microcredit loans but happy to begin grants. We hope this new beginning will help the village become more self-sufficient. All the best for your new beginnings in 2013 too!

The only way we could think that she was sick was changes in moods. I initially thought she was having a kind of depression because she kept complaining about the difficult kids at the school where she was teaching. She then lost interest in cooking and suddenly lost her ability to speak English, and then she had difficulties speaking German. All this happened in a three-week period in December. I still thought she was having a depression and wanted to take her to the hospital, but she refused. Monika hated hospitals and never took medicines. When she was not feeling well, she took herbs.

Her family was also concerned, especially when she told her father that she had once seen strange things when she was driving. (She did not tell me this because she knew I would urge her to go to the hospital, and her father could not tell me this because he does not speak English.) When her father told her brothers, they called an ambulance and forcibly took Monika to the hospital. There they took tests of her, and she was diagnosed with brain cancer. The changes we were seeing meant that the tumor was growing day by day and pressing on the brain.

She was then transferred to the biggest hospital in Austria (in Vienna) where there is a cancer institute, and fresh tests were taken, including a minor operation to get a sample of the tumor. They told us that surgery to remove it completely could damage the brain, so they recommended a combination of radiotherapy and chemotherapy. We had to wait [at home] for the wound [from the operation] to heal before the recommended treatment could be started, but on the fifth day after being discharged, she fell into a coma and was readmitted. She passed away in hospital within a week.

Now life has completely changed, and I have to shoulder many responsibilities. I wanted to take Isaac to Moshi to stay with my mother for a while, but the authorities have not approved it because he is Austrian [and Tumaini and

Monika never married]. They have their own regulations for dealing with minors of Isaac's age. I have to show proof of subsistence (a job) among other things. In the meantime, I gave "temporary custody" to Monika's brother although I live with Isaac. I hope to be able to negotiate travelling with Isaac sometime soon because it is very difficult having to live here. The house is full of Monika, and he keeps remembering her.

That is all for now.

Our hearts broke for Tumaini and his little boy. Understandably, not much had gotten done on the land purchase.

We heard from Salma in February that the poultry project was going well and the first batch of chicks had been sold. She said that 40 percent of the profits were used for two more poultry projects. We were very pleased about this but less pleased to find that Melki had taken the remaining 60 percent to start his own poultry project on his own land. What? We sent word that we were unhappy to hear this, and that he could count that his yearly payment from us.

We were still waiting word on the land purchase, and in March, I received this email from Salma:

> For the land, the owner is waiting to hear from us on when we will be ready to finalize the deal so she can come to Moshi from Dar es Salaam. It will be real useful if we can do it soon, probably right after Easter because she has been waiting for quite some times now. Let me know when it will be convenient for you and will work with the logistic here to finalise the purchase.

Alas, I had no news for her about getting added as trustees to the AVPT and no idea when that might happen. But in April, thanks again to Tumaini's initiative and hard work, Dale and I were finally added and approved as trustees. We received from Tumaini a copy of the official Notice of Change of Trustees.

We were now ready to go ahead with the purchase. Salma found a lawyer in Moshi to do the documents and finalize the purchase. Everything was in place. I wired Can$7,000 of the total cost of $9,000 to Melki for the purchase. The remaining $2,000 needed was in the AVPA account at the Kikilora credit union. On August 16, the deal was done, and the AVPT now officially owned land!

Over those months of waiting, there was much ado about everything that the land could be used for. In May, Salma emailed us a detailed proposal by Tumaini that included several possible "plans." The first was to renovate the existing three-room structure on the property as a medical dispensary and to add three new rooms and a veranda that would used as a waiting area for patients. The six rooms would be a lab, a store, a chemist shop, a reception area, and two rooms for the clinical officer and nurses. A two-stall toilet facility would be installed in the small structure behind the building.

The second plan was to build a two-bedroom staff house for the clinical officer. The two bedrooms were if the officer had a family, which might encourage them to take the position.

Plan three was to construct a volunteer house for people who would be willing to work temporarily at the medical dispensary. One room in this building would be used as an office for the AVPT, in which to keep documents and hold meetings and training workshops.

The final plan was to build a coffee shop that would provide employment opportunities for the villagers. It was to be used to sell snacks and soft drinks to patients and locals at a reasonable price. The AVPT would not run the shop itself but would rent it out to young businesspeople who would be in charge of it.

This proposal was followed almost immediately by a revised proposal from Tumaini. This one put forward five different uses for the land, most focussed on women. First, the idea of using the existing structure as a medical dispensary was jettisoned, and instead, Tumaini proposed renovating it as an office for the AVPT.

The second was to build a multi-purpose warehouse on the land in which women's groups could store perishable and non-perishable produce for eventual sale directly to buyers in Moshi.

The third idea was the establishment of a model/illustrative vegetable garden and a model poultry project. The vegetable gardens would teach the Okaseni women the rudiments of growing more lucrative vegetables to increase their income beyond the current repertoire of banana and beans. The poultry project would teach the women how to raise chickens by themselves for market or home use. The security guard would be encouraged as well to grow his own vegetables "as a bargain for his salary package."

Security guard? Salary package? Oh. That turned out to be the fourth idea. A security guard was considered essential given the many buildings and projects proposed and would obviously need a house in which to stay.

Idea number five was the construction of a multi-purpose meeting place. The women involved in the above activities would need a place to get together. The building would accommodate between fifty to sixty people and be used for AVPT meetings, seminars and workshops about gardening, marketing, for microcredit loan activities, and for women's group meetings in general.

Here was my reply to Tumaini, Salma, Peter, Melki, and Robert:

> I have read the proposals and thank you for your work on them, Tumaini, much appreciated.
>
> Dale and I are concerned that the proposals
> * do not reflect the AVPA's current goals regarding women and the microcredit program. We are not supporting these two ventures anymore.
> * are much too large and ambitious for the AVPA (which, as you know, is very small and minimally funded). The scope of buildings, staff, and expenses is completely beyond our capabilities.
> * do not include any ideas from the villagers themselves. We would like to get their own ideas and not to impose a grand plan on them.
>
> Our idea was to use the land for small businesses that the villagers could operate to make money; for example, a place to manufacture building blocks, etc. We like the idea of a coffee shop. However, we would prefer that the villagers be consulted.

We would like to thank you again for the proposal. We look forward to hearing from you.

In August, we received an email from Melki saying that an Okaseni meeting was planned soon to get ideas from the villagers about the land and building. In September, we received the following email from Salma about the meeting:

> Warm greetings from here! The village meeting went successfully, with a lot of good ideas from the villagers. Below are three ideas the villagers proposed:
> - Their first option was to renovate the current house and start operating it as a medical dispensary.
> - Part of the land, they were thinking to start an internet café. They hope it will help them to start a computer class for young people and hopefully charge people [for] using the internet.
> - And lastly, to start a small vocational training centre for making stuffs and for teaching other young people either carpentry, welding, and electricity.
>
> These are the ideas they have proposed. Looking forward to hearing more from you.

I sent Salma an email of thanks and a request to hear more about a final decision. After several weeks, I had still not heard back, so on October 1, I sent Salma and Melki the following email:

> Thanks again for your message, Salma, about the village meeting. We haven't heard back from you, and we need to find out what the final decision is for the land and the building.
>
> As we mentioned in our earlier email, we were very pleased that the villagers would like to use the building as a

medical dispensary. Please tell us what has been done on it, if anything.

We must disburse the rest of the annual funds soon so that we can submit our annual report to the government. Do you need funds to improve the building and set up the dispensary? If so, could you please let us know your plan and the costs immediately. We would be happy to use these funds to improve the building, or we could use them to pay school fees and/or give business grants.

If we do not hear from you about this, we will have to give the funds to another charity. The funds must be used as soon as possible so that we can tell the government what we have done with them. We look forward to hearing from you.

Melki sent us the following email soon after: "Thank you for your support. After consulting district medical officer, he allow us to go on what we are planning. So I attach cost of renovation latrines building [and] of house."

I read the estimate Melki had attached to his email. Here is my reply:

Many thanks for your message and the estimate to renovate the building on the land as a medical dispensary. We appreciate the work that went into the estimate. However, the total is about US$15,000.

As you know, we are a very small organization with limited resources. We do many small fundraising events throughout the year, which are difficult and hard work. All the people who help the AVPA work for free, including Dale and me. As well, Dale and I pay for all the expenses of the organization, such as mailing, internet costs, and computer supplies. We also pay for our trips to Okaseni, which are very expensive.

Our fundraising usually brings in about $5,000 a year. An exceptional year would be about $10,000, but that is very rare. We had the very large expense of the land purchase for 2011, 2012, 2013, as well as other expenses for those years, including medical dispensary supplies, grants, teaching materials for the elementary school, and school fees.

The funds that we have left for 2013 would cover only about one-third of your request. We have no more funds beyond that. Please let us know what you would like us to do.

Several days later, we received a revised estimate. The total cost was about US$3,500, which was much better. (Nice try, Melki. The difference in the two estimates likely meant padding and subterfuge to the extreme.) On October 29, I wired the remaining funds we had for the year, which nicely paid for the renos and annual school fees. The renos proceeded into the next year.

The other big project of this year was the grants program. Over the year, we received updates from Salma about these three grantees. Salma was doing a satisfactory job this year as our assistant and chief liaison to Okaseni, for which we were very grateful. Paying her a monthly stipend helped a lot.

In March, we received this message from her:

Many greetings from Tanzania. I was real shocked too with the death of Monika, plus recent email from Tumaini about the causative of her death. I can't imagine the current situation Tuma is in now especially as a foreigner there. Hope he will find the way to overcome this in a near future.

Updates for Okaseni, I had the opportunity to meet with Mama Augustina and [she] was able to share with me more on how she spent the remaining money. She is still continue selling bananas for people who make the local brew [beer] in Okaseni, and taking banana, ripe banana and avocados to town. She is doing well.

Renatus have been working with his extension on the melting place (foundry) and the progress is good. I'm impressed with each the individual progress but it will be good to have the written [records] for each of them in the near future, just to find out more how much they spent to purchase goods, how much they sell it and how they can improve their business. Such close follow ups with the stuffs they are working will be useful for them and will keep the records for the AVPA project as well.

Mama Marietha, she was away the day so I could not find about it.

The promised "written records" never did turn up. We were pleased to get this message from Salma, however, and were much happier with the grants than the microcredit program. In October, she sent news of Mama Marietha:

Mama Marietha is also doing fine. She continues to add some more products on her shop and hoping to expand as per demand of products within the village.

I appreciated Salma keeping in touch with us about both the grants and the proposals about using the land/building.

Other random but noteworthy events happened throughout the year. In January, a Bowen friend started a theatre school in the large basement of a commercial building in Vancouver and asked for Dale's help to fix it up. She was very busy and had begun to realize what a big undertaking it is to start a project/business like hers. Or ours.

"Not many people could do what you have done, starting the AVPA," she told me. "Doing something like that is very rare and quite an accomplishment." My heart sang to get recognized for that because most people don't seem to have a clue. They are always keen to give me ideas though. (Everyone's got a good idea!) I appreciated her kind words very much.

In April, we went to a fundraiser in Chilliwack thrown by Vivien, the woman who was helping the orphanage in Moshi. It was an impressive and well-run event, including a dinner, silent auction, and PowerPoint presentation. She did have some advantages compared to us on Bowen (access to cheap, full-service facilities and an enormous number of personal connections across many fields). However, it was a boost to my spirits to see her do so well.

Also in April, we held a board meeting on Bowen to which Kerri, our new board member, and Valerie came. It was good of them to make the effort. As always, it was a lot of paperwork but useful. I also wired a six-month payment this month to Salma and did spreadsheets and financial updates. I attended a grants workshop on Bowen, which provided the opportunity to do a practice grant application, but again, grants seemed like a time-consuming rabbit hole for a one-person band. Anyway, the mere thought of AVPA paperwork was beginning to make me nauseous.

Despite all the AVPA accomplishments this year, my shift away from the project that had begun in 2011 continued. Time opened up more for me with the failure to find a foster kid to help, and I had room to let other things into my life. In February, I volunteered to help with "Broadway on Bowen," a musical revue of fourteen songs with twenty-seven actor/singers, including about ten kids and teenagers. It was a massive undertaking, and I was assigned to help the emcee with his seven costume changes and then pitched in wherever I could. The show was a mega hit on Bowen and a fabulous experience. I was given a shout-out at the afterparty and a bottle of wine for my help.

I began reading for an hour every day after lunch, beginning with a biography of Frida Kahlo. Her life was so difficult, yet she had enormous joie de vivre and elan. I loved her. We had many lovely hours together, Frida and I. I also started a massive tome by Steven Pinker called *The Better Angels of Our Nature: Why Violence Has Declined,* which detailed the astonishing progress humanity has made over the millennia. It was a revelation and forever changed my view of humanity.

In June, I volunteered to walk with Laura, a blind lady, once a week in Vancouver's West End, a gorgeous, older neighbourhood on the waterfront with huge avenue trees, elegant, aged apartment blocks, many newer high rises, and a beauty that utterly bewitched me. I felt that I should be paying Laura for the pleasure of walking each week in that urban paradise.

I did a massive clean-out and retrofit of house stuff, clothes, shoes, and such. For the first time in about two decades, I had time to go to plays, art galleries, and movies, as well as to the United States to visit friends and relatives. My social and leisure life burst forth, and I danced for joy.

Ironically, this year was a terrible one for me personally. The unexpected collapse of several long-standing, dearly held relationships was catastrophic. Several people changed so dramatically that I had to re-evaluate having them in my life. It was very painful and sad to emotionally and mentally say goodbye.

The year ended in Lauterbrunnen, Switzerland, where we went to celebrate Christmas and the New Year. It was a magical holiday of snowy Alpine mountains, sparkling lights, European charm, and the many kindnesses of Brigitte, the Hotel Jungfrau owner. This year was the beginning of a new era in my life as the "setting aside" of the AVPA started to gel. This change was surreal at times. After having poured my heart and soul into the project, it was oddly like venturing onto a new continent yet still seeing movie images of my old life. I was reminded of the words of Goethe: "Talent develops in solitude, but character develops in the storms of the world."

I guess this year (and every year of the AVPA), as I did in Africa in 1975, I was developing a whole lot of character.

CHAPTER 8

2014, YALE, GRANTS, AND CASH

1975

We left Ibadan and our kindly host and headed west, crossing into Dahomey (now Benin), a former French colony. Roads throughout this part of Africa were mostly dirt or gravel. We were getting yet another ride with some local ex-pats when the road suddenly morphed into massive slabs of concrete. I can still see it in my mind's eye. It was a shock, like coming across a Tiffany's jewelry store in the middle of the Sahara Desert. The driver told us that it had been built by a former prime minister who wanted a good road into the capital to save wear and tear his twenty or so Mercedes Benz cars. Hmm . . . I thought. Why would he want twenty Mercedes? Why didn't he just keep the cars in town? Why was the road out of concrete and not asphalt as in Canada? Ever naive, it was years before I finally realized the answers to these questions. I eventually also discovered that those who are rich and powerful like to keep money for themselves, and they like nothing but the best—for themselves.

2014

This year consisted of one big project after another. With conferences, purging papers and files, fundraising, and renovations, it was busy and rewarding, with the usual dose of fun, drama, and difficult people.

My first project was finishing the financials and other tasks for the AVAP and getting it completely up to date, a huge job. I started on January 13 and didn't finish until mid-September, with many interruptions and other projects surfacing throughout the year. It was mind-boggling how much time it took and made me realize, yet again, how immense an undertaking the AVPA was. I filed, compiled, entered masses of documents and info into the computer, wrote reports, and turfed umpteen bagsful of stuff. The relief and joy of getting everything done were enormous.

The second big project was going to conferences. On New Year's Day in Switzerland, one of my resolutions for 2014 was to get off Bowen more. It was a lovely place for sure, but too much time there without a foray into the outer world was too much. How about conferences? I asked myself. I should go!

When I was researching how to help foster kids in 2012, I came across a group called the Legal Education and Action Fund (LEAF). It was a national organization with the mission of furthering equality for all in Canada, especially women and the disadvantaged. They were holding their AGM in March downtown at the ritzy Hotel Vancouver. Many of its members were lawyers and most were women, and they cared about social justice. How good was that?! I felt that a stay in that beautiful hotel hobnobbing with like-minded people would be just the ticket. The AGM was a breakfast meeting on March 4, International Women's Day. I registered and was excited about going although very nervous. My youthful shyness had resurfaced.

On March 3, I headed into Vancouver for my overnight stay before the conference. The hotel opened in 1939 and was still endearingly old-fashioned albeit with a regal, classic ambience. I wandered around, had dinner, and then had a swim in the lovely pool surrounded by many large windows. Then off to bed.

I got up at 6 a.m., got into my good clothes and headed down to the conference room, still anxious. It was all well and good to work at home by myself on the AVPA in peace and quiet, just me and my computer in these post-retirement days, but it was sometimes daunting to venture out into the world and do different things even though I did want to. I steeled myself and entered the conference room and busied myself checking out the silent auction and making a couple of bids, then found a spot at one of the tables. The person on my left was a man (!), a rep from the Notaries of BC organization. On my right were three older women who had been on the LEAF board in the '80s. Very cool! One was in poor health and kept checking her blood pressure although she did eat a lot of breks. Another was involved with a book charity for Tanzania. She said they could take books to Okaseni if we wanted.

I realized all was okay. Nobody paid any attention to me though the people at my table were very nice. My nerves calmed down. This event seemed like an excellent rehearsal for another conference I was planning to go to in April, which would likely be much the same.

At 7:30, breks was served: very tasty poached eggs with greens and potatoes. We tucked in appreciatively. The program started. A lot of local high-powered types were in attendance. Gregor Robertson, the mayor of Vancouver, and MLA Jenny Kwan, and other NDP government people were there. Gloria Makarenko, a local television anchor, was emcee. There were many introductions, greetings and thanks to one and all. An all-female tap dance troupe did a rousing *History of Women* performance from the Suffragettes, to Rosie the Riveter, to hippy chicks, to Lady Gaga. It was priceless.

The keynote speaker was Samantha Nutt, a doctor, professor, wife, mum, and the author of a book called *Damned Nations*, in which she recounts her harrowing experiences in war-torn countries and describes how aid from the West can be more effective. She gave us an impassioned speech about helping women in war zones and suggested we donate monthly to LEAF. "Instead of buying a goat," she said, "you should buy a lawyer." Too good. I later signed up and donated monthly to LEAF for a year or so. I also bought her book that day.

By the end of the event, I was exhilarated. It had been invigorating be with people who cared and were doing something. I was pleased I had gone, nerves and all.

In April, I attended the Global Health and Innovation Conference in New Haven, Connecticut, the home of Yale University. This conference was hosted by Unite for Sight, an organization that funds eye health efforts in the developing world. I had received a random email about the conference through the AVPA website in January. The keynote speaker was Jeffrey Sachs, founder of the Earth Institute and author of *The End of Poverty* (see Introduction). It was this book that inspired me to take a multi-project approach in Okaseni village, rather than focusing on just one thing. I knew I had to go.

The conference also provided the opportunity to present a social enterprise pitch. Here is the description they sent out:

Social Enterprise Pitch

The 2014 Global Health and Innovation Conference will include special sessions where selected participants will present their new idea in the format of a 5-minute social enterprise pitch. Following the pitch, there is a 5-minute period for questions and answers, as well as feedback from the audience. This will provide participants with an opportunity to formulate and present their idea, collaborate with others interested in their idea, and receive feedback and ideas from other conference participants. Professionals and students are eligible to submit a social enterprise pitch.

All of the presentations will be ideas that are being developed, meaning that the ideas are in the brainstorming, early development, or early implementation stage. . . . The goal is a dynamic session in which participants and speakers will network and collaborate about the innovative ideas, and the hope is that we will see many of these ideas effectively implemented in the future. . . . We welcome submissions pertaining to all fields relevant to global health, international development, and social entrepreneurship.

Hah! I thought. I can do that.

To be considered, you had to submit an abstract at the same time that you registered and paid to attend. Non-attendees would not be accepted for a pitch. (No worries, I was elated to be attending.) The specifications of the abstract were given. It had to be 250 words maximum and follow a strict format. Also included was an example of a poor pitch and instructions on how to improve it.

No problem! I thought. I am so on this. The writing I could do, and the formatting was easy. I might be nervous on the day, but I knew I could do the presentation (my teaching and acting selves would not desert me). Finally, by sheer good luck, I had an idea.

By 2014, we had accomplished a lot in Okaseni. Some projects (microcredit and grevillea trees) did not work out, and we abandoned them. A major accomplishment was the land purchase in 2013, with renovations well under way this year. I had begun to mull over what we might tackle next. We did a lot of projects for the common good: electricity, water systems upgrades, the coffee and grevillea tree nurseries. We also did targeted ones: school fees and materials for needy kids, grants for small business owners, and the workshop and materials for the teachers. We sent the shipping container with books for kids, sewing machines for women, and bikes for the council (alas). Now perhaps a still focussed but wider group could be helped. Perhaps we could do pensions for the elderly in Okaseni.

I emailed Melki to get an updated population total for Okaseni. The current number of senior citizens was about nine hundred. He also mentioned, to my dismay, that the total population was now nine thousand, an increase of over 100 percent since 2007. My knees buckled. We were having a hard time providing basics for four thousand people. How could we hope to help nine thousand in any meaningful way? I was already demoralized enough at this point about the AVPA, but for now I had to set that aside and get on with my pitch.

I began to research the topic and discovered a book called *Just Give Money to the Poor*. It gave an overview and analysis of cash transfer programs in the Global South, countries such as Mexico, Namibia, Indonesia, and Brazil.[1] These programs were a recent phenomenon, starting in 1997.[2] The West has been giving aid to the poor since the 1600s, when in 1601 England passed one of the first ever "poor laws."[3] Over the next centuries, these laws proliferated, and the idea of providing for the poor became more acceptable. Today, financial help is routine and unremarkable. In Canada, cash transfers include pensions, disability payments, unemployment insurance, workers compensation, and the 2016 Canada Child Benefit brought in by Prime Minister Justin Trudeau. Both federal and provincial governments provided cash benefits during the covid shutdown in 2020 to 2022.

Cash transfers tend to stir up a lot of antagonism, especially in those sensitive souls, the wealthy. "The rich and powerful always argue that poor are at least partially responsible for their own poverty and therefore unworthy of support."[4] (It makes you wonder if the heartless have a monopoly on getting rich.) Another myth is "If you give people money, and especially poor people, they will sit down and become lazy."[5] These beliefs have been disproven by research,[6] and most industrialized societies no longer operate under such delusions. Even some of the ultra-rich today have started their own charities and foundations to help the less fortunate.

As the authors of the book discovered, cash transfers work dramatically. For example, poverty was cut in Brazil from 28 percent in 2003 to 19 percent in 2006.[7] Contrary to the fears of the rich, the recipients spend the money first on food, medicine, and then on clothes and shoes for the kids, as well as school supplies. With cash transfers, the poor have better health outcomes, and kids stay in school.[8] The community at large benefits as well, because most of the cash is spent locally on goods, services, and food, which stimulates the regional economy and is especially beneficial to small farmers,[9] which in turn helps prevent more poverty.[10] The positive effects of cash transfers multiply over time. "Poverty stretches out over generations," and poor children are unlikely to get out of poverty when adults, but cash transfers do help succeeding generations get off to a better start.[11]

As well as the cash itself, the dependability of the transfers is a huge boon. Assured of ongoing basic support, the poor might invest funds in materials and supplies to start a small business or improve their agricultural harvests. They might buy a work animal or hire someone to tend their crops while they find a job that will pay more (and also provide work for someone who might be even more poor). They can leverage the $1 into $2 income.[12]

You have probably heard the old saying, "Give me a fish, and you feed me for a day. Teach me to fish, and you feed me for a lifetime." Cash transfers do not teach. The poor already know what to do. They just don't have the money to do it. With cash, they can get the fishing rod, the net, and the bait, and head to the lake.

So I had my topic. After hours of work on those 250 words, I registered just in time for the conference and submitted my pitch abstract:

CASH TRANSFERS FOR OKASENI, TANZANIA

- **Problem**: The development projects we are doing in Okaseni, Tanzania, do not always reach the poorest villagers or compensate those who provide a valuable service to the village.
- **Solution**: We will initiate a cash transfer program.

- **Innovation**: Selected villagers will receive modest cash transfers every month on an ongoing basis. Recipients will be the 200 oldest people in the village.
- **Based on evidence**: When cash transfer programs are implemented, recipients spend the funds on the health and education of their families. Also, the funds are spent locally, so the community prospers, and economic growth occurs—a virtuous circle. One dollar of cash can create two dollars of benefit.
- **Expected impact**: The recipients can buy more and better food, pay school costs, and generate extra income.
- **Management and financing**: We have a dedicated team on the ground (the village chairperson and our assistant manager), and we have a financial transfer procedure already set up. The funds will be wired directly to our account at the local credit union, and recipients will pick up the funds there every month.
- **Stage of idea**: The villagers will decide which seniors will receive the funds. We need funding for monthly cash transfers of $10 to 200 seniors..
- **My "ask"**: We are asking for funding of **$25,000** for a pilot project of one year.

I then tried (unsuccessfully) to wait patiently to hear whether I had been accepted. In February, I received an email from Unite for Sight: "Congratulations! We have selected your social enterprise pitch for presentation at the Unite for Sight 11th annual Global Health and Innovation Conference at Yale University on April 12 to 13, 2014. We receive many excellent submissions, and the selection process is competitive."

Yippee!! I was ecstatic. Although I had no idea what the conference would be like or who would be there, I hoped to get information about funding and meet possible donors. I love universities and colleges and have spent joyous years there taking random courses and getting my BA in English and my MA in theatre (some of the best years of my life), so I was excited to be visiting Yale. The hotel that I booked in New Haven was within walking distance of the campus and seemed pleasantly old-fashioned and comfy. Dale was not coming with me as he doesn't like cities. It had been years since I had travelled by myself and I was nervous, but, as always, the thought of a journey to new and different places was intoxicating.

In the early morning of Thursday, April 10, I bid a teary goodbye to Dale at the Vancouver Airport and boarded my 7:00 a.m. WestJet flight to Toronto (four and a half hours). There I transferred to the flight to La Guardia Airport (one and a half hours) in Queens, New York. The "shared van" that I had booked picked me up there and took me to the hotel in New Haven. It was 8 p.m. local time, ten hours after I left Vancouver. The hotel was as appealing as I expected. I settled in, phoned Dale, then sank into a deep sleep in the yummy bed.

Friday was a free day and I was keen to explore the university and the town. I first beetled over to the campus and arrived at an esplanade lined with buildings that were very beautiful and very old. This I had not expected. I suddenly felt back in England as a child, when my Mum and Dad took us kids to all manner of ancient, medieval, and later buildings, towns, churches, castles, and cathedrals. Was I in a time warp? Then I remembered that yes, Yale *was* old, 313 years exactly in 2014.

I was enchanted. To my right was a three-storey building made of large whitish stone chunks that looked like marble. Exquisitely detailed workman-ship was everywhere: curved arches over every window, miniature Greek columns dividing the glass in the windows into panels, trim in a different stone along horizontal and vertical lines that broke up the starkness of the white stone. Larger Greek columns stood sentinel beside the entrance, and a tall, Gothic arch soared above the large wooden doorway. I peeked inside. The small foyer sported rich wood panelling, and the narrow hallways and staircase led off to little classrooms and offices. It was all deliciously *not* modern and seemed to embody the eternal desire and passion for learning and discovery.

The campus abounded with many such beautiful structures. During my explorations, I did not see any modern architecture to my great delight, so the sense of time travel remained unbroken. Adding to the beauty of the archi-tecture were the gracious, aged trees, the various shrubs, the innumerable flowers, all in their spring glory and rustling gently in the light breezes. The atmosphere was bewitching. Yale seemed timeless in its beauty, not bound to any era, but instead like an ageless archetype of the perfect, ideal university.

I felt carried away to a kind of heaven for those who love books, study, and contemplation, like moi. How lucky was I to be there? How fortunate was I to have experienced and reaped the benefits of a first-world education? Life's unfairness reared its evil head, and I vowed to keep trying to help those school kids in Okaseni.

After my amble through campus, I headed over to the Yale Centre for British Art, where I especially liked the Turners, and then to my final stop of the day, the Beinecke Rare Book and Manuscript Library, where I saw a special display of book blurbs across the ages. Who knew that would be so good? Both places were treats for the eye and the mind. I headed back to the hotel, thankful for the day and its many beauteous sights, despite that dismay that had surfaced about the gargantuan disparity between Africa and this smashing college town.

The conference started the next day, Saturday, April 12. The number of sessions and speakers was breathtaking. Sponsored as it was by Unite for Sight, it focussed deeply on health issues. Topics included mental health, evaluation of systems in health care, ethical dilemmas in medical education, dental training curriculums, and a writing workshop for the global health field. These were just a small fraction of the morning offerings.

Also on Saturday morning were two pitch sessions. I went to the one called Philanthropy and Investment. The topics were the role of government funding, reimagining philanthropy, investments in AIDS treatments, and social return on investment. I enjoyed these presentations and was unsurprised that raising funds was always an issue. The other sessions I went to that day were a presentation on markets and public/private partnerships and a workshop on hard financial choices for social enterprise start-ups. They were all good. As you know, I like the topic of money.

On Sunday morning, I went to the keynote speakers' session at 8 a.m. (5 a.m. Vancouver time, groan) to see my hero, Jeffrey Sachs, the founder of the Millennium Village Project (MVP). The MVP had not been a huge success and was criticized for insufficient evidence of results and the diversion of funds to debt payments and crisis management. It was never upscaled in any impoverished area or country, so the experiment, although well-meaning, was both expensive and disappointing. My concern with the MVP was that it could have consulted more with the villagers although I liked and adopted

Sachs's idea of tackling everything in the village. In Yale that Sunday morning, Sachs talked instead about the UN shift to sustainable development goals, which emphasize coping with and mitigating the effects of climate change in the developing world. I was pleased to see him in person as he *had* tried to tackle the problem of world poverty. I admired him for that and was grateful for his template of providing a kind of universal aid to a village.

My own pitch was in Harkness Hall early afternoon on Sunday under the title of Community Based Social Enterprise Pitches: Ideas in Development. The room was not large but theatre style with raised seating. About thirty people attended, all looking rather solemn. I was again quite nervous but had spent so much time on my pitch and practiced it so often that I was somewhat sure I would not totally fall apart. The moment arrived. Fortunately, the PowerPoint presentation worked, my trusty laser pointer was at hand, and I was off and running, so to speak. Here is what I said:

> Thank you very much for the introduction. I would also like to thank the members of the academy, um, I mean Unite for Sight for this incredible opportunity. I feel like I have won an Oscar just standing here. [No one laughed.] I'm the director of the Africa Village Project Association, a very small NGO that my husband, Dale, and I started on 2007. We live near Vancouver, Canada.
>
> We have adopted Okaseni village in Tanzania and have followed the Millennium Village model pioneered by Jeffrey Sachs. We have worked on everything in the village and have raised and disbursed a total of $75,000 since we started. One hundred percent of the funds raised go to the village.
>
> We have always asked the villagers what they would like us to do. One of the things they requested was bikes. So we sent a shipping container with bikes, among other things, in 2008. This picture shows some of the village council members on some of the bikes we sent. The problem we have discovered is that sometimes the projects we do don't always reach the poorest people in the village, and this is an example. Granted, nearly everyone in the village is poor and

needs help, but it was disheartening to see that the political elite in the village got the goodies.

So our innovation is that we would like to start a cash transfer program. It turns out that cash transfer programs are quite effective as documented in this book, *Just Give Money to the Poor*. [I held my copy of the book up.] The authors found that the poor are quite canny with their money and can generate up to US$2 of income from US$1 cash. However, the authors did discover that to be effective, cash transfers must be at least 20 percent of the average daily income, which in Tanzania is about $1.25 per day. They also must be consistent and reliable over time.

The impact we would expect in Okaseni is that the villagers will be able to improve their lives by using the cash transfers to buy more and better food for their families, possibly pay school fees, and even generate more income.

For financing, well, financing is our ask. We would like to give $10 [US] per month to the two hundred oldest seniors in the village, essentially a pension. So we are seeking funding of $25,000 [US] for a pilot project of one year. For management, we already have a team on the ground in Okaseni. Melki Mushi, the village chairperson, and Salma Khatibu, our assistant manager, have been with us since the get-go and are reliable and hardworking.

The stage of the idea is that we are almost good to go! We need to find out who the two hundred oldest people in the village are and get them interviewed and registered at the local credit union, which is where they would pick up their pensions.

We feel this is a great opportunity for a funder to find out about cash transfers. Who knows? Cash transfers could be the cutting edge of aid. It's a chance for a funder to find out how they work right from the beginning.

Thank you so much from me, from my husband, and from the villagers of Okaseni.

I was the third speaker in this session, and as I listened to the five pitches after me and remembered Saturday's pitches, it became very clear that nearly *everyone* was asking for money. Oh dear. It brought home yet again that fundraising is extraordinarily difficult and painfully time-consuming and yields meager returns. What was I thinking about this conference? Was I hoping Bill Gates would be lurking in the back of the room, wads of cash in his pockets, waiting for the perfect pitch? Well, maybe not. But I should have realized that the conference was probably not going to be an opportunity to find funding. On top of that, I had discovered at the Sachs presentation that morning that most of the attendees were students, poor and starving too no doubt. I was disappointed and embarrassed too about my eternal naïveté.

But I was glad I had gone and enjoyed it immensely. It had been quite the eyeopener. I was relieved my pitch had gone well and decided to keep it on hand just in case I ever did meet Bill. My plan to go to conferences was a good one although I haven't yet been to another.

On the Okaseni front, we were pleased to see that our decision in 2012 to start paying Salma a monthly stipend was an excellent one. Roles and boundaries were clear, she did not feel taken advantage of, and her behaviour improved dramatically. She was diligent about keeping us updated on various Okaseni happenings. She did a great job at the administrative level, and we were very grateful and deemed this a success.

The grants program continued fairly well this year. In March, she sent us the following message:

> For the grants, Renatus is doing great. He is current busy in Dar es Salaam now to deliver some of the products to his customers and trying to get more market. I talked to him over the phone and very happy to have that opportunity to expand his working place and the business in general.
>
> Mama Marietha is also doing well, continue running her shop and still have plan to expanding it. Mama Augustina is still working on her small business and working on her farm at the same time too. The rain season have just started and most of the villagers are on either their farms or working as a part time workers in other people's farm to earn a little.

Hope this explanation helps, Sheena, if you would like to receive any additional information, please let me know, and will be happy to provide it to you.

In October, we received this email from her:

Updates for grants was on my list to report to you, below are updates for what is going on for the people you gave them grants and some plans in the near future.

Renatus is progressing well with his business and is now getting some more orders in Dar es Salaam. He already extend the building on the melting side and continue to work hard to finalize the roofing part. He said it will take sometimes before he start doing that as he used the grants money to generate more income and finalize the building. He also said in the future he would like to receive another grants but will let me know when he is ready for that. . . .

We have also discussed this with Mr. Mushi about the important of evaluating their progress at the end of this year, and probably soon next year to identify some other groups or people for possible grants. Let us know your thoughts about this, Sheena!

We appreciated these updates but never did receive any progress evaluations or the names of any other groups or people who might qualify for grants.

At the end of October, we received another email from Salma that all the grant recipients were doing well. She mentioned that Mama Augustina had used part of the money to add a room to her house. Mama Augustina was very happy with this and told Salma to thank us on her behalf for making it possible for her.

It was good to hear all was going well. Mostly, that is. We were dismayed to find out that Mama Augustina had added a room to her house with the grant money. To be charitable, it seemed a lack of understanding of a business grant (*not* free money) as neither Salma nor Mama Augustina was reticent about telling us about the room. As with the microcredit program, our inability to monitor things from the other side of the world was a major handicap.

Salma did, however, do a great job on keeping us posted about the renovations on the dispensary building. In her March email, she gave us the latest:

> Just had a talk with Mr. Peter Mchau yesterday and he is so happy with the progress of the building and also told me he managed to send some few pictures to you too. I was pleased with it! This afternoon, when I was talking to Mr. Mushi, the mason are going to finalize the plastering outside walls, at the corridor, toilet and putting doors and windows too. Is real exciting and can't wait for its accomplishment and see its sustainability too. It will be a BIG help for the Okaseni villagers and again I would like to thank you and Dale again for your generous support always!

We were so pleased to hear the news. Peter Mchau did indeed send us some pictures of the renos, including several of the latrine. Great excitement all round. Whoever would have thought latrines would be a big thrill? It was a big deal and probably the best one in Okaseni. The pit was about 30 ft. deep, and the out-building itself that housed the latrine had two stalls, each with a squat toilet and flushing capacity. The villagers had wanted a separate building for the latrine, with these state-of-the-art toilets, recognizing the need for hygiene in a medical setting.

If a loo can be called dazzling, this one was. The villagers were extremely proud of this accomplishment. It was one of the best projects the AVPA ever did.

The final project of the year was fundraising, the ongoing project that never ends. Our only independent event was a book and bake sale at BCIT in February. Dale, Valerie, Kerri (our new board member), her daughter, and I staffed the table. We all donated baked goodies and books, as did Sarah, Valerie's daughter, friends on Bowen, and folks at BCIT. Cocoa West, the chocolate shop on Bowen, donated a box of chocolates for the draw, which a student won. We made over $610, including sales on the day and donations that came in before and after. The sale was also, as usual, a lot of fun.

This building would become the renovated dispensary.

The latrine pit was enormous. You can't see too far down
the pit in this photo, but it was 30 ft. deep.

This small out-building behind the house was renovated as the latrine.

Inside the latrine building was probably the best toilet in Okaseni.
It was a flush toilet and had its own water faucet.

The second fundraiser of the year was the independent Rotary Variety Show on Bowen, held in November. I volunteered to manage it, missing the AVPA roller coaster, I guess. We were promised a portion of the gate as a donation to the AVPA. The show featured singers, dancers, a skit about a psychiatrist, teenage violin and cello musicians, and was a huge amount of work. From May until December, Dale and I devoted ourselves to putting this show together with an amazing group of talented, dedicated, hardworking people. But as always, there were a few difficult ones, some of whom were so rude and hostile that I avoided them for several years afterwards. But the show itself was a rousing success, and I was praised to the stars for my stellar management. It was disappointing though, because the donation we received from the proceeds wasn't much, and after all that work, I had been hoping for more. Still, it *was* fun, some of the most fun I had had since I retired.

In the fall, I went to another fundraiser on Bowen (not mine for a change) for a private middle school. I chatted to a woman there about fundraising and told her about my waning enthusiasm for the AVPA, especially the tedious administrative workload. She suggested trying to find an existing group (a church, Rotary Club) that might want to take it on. I perked up a tad and decided to start looking . . .

I still went to Rotary meetings this year, and one of them featured a guest speaker whose topic was ageing. (Most of the Rotary members were retired.) He strove to present a positive view of getting older and gave us handouts of uplifting poems and quotes. But his idea of ageing left me cold. He suggested that you "harvest your life" and ask yourself a lot of questions, like what is life for and how should you live and what have you learned. Hmm . . . I had already been asking myself those questions nearly every day of my life since my teens. It seemed a bit late in the day to wait until getting older to start asking. I have found that nothing really changes as I get older. I still want the same things: to love and be loved, to have satisfying work, to travel, have adventures, and learn stuff. Still the same old me. He also said he thought the baby boomers would profoundly change the concept of old age. Yup! Enough with the harvesting—I want to keep sowing!

As I looked back on this year, I noticed the issue of money was ubiquitous. In 1975, I saw how government money was put to ill-use in Africa, building a highway that would benefit only a few. In 2015, I was helping a country also in Africa in which the members of Parliament (MPs) made US$98,000 that year[13] while the median annual income was $1,800.[14] This is 1.8 percent of the MPs' take. I was visiting from my home country where the MPs made $167,400 that year[15] while the median income was $48,000.[16] This is 28 percent of the MPs' take.

How outrageous is that disparity? Tanzanian MPs are getting their money from somewhere, and if there is money in to pay them such hefty salaries, there is money to instigate cash payments. Although corruption and poverty are strongly correlated, Namibia and other poor countries are even now making cash payments to the poor.[17]

Industrialized countries have been spending money to help the poor for centuries,[18] yet many people are still against it. Margaret Thatcher and Ronald Reagan were fomenters, although not the first, of the idea that government should spend less, do less, and be less involved in citizens' lives. In actuality, this meant not supporting social programs, giving tax cuts to the rich, and increasing taxes on lower-income folks. Their nefarious policies led to the disasters of the 1990s (see chapter 1) and have contributed to the many ills of today, especially the refusal of the one percent to pay taxes for the public good that they enjoy along with the rest of us.

Governments are good at universal programs (see chapter 7). Industrialized countries are proof of this. Poorer countries can follow suit. The World Bank, International Money Fund, and United Nations can encourage developing countries to do so by using money not to buy high-end cars and build high-end but short highways, but instead to implement high-result programs such as cash transfers.

Please, WB, IMF, UN, put us little NGOs out of business. We can make some small difference here and there, but for optimum effect and massive benefits, you biggies need to step up and do something worthy—now.

CHAPTER 9

2015, DISPENSARY AND
SOCIAL ACTIVISM

1975

When Ralph and I reached Dahomey, we headed south towards the West African coast. After our journey from the Mediterranean Sea, down through the Sahara, the Sahel, and into Sub-Saharan Africa, we were now getting close to the Gulf of Guinea. Before we even saw the ocean, I swear I could smell its saltiness and feel the heavier air, dense compared to the air inland. We arrived in Cotonou, a pleasant coastal town, and I was delighted to be back on the water, child of the Canadian West Coast that I am.

We now turned west, crossed into Togo, and followed the coast to Lomé, the waterfront capital of the country. Ralph had started feeling ill earlier but was now feeling worse. We realized to our dismay that he had malaria. Fortunately, the prophylactics we were taking against malaria were also a treatment for the disease, but he was in no condition to keep travelling. What to do? No kindly ex-pat had found us and offered us free room and board. We could not afford a hotel. We thought that, since Lomé was a capital city, we might try a consulate.

There was no Canadian consulate in town, but there was a British one. Perhaps they would help someone from the colonies? The African officials there reluctantly but kindly let us stay and ensconced us on the second floor in a modest library. The building itself was older, but the library had several large windows that made it feel open and spacious. Many tall bookcases stood against the walls and shorter ones stood free. We slept on the floor and stayed there for four days, with Ralph unable to do much. I checked out the books and read a lot. Every day, a middle-aged fellow came through the library dusting all the books and shelves. The library seemed barely used, but every day he continued to do this task of dignified upkeep. I was moved by his caring.

There was a café across the street where I went for meals and got food to take back to Ralph. This café both of us will remember forever because it loudly played continuously every evening the same two songs: "Wake Up, Little Susie" by the Everly Brothers and "Kung-Fu Fighting" by Carl Douglas. I never knew it was possible to hear the same two songs blaring out over and over again and still keep your sanity. Ralph told me, "The juxtaposition of the two was as bizarre as it was grating and permanently etched into my malarial-fever dreams."[1]

I was sitting one evening on the patio of the café (before the music started) watching the townspeople saunter by, chatting, friendly, greeting one another in the pleasant coolness of the hour. It was a lively scene, and they were beautiful to watch. A strange feeling slowly began to move over me. I realized that it was a massive wave of homesickness, an overwhelming longing that was deeper than tears. Oddly, it wasn't for my family or my language or my flat or the local Coastal Mountains or my beloved city of Vancouver. It was for my ethnic compatriots. How strange. It was a visceral and spontaneous reaction that I had never felt before and never did again.

At that moment, I knew I was done. I wanted to go home. The trip was very hard and had been since we debarked in Tangiers. I didn't want to do it anymore and could have gotten on a plane for home that very day. Ralph wanted to continue but agreed we should head to Dakar in Senegal and fly home to Canada from there. So began the final stretch of our journey in which I counted down every single remaining day. But we still had far to go before we would get home.

2015

On Thursday, January 8, I held a protest against extremism at the ferry terminal on Bowen following the mass shooting at the Charlie Hebdo newspaper office the day before in Paris. I wrote the following article about it and submitted it to the *Undercurrent*.

On the morning of Thursday, January 8, I held a vigil in Snug Cove in honour of the people killed in the Wednesday attacks in Paris. It was just me on that very cold morning, and my little sign, "not afraid." In Paris on Wednesday night, people held up beautiful lighted panels that spelled out the phrase "not afraid." At the Vancouver vigil, there were smaller signs saying the same thing. I have always felt this way about terrorism and its perpetrators, and I wanted to make the same statement at my vigil. Terrorists want us to be terrorized, thus their name. I feel that we must not be. By refusing to be, we strip perpetrators of their power. Don't even use the word. Call them what they are. Use the word "murderers" instead.

Why do some young men take this destructive path? The two brothers in Paris had been abandoned as children and lived in poverty. Poverty itself is dreadful, but a more dire result is the disengagement of the poor from society. An us/them, class-war mentality arises, quaint as the idea seems to us egalitarian Canadians. France, one of the richest countries in the world, has not done the best job of integrating immigrants into its society and should do better to give hope and better opportunities to all its citizens.

Bowen Island is surely one of the most privileged places on the planet. Our immense good fortune behooves us to look beyond our gentle shores to the world at large. We have a responsibility to the greater good. If you feel moved to do something, here are some suggestions.

To help stop home-grown radicalization, take action to help local impoverished immigrant families in the Lower Mainland. Check out the Mom2Mom Child Poverty Initiative (m2mcharity.ca) and the Vancouver Sun Adopt-a-School program (vansunkidsfund.ca). You can donate and/ or volunteer to help vulnerable kids get a good education and basic resources and to feel that someone cares.

Refuse to be afraid. Do not utter the "t----" word. Don't let politicians stoke your fear. Contact our MP (John Weston) and MLA (Jordan Sturdy) to instead request better government funding for social services and mental health programs. Tell the media to stop their incessant coverage of brutal groups and relentless replays of men about to be beheaded and psychopaths shooting off weapons and ranting about their violent ideology.

Remember that we live in a world far better than ever in the history of humanity, and that even the radicalized will eventually become modernized. Read *The Better Angels of Our Nature* by Stephen Pinker for the good news. In the meantime, be not afraid.

I protest extremism in Snug Cove on Bowen.

This humble deed was one of my first ever of social activism. I cannot begin to tell you where the motivation or inspiration came from. A kind of spirit moved me when I saw this terrible news, and I wanted to do something, make a statement, take a stand. I was always moved by current events and tragedies and woes but was also shy and reticent. This time, I just could *not* do nothing. It was gratifying, and I got many accolades from Bowen folks for this. I could never have imagined where this humble action would lead me.

I did some work on the AVPA this year including holding two board meetings in January and December and the AGM in September. There wasn't much to report, and I didn't do minutes. I did a presentation at Sky on Bowen about the project but unfortunately was not able to do my PowerPoint presentation because the Rotary person who was supposed to bring the equipment didn't. Instead, I held up my speaking notes in hopes they could see the pix. Sigh, this did not go well. We did a bake sale at BCIT in May and made only $232.00. It was too late in the year and the campus was deserted. I met a young woman from BCIT called Jen who wanted to get involved and then vanished. Too bad! She seemed like a find. I worked on catching up on everything AVPA, so I could then do just the bare minimum. My dear friend Leah was helpful and said the AVPA was a huge undertaking. I so appreciated her understanding and kind words.

This year, we made our fifth and final trip to Okaseni. I also booked a side trip to Switzerland. I was unwell before we left but hoped that I would recover by the time we had to go. I did not.

TRAVEL JOURNAL
Monday, May 25
Our flight to Amsterdam left Vancouver at 4 p.m. It seemed a very long flight. Feeling ill was not a great way to start the trip, but I was hardly afraid at all and sailed (flew?) through the flight with the greatest of ease. It was still astonishing to me that all my work getting over my fears had paid off in spades and that those techniques worked. Hallelujah!

Dale slept quite a bit, me not so much. I watched two movies, *Pride* and *The Imitation Game.* Both were excellent. *Pride* was about a group of gays in London in 1984 who were fighting for social justice and equality for LGBT folks. At the same time, the British coal miners were on strike to protest the evil policies of Margaret Thatcher, who was trying to break the union. One of the gay guys, Mark Ashton, has the idea that they should support the miners and raise money to help them as they of course are not able to work. The miners are getting bullied like the gays, Mark says, so the gays should do something to help! They do raise some money, but when they try to find a way to give it to the miners, they are completely rejected by everyone. So they decide to give it directly to a coal-mining town and find Onllwyn, a wee town in Wales, by checking out a map of the British Isles.

They have their own bus, so they pile in and trundle up to the town to give them the loot. The miners completely reject them, but their wives are more on the ball and welcome the gays, accept the loot, and berate their husbands into being more gracious.

It's very touching. They all become friends and have some fabulous times with each other: dancing, partying, going to gay dance clubs (well, the women anyhow). Back in London, the gays continue to support the miners. But in the end, the miners go back to work at a greatly reduced wage, and that is the end of their association with the gays.

Several months later, the gays are getting ready to put on the Pride Parade in a London park. There is an argument over banners: Mark's group wants to carry their "Support the Miners" banner, but the organizers say they don't want the parade to be political. All of a sudden, a bus pulls up and the Onllwyn miners and their wives come flooding out, whooping and hollering, carrying the local union banner, and rushing to take part in the parade. The gays are gobsmacked. Hugs and more hugs! The organizers are flummoxed. Then another bus pulls up, and another. More miners with more banners pour out to join the parade. It's brilliant! They are there to support the gays as the gays had supported them. The gays are of course on cloud nine, and the organizers say that they and the miners should lead the parade.

It was just the best ever. The tears were zipping down my face. What an amazing story, and true apparently. It was so ironic that in the end, they tried to help just one little village. (Hey, just like us!) They did a bit of problem-solving at first to even find a village. (Hey, just like us!) They did their best despite lots of challenges. (Hey, just like us!) And they accomplished more—*much more*—than they could ever have imagined. (Hmm . . . not like us, yet.)

What they did was further the cause of humanity at its very best. They showed that a little kindness goes far, that just even having the *idea* to help someone and doing even what little one can is monumental and can have tremendous results. I didn't think I had ever seen that idea expressed so movingly, and the fact that it was a true story was breathtaking. Talk about inspiring. It encouraged me to keep helping Okaseni. The AVPA seems too much for one little person and so miniscule in the face of so much need, but the movie heartened me, and I was incredibly moved. At the end of the movie, it said that Mark Ashton died of AIDS two years later at the age of twenty-six: a short life but so well lived.

The Imitation Game was good too and, coincidentally, the same theme. It was also a true story and also set in England. During World War II, Alan Turing, an odd but brilliant chap (also gay, by the way), creates an early computer-like machine which deciphers the German enigma machine code and thereby saves the civilized world. The movie is another testament to the power of one person, like *Pride*, where all the action was driven by one passionate, creative, and active young person. Turing's dear friend Joan tells him he has saved many, many lives, and helped immeasurably to win the war, and that without him, the world would have been a much worse place. The movie was wonderfully acted, and the writing was excellent. It was amazing to think that so much can hinge on just one person.

Tuesday, May 26

We arrived in Amsterdam at 10:30 a.m. local time. We caught the shuttle to the Best Western where we were booked and begged them to take us in early. They said yes for which we were very grateful. We spent the day resting and getting ready for our flight to Tanzania tomorrow morning.

I got to bed by 11 p.m. and slept well for the first few hours but then was wide awake for two hours until we had to get up. It was a very worried two hours, fretting about how ill I felt and how I just did not want to come on this trip. It was so far to go, so expensive, and so difficult, and I was worried about Dale, although he seemed fine and was healthy enough to cope. I just wanted to stay home with the kitten and not go anywhere. I wondered if I were depressed because of not feeling well as I was not my normal cheerful self. How could I not be excited about travelling anywhere, as is usually my wont? It was an unhappy two hours.

Wednesday, May 27

The flight to Kilimanjaro left at 10:15 a.m. I was beat and unwell and spent most of the time resting. We arrived at the Kilimanjaro Airport at 7:45 p.m. Tanzania time and were at Bristol Cottages by 9 p.m. We had made it.

I got to sleep right away but woke at 3 a.m. and could not get back to sleep. Another hour of worries prevailed, this time about how I actually did not want to do the AVPA anymore and would have to announce to the villagers that their time was up, and it was sayonara, baby. It was a very depressing hour. I thought about how on earth I was going to get through the visit and came up with a game plan for coping: try to do interesting stuff so the time would pass quickly until I could escape. I finally dozed off and slept till 6 a.m.

Thursday, May 28

This was a restful morning. I wrote a lot. Dale read and did some emails to let Melki, Salma, and Nuria know we had arrived. I talked to Dale about scaling back the project and how disheartened I was feeling and that this would be our last trip to Tanzania and that I was going to tell the villagers the AVPA was done but that I was sad about having to do this.

"No way!" Dale said. "Don't tell them that. No need. It might not be the last time anyhow. We can still come back. We can still do stuff, even if it's minimal. We don't have to end it." I thought this probably the more circumspect plan of action. We decided to turn the dispensary over to the villagers, and Dale sent Tumaini a text to let him know. Suddenly, I was momentarily happy to be here, my affection for my dear little project was revived, and all was good with the world. I still felt ill though.

About 2 p.m., Melki arrived. Despite everything, it was nice to see him. It was funny how familiar it all was, as we chatted about a schedule for our visit. Melki was not happy to find we were staying for only five days.

Nuria and her kids arrived soon after, all bundled up in burkas and hijabs like three little Muslim fairies in Disney's *Sleeping Beauty*. We were so happy to see them. They are one attractive family for sure. They were thrilled to see us, and Nuria kissed and kissed me. As usual, Anisa talked non-stop. She showed us her thesis for her degree, which was very well done. Fatema seemed more herself. She was quite pretty and I thought she had realized that. She was in a different school from Anisa, which must have been freeing for her. Nuria was very shy and kept saying she wanted to go. Her teeth were very bad, dark and rotten with some missing. (When we got home, we wired her money to get them fixed. Afterwards, she looked like a movie star.)

They were so appreciative of everything we had done. Nuria cried. It was disconcerting to think we saved these girls from unfree lives, to put it *mildly.* It is surely one of the best things we ever did. We had a picture-taking fest, and they all hugged and kissed me again. I went back to the room for something, and Dale told Melki the story of how we met them and tried to help them. Dale told me Melki seemed impressed. Hah! Nuria cried as I did a re-tell when I got back. They were such a blessing in our lives.

They could not stay long. As I walked them to the gate, I told them briefly about a dear family member I had lost and how happy I was that they were in our lives. More tears from Nuria. She invited us to their place for dins on Saturday.

The beautiful and dear trio of Anisa, Fatema, and Nuria whom we have helped since 2008.

Melki seemed a bit morose after they left. We talked our idea for pensions, and he perked up immediately. We kept saying again and again that it was just an idea and very expensive and that we would likely never get funding for it. We also mentioned some projects we were not going to be able to do. Melki seemed crestfallen by this news. Later in the conversation, he gave us a list of the projects he wanted us to do. They were all the ones we said we could not do. Sigh. Why would he bring those things up? It was completely unrealistic, and I wondered what he was thinking. (I later realized it was a power ploy, albeit weak.)

He finally left. Dale and I enjoyed the soothing quiet of the courtyard and then had dinner. At about 6 p.m., Salma arrived. She told us about the dispensary, the attempt to get a clinical officer to staff it, and all the work Melki had done. She also talked a lot about the one volunteer she had managed to find for the dispensary and how hard she had worked with that person to get her to do anything. I began to wonder how much work she herself had actually done over time given her emphasis on that one little volunteer.

But I was happy to see her, and she was friendly but hardly looked at me. I had no idea why, but it did not seem like a good thing. Was it guilt? Embarrassment? Her info about getting a clinical officer at the dispensary showed she had done some research as well as just sent chatty emails. She also told us that Melki had not taken the poultry money as she told us in an email last year. That was a relief. But I realized later that he had probably indeed taken the money, but when I emailed back our extreme displeasure to Salma, Tumaini, and Peter, Melki got the message to cease and desist. Or at least that is what Salma seemed to have told us. Trusting as always, it never occurred to me to check this out by going to his property to see for sure. As I write this, it seems very possible that he did not stop.

I told Salma that she was currently our biggest expense and asked her if she wanted to continue working with us. She said yes, and that she had more ideas for other things to do. The status quo reigned, I guessed.

Friday, May 29
We received an email back this morning from Tumaini about turning over the dispensary to Okaseni. He suggested a church, which I was categorically

against. Dale and I discussed our options, and I finally said we should just get our names taken off the AVPT constitution and let them get two villagers instead. That way, we and the AVPA would be completely removed. We agreed that was a plan.

Melki was supposed to arrive at noon with a cabbie to take us to the Okaseni to see the dispensary. He arrived at 1:20 p.m., kind of smirky that he had made us wait so long, I guessed. Sigh. We finally left, Melki just ignoring us and talking to the cabbie. Sigh again. When we got to Okaseni, I was dismayed to see how unkempt and uncared for it looked, shabbier and more rundown than it had been and awash with poverty. It was discouraging to think that all our efforts and hard work were being swamped by a tsunami of worsening conditions. There also seemed to be more young people everywhere, late teens, early twenties, so many. It was evidence of a skyrocketing birth rate and very rattling.

At the village office, some council members and other villagers were holding a meeting about an upcoming election. The leader said the AVPA meeting that we had scheduled for Sunday would have to be cancelled. Disappointing.

We walked down to see the dispensary and were delighted. It was beautifully done and aesthetically gorgeous. The outside doors are heavy and metal, with pretty decorative features.

The interior had been completely revamped, so there are now four rooms: the doctor's office, the lab, maternal health room, and a storage room for drugs. The inner doors were massively thick and made of resplendent wood, and the windows were wood trimmed with safety bars on them that looked like stylish décor. The walls had been painted a cheerful yellow, and the upper wall vents were an intricate Arabic design. We were exhilarated, especially to see that the most recent things we had sent money for were almost completed: the windowpanes and electricity.

We then went outside behind the dispensary and admired the his and hers loos in the small out-building. The squat toilets were stellar, sparkling white, and had flushers. Now wonder the villagers were chuffed to bits.

The renovated dispensary and latrine were breathtaking. The surrounding plants and bushes had been removed so the building was more accessible.

We saw Mama Marietta as well, who proudly showed us her store, now selling beer and wine. She had also opened a canteen in the next room and hired a young woman to do the cooking. We were deeply impressed that she was able to provide someone with a job, just what we hoped the grants would do.

We walked back to the office where the councillors' meeting was still going on. I asked them if we could hold our meeting right then. The group was fine with it, so I was off and talking.

Melki was pleased to show us the inside of the dispensary, with the four separate rooms off the hallway.

I first thanked them for everything. I then listed some of the projects the AVPA had done in Okaseni and said we had spent about Can$80,000 total so far. There was a shocked silence, and I could tell they were all thinking, "$80,000?! Where did all the money go? Why isn't there more to show for it?" It was quite uncomfortable. Melki looked very sick all of a sudden as the group started eyeing him suspiciously.

I soldiered on, quickly changing the topic, and telling them Dale and I wanted to turn the dispensary over to them. We would resign from the AVPT board and suggested they replace us with two villagers. We wanted them to take it over, please! This went over very well with applause and smiles all round. I said we liked their idea of renting a truck (remembering Peter Mchau's warning about buying trucks for villages) to transport local produce to Dar and would be pleased to fund this venture. That also went over well. They asked us questions about the dispensary and the water system as well. All and all, I think they were pleased. I was too, especially that we had been able to even have a meeting.

We got back to the hotel barely in one piece. We had some curried chicken and rice for dinner. I was so tired and unwell that I went right to bed and slept for nine hours straight.

Saturday, May 30

I felt somewhat better today. I worked on an agenda for a meeting with Melki and Salma in lieu of the big village meeting tomorrow that got cancelled. Dale read and rested, taking it easy because he had an upset tum.

At about 3 p.m., Anisa arrived with a little tuk tuk, or "auto-rickshaw," to take us to her house for dinner this evening. I absolutely refused. It was very tiny with only canvas walls and doors and no seat belts. The cabbie from yesterday came too, so I went with him. Anisa came with me. Dale, however, hopped into the tuk tuk and off they puttered down the road amidst a lot of cars to Nuria's house. We followed them. They were very slow, but we all arrived safely.

It was sweet to be back at Nuria's. They were happy to see us and so gracious. We chatted merrily away and had snacks and juice. It was good to hear Anisa was doing well in school. While we were talking, a little black boy came into the room and whispered to Nuria. She got up and left. I followed her and the kid into the kitchen where she was wrapping some eggs up in newspaper. She told me the boy was the son of a couple who had rented the small mud shack behind her house. They were drunks, abusive to the kid, and complete messes. Eventually, they just up and left and abandoned the kid, who was about six.

Nuria took him in. He was in bad shape: malnourished, sick, and with worms in his feet. She decided, however, that she was going to take care of him. She told me she did this because of us. We had done so much for her and her girls, and she wondered how she could ever repay us. Then this little boy turned up. She thought, "This I can do, like what Sheena and Dale have done for me. I—even I—at least can do this." She said Arif did not want to take him in, but she told him she would pay for everything: meds, health care, clothes, schooling, food. The egg business she started with money we had sent her allowed her to do this.

I was stunned. My eyes filled up with tears as she told me, and a kind of wonder and stillness came over me. How could humble little us, just bumbling along trying to be helpful, have not only to have saved two girls but also this child of misfortune? It was surreal and became beyond tears.

We went back to the front room for more pleasant chatting until the conversation veered to Arif, Nuria's husband and the father of her kids. They told us that Arif was awful, very abusive. Anisa said, "You cannot spend one day with my father without crying." Both girls wanted to escape as soon as possible. Nuria said that after they could support themselves, she would take Kevin (the boy) and get the heck outta Dodge. It sounded like she would even abandon the house, which she inherited from her mum, if she had to. She said men like him talk a good line, but in private they are not good. I really felt for her.

Arif himself turned up after a while, and Dale and I were mildly pleased to see him. The others, not so much. They didn't even acknowledge him. Nuria went off to prep dinner and Fatema to pray. The rest of us had an interesting talk about politics and African economies, and I found out more about Tanzania than I wished. It wasn't a surprise but very depressing to hear about the corruption, lack of rule of law, and mismanagement. Anisa said that to improve the economy, Tanzania should stop all imports and develop its own manufacturing industries. I thought this a stellar idea. It would be hard to pull off and would require an efficient government, but they could definitely compete with China as they had so much cheap labour.

They took us on a tour of their yard where we saw Nuria's amazing chicken/egg compound and chicken house that we had funded. The house was about the size of a small shipping container and built out of sturdy cinder blocks with openings for windowpanes. She said she wasn't going to raise broilers anymore because it was too tricky and too much work (including killing them, ugh). Instead, she wanted to rent the house out, but it needed a kitchen. We told her to get an estimate for the work, and we would help her pay for it. They all seemed very grim about that: stern, impassive faces. Perhaps they didn't want to show their immense glee and excitement. If so, they did a very good job of it, although at one point, Anisa gave us a beaming smile.

I admired Nuria's hard work, resourcefulness, and persistence. She always seemed undaunted by her many challenges although she suffered immensely, but then she just got on with it. She was beyond admirable.

We walked down the road a bit. It was a nice neighbourhood in a way, but with the usual hodgepodge of garbage, small stands of veggies and other foods for sale, a tiny canteen, shabby houses, and then, oddly, several huge mansions under construction. The roadside was lush with greenery and masses of tropical flowers, it being the rainy season right now. I appreciated the beauty despite the many signs of extreme poverty.

Back at the house, Dale and Arif talked a lot about wood splitting, jobs, cars, manly stuff, while I listened politely. Nuria and Anisa worked busily in the tiny kitchen.

Dinner was good: delicious salads and a chicken that had been running around in the yard the day before intact. It was very, very chewy. Dessert was a delectable chocolate cake made by Anisa. After dinner, we talked to Fatema about what she wanted to do after she graduated from high school. We said we would help her. She was quite artistic and wanted to go to design school. That seemed like a good idea, but Anisa voiced her opinion and said Fatema needed to decide *right now* and study something practical. Oh, dear. But as Dale said, Anisa was probably a match for Arif.

By 8 p.m., it was time to go. Arif said he would drive us home. We said goodbye, tearless on my part still, but they were loving and appreciative. It was odd. They were very dear, but I think I was still in a state of shock and kind of frozen.

Arif drove us to the hotel; Nuria came too holding Kevin on her lap. It was familial being with them, comfortable and warm. Their friendship and appreciation meant even more to me now since my recent personal losses. They dropped us off and drove away into the night. They had made this a memorable day.

Sunday, May 31

I was on a mission to finish my agenda for our meeting at 11 a.m. with Salma and Melki. They arrived eventually. The meeting was good. We went through the agenda systematically and discussed every possible project we could work on. We decided to take the funds we had on hand and divide it three ways for the dispensary, the school fees, and the water system. We made a prioritized list of future projects. All round agreement, all good.

After the meeting, we chatted a bit. Melki asked me about the total amount of money we had spent in the village as I had mentioned in the village meeting yesterday. It sounded like the villagers *did* have some questions about where all that money went. Perhaps they suspected him of absconding with it. I realized that they might not have known about or remembered the many smaller things we had done, like paid school fees, taught the teachers' workshop, and such. (Hmm . . . how foolish it was of Melki not to have told them. I just assumed he would.) Anyhow, I told him we would write a list for him.

When they left, Dale and I listed the projects (that we could remember) with costs (that we could estimate). We texted Melki to come tomorrow morning so we could give him this info. I thought perhaps we could do a poster when we got home that he could put at the village office and the dispensary. It would list everything we had done and the costs.

We were leaving the next day, so we organized, packed, and checked out our money sitch. We had given a lot of our US$1 bills as tips and saved $200 to give to Nuria if she could visit us tomorrow. It had been a fruitful day. Surprisingly, this trip was going okay for me, despite not being well. I was not expecting much and just wanted to turf any responsibility for the dispensary and not suffer any drama. All good up to this point.

Monday, June 1

Departure day! I was so glad to be going. Being in Tanzania was always difficult with many things to worry about (mosquitos, meds, water, heat, drivers, poor quality food, and so on). I was also concerned about Dale and not letting him get harmed in any way. It was so far so good although, unfortunately, he still had his cold. I still felt poorly.

We wanted to be packed and ready to go before Melki arrived at the appointed time of 11 a.m. As usual of course, he was not on time but three-quarters of an hour early! This was a first and even more annoying. He always was a pain until we started paying him, and then he improved a lot. But this trip he was back to his old self. Always bewildered by such behaviour, I could not figure it out. Maybe as Dale said he was upset because we were helping Nuria. Anyway, it was a royal pain and very off putting.

Dale went out to meet him and I stayed in the room and finished packing. At exactly 11 a.m., I went out to join them. We gave him the list of projects and costs we had compiled so he could tell the villagers. I told him I had receipts for everything. He started suddenly and seemed for the first time to get receipts. There *was* a reason for them, and my obsessiveness about them didn't seem so weird. They were proof of expenditures so that he wouldn't get his ass fried by his constituents. Hah, vindication!

We also told him we would do a poster listing the AVPA projects for a sign that he could put up at the dispensary and the office. He seemed better today, more subdued but more pleasant. Maybe he did get all bent out of shape that first day because he realized we like Nuria and her family very much and probably more than him. He left about noon.

We were getting ready to vacate the room when Das, the receptionist, said we could stay in it for free until we left for the airport this evening, which was very kind of him. The staff there had been very good overall. I gave my runners and some trinkets to Happiness, our cleaning lady. She seemed mildly pleased. I realized that nothing escapes anyone in this place, and all the staff knew Happiness had gotten something. There was a lot of hostility after that until we put our extra US$1 bills in the communal tip box. Then everyone became much nicer again.

It was very difficult. We had so much. They had so little. They were doing their best and trying so hard. The situation was unbearably unjust. I felt terrible, but at least I was trying in a very small way to change that (no pun intended). Tips did help.

Nuria arrived at just after lunch.

We had an illuminating visit. We gave her the US$200 we had set aside for her. It was heaven to talk just to her and not be interrupted constantly. She told us about a support/microcredit group that she had set up in her neighbourhood. Fifteen women got together every month for a meeting to give short-term loans, support each other in difficult times, and raise funds for the group itself. They would buy something in bulk, such as cooking oil, and then each person would buy one-fifteenth of it at slightly more than the original purchase. The extra money went into a communal fund. They also each had to put about US$4 into the fund every month. What a great idea, I thought. Turns out it was Anisa's. She got her mum going on it. As Nuria talked, I realized we were responsible for that too. The expanding circle of help now included fifteen women, unknown, unmet, unaware probably of us. (Hmm, maybe not. Nuria might have told them.) It was mind-boggling. Had Dale and I created a virtuous circle? In my most extravagant dreams, I could not imagine having an effect like that on anything *ever*. But truly, if we had not paid for Anisa's schooling, she might never have learned about microcredit and then given her Mum the idea or encouraged her to start the group: a virtuous circle of goodness indeed.

We said goodbye to Nuria at about 3 p.m. She cried when she left and could hardly look at us. She was such a sweetheart. She said she and the girls call us "Malaika" (angels). Our lives were immeasurably richer because of her. I also realized later that, thanks to the funds we had sent her for her chicken/eggs business, she was also able to pay for Fatema's schooling. (She hadn't contacted us recently for money.) Sooo good! Again, my mind was boggled. I felt dumbstruck by it mostly and then overcome with a painful wonderment.

We rested some more and then got loaded into the hotel van to go to the Kilimanjaro Airport. The plane left just after 9 p.m. It was a long flight but smooth and fortunately with the only one-hour time change only, a big blessing. I was still not well.

Tuesday, June 2

We arrived in Amsterdam about 7:30 a.m. Beloved Schiphol, our home away from home. We wended our way to the waiting area for our flight to Zurich. It was downstairs beside what looked like a very big parking lot, with a myriad of small planes instead of cars scattered around seemingly at random. We hoped there was some organization there somewhere. It was a three-hour wait but very pleasant, resting, doing sudoku, and chowing down lunch.

I had time to ponder and marvelled at how well the AVPA was going. Progress had been slow because of the massive land/building/renos/dispensary project, but it had been steady. It was a thrill to see what Mama Marietha had accomplished with the grant we gave her. Ditto Renatus who, according to Salma, was doing very well. (He had been away while we were there.) It was gratifying and made me somewhat want to keep on trucking.

At noon, we crammed into a huge bus with many other passengers, their luggage, chickens, and goats. No, just kidding. It was standing room only though and did have an African vibe. The bus took us through the maze of planes to a nice little KLM one that was roomy and fast (just under an hour and a half).

At Zurich, surely one of the most sterile, unwelcoming, characterless airports we had ever been in, we took a cab to a nearby hotel where we spent a quiet evening in prep for our journey to Lauterbrunnen tomorrow.

Wednesday, June 3

We trundled out this morning and headed to the train station. A very crabby service lady was no help at all and then proceeded to fill out our Swiss Pass cards for us as if we were without a doubt the stupidest people *ever!* We nicely caught the next train to Bern where we had to transfer to the Interlaken train. While we waited, we wandered around outside in the sunshine. Although it was mid-town, few people were out and about. A fellow was selling alternative newspapers, and I bought one, pleased to be able to support the cause.

I realized later with a marvelous shock that I had had the opportunity to redeem myself for not buying the newspaper from that Utrecht train-station guy in 2012. I was so, so grateful for my second chance.

We hopped onto the train to Interlaken and there onto the little train to Lauterbrunnen, where we arrived safely but rather beaten. Our lodging, Chalet Horner, was in the centre of the village and just too cutely Swiss. It was a large, beautiful house, half of which had been subdivided into five separate tourist flats. The building was older and a tad rundown but had an Olde World charm. We could not get a continuous booking there for the eleven days we would be in Lauterbrunnen, so after six days there, we had to move to the Hotel Schützen for two days and then back to Chalet Horner for the last four days of our stay.

Our flat at the Horner was called the Jungfrau. It was very small. Two twin beds just fit in it, and around the corner by the door was a sink, hot-plate, some dishes, and silverware. Around the corner on the other side was the bathroom, barely wide enough for a clawfoot bathtub and long enough for the toilet and sink too. The beds were very comfy, très important. The flat was a few feet above ground level, and a small balcony was suspended outside that faced the Jungfrau mountain—spectacular!

We checked in with Theresa, the owner, who was a widow and a bit dour but kind and helpful. She left all manner of goodies in our flat: chox, packets of coffee and tea, cheese, crackers, and candies. She was a good businessperson and had done well to remain independent with a viable source of income. All and all, the flat was just fine and not hugely expensive, given Switzerland.

I was feeling marginally better today despite the travelling. Happy, happy day!

Thursday, June 4

How good it was to wake up in Switzerland and have slept so well in that cozy, comfy room in an authentic Swiss chalet. I was so grateful to be there. The relief at being in one of the most developed countries in the world and to be feeling better was indescribable. Being ill on this trip had not been fun, and if I had needed medical care in Tanzania, it could have been a disaster. Switzerland, with its excellent health system, offered peace of mind and a sublime opportunity for rest and recuperation. Also, the wee valley and village were so dramatic and stunning that anxieties just could not take hold. They were a balm to my shaken-up body and trampled-on psyche. It was heaven.

The day stretched before us with no meetings, no drama, no hostile or contemptuous people to have to deal with. I took it very easy today, wanting only to rest. After a nap and lunch, I perused the books I had brought, *Survival of the Nicest* and *One Summer: America, 1927*, which looked perfect for recovering from Africa and illness in a romantic Swiss village in the Alps. Dale still had his cold but slept thirteen hours last night and was feeling better and more cheerful today. I made chicken legs for dins and felt so hollow inside that I kept eating and eating. I also ate a lot of chocolate, a necessity of life, non? I felt a little better.

In the evening, Dale started to read *One Summer: America, 1927* and got hooked. I walked over to the Hotel Schützen to find out about checking in. They were very unhelpful people. I hoped our move there would work out. We were so tired and out like lights by 10 p.m.

Friday, June 5

I woke up about 6 a.m. absolutely exhausted, far worse than yesterday. I might have still been going on adrenalin yesterday, which ran out overnight. I dragged myself up at about 6:30 a.m. to get on Swiss time.

This was a day of major R & R for me. I read, wrote in my journal, and napped. Dale went for a short hike, so he was feeling better. I sat on the balcony and chatted with the neighbours on the balcony next door, telling them about the AVPA. They had lots of stories of various people *they* knew who had done something similar. I mentioned that I was going to write a book called *How to Adopt a Village in Africa*. One of them said, "Oh, good idea! People might not believe you if you just tell them, but if you write it, they will believe!" I thought this a bit odd. Did they not believe me?!

After dinner, I went for a short walk although I had to force myself out. It was a beautiful evening and worth the effort. Back at the Horner, I read some more then sank asleep.

Saturday, June 6

We had breks outside this sunny morning on our petite balcony. We could see far down the road past the church and noticed some people walking there in bright orange workers' vests. I thought they were construction workers, but then we could see they were walking with cows, taking them to the summer pastures I guessed. I jumped into my clothes to take a look. Dale tore out of there ahead of me and got a couple of videos of cow bums and the backs of people walking through town.

In the afternoon, I settled on the bed to read. It was going swimmingly. *Survival of the Nicest,* by Stefan Klein, was a bit so-so and hard to read but had a positive, encouraging take on humanity. *One Summer: America, 1927,* by Bill Bryson, was delightful as are all his books, interesting and artfully written. I hardly ever have time at home for long, leisurely chunks of reading, so it was a joy to have hours to devote to one of my great loves, devouring books.

Dale went for a hike along a footpath outside of town. A big storm began to brew and right in front of him, a small flock of little goats got all perturbed and ran down the hill to their mums' shed. He got two darling videos of them scampering down, their little bells tinkling in magical chimes. He got back just as the rain started, and we enjoyed from the shelter of our little balcony the tremendous thunderstorm right in front of us. We saw dazzling bolts and diffused flashes of lightening and heard thunder so loud I had to plug my ears. It pounded rain, so heavy it looked like hail. What a crazy mix of weather. Tanzania must have gotten the memo for Switzerland (very cool, not much sun, a bit of rain), and Switzerland got Tanzania's (very hot, blazing sun, monsoon-like rains). The massive bolts took turns zapping the huge mountains and cliffs, even setting an outcrop on fire on the west cliff. I love thunderstorms although I did move off the balcony to just inside the flat. Still the same good view though.

After all that excitement, we were even more tired and quickly fell sound asleep.

Saturday, June 7

We did a gentle walk this morning, the first walk for me of any seriousness since leaving Canada. I was definitely on the mend. After lunch back the

Horner, Dale did a walk part way up the Wengen trail. I thought he might
be in love with one of the goats up there. Loath to bestir myself, I lay on the
bed for hours reading, so glad I had brought those books. It is always a crap
shoot packing stuff for trips. Some dress or sweater I might have my doubts
about bringing turns out to be the thing I wear most. Books might be heavy
but who can live without them? I am always aiming for perfection and never
attaining it. The packing gods are always busy when I call.

In the evening, I chatted on the balcony with the neighbours on our left
and our right. We said goodbye to all as we were moving tomorrow to the
Schützen for two nights. It was a bit sad to be leaving.

Monday, June 8

We charged around packing this morning so we would be out by 10 a.m. as
requested by Theresa. She kindly let us leave our gear in the Horner vestibule.
It was a desultory day, a bit of lunch here, a little hike there (for Dale), an
enjoyable read in the internet café (for me). I took some moments to revel in
having found the lovely Chalet Horner, the perfect size for Dale and me, very
clean, and reasonably priced, with a great view. I was unexpectedly surprised
to be enjoying this trip. I had not wanted to come, but Switzerland turned
out to be full of happy surprises and good experiences.

The Swiss were amazingly generous in many small ways. Again and again,
people gave us little extras or did not charge us for things. Perhaps it is the
sign of a very rich country but also an equal one in which people don't resent
each other, or feel excluded from the prosperity in the country, or feel com-
pelled to suck up as much money as they can from the rest of the populace.
It makes for a pleasant atmosphere and happy day-to-day interpersonal
exchanges. Way to go, Switzerland!

It was so different from poorer countries where corruption is rife and theft
common. There, it's survival mode to the max. I did get it, but it was hard
to always be sympathetic when you are trying to help and getting gouged
and ripped off at every chance. The hurt was caused mostly by Tumaini and
Melki, who accompanied their possible misdeeds with a huge glob of contemptuous misogyny. It made me even more appreciative of the generosity of
the Swiss.

Dale came back from his walk, and it was time to go to the Schützen. You could check in there only between 4 p.m. and 8 p.m. and check out only between 8 a.m. and 10 a.m. The owner seemed not to care about the place. He lived in Interlaken, barely staffed the place, and hardly ever visited. I had never before been in a hotel that had the air of a morgue or funeral parlour. Quite odd.

We got checked in by the lone hotel clerk and then went out for a delicious dins of rosti, that delectable dish that became a staple for us this visit. When we got back to the hotel at about 8 p.m., the hotel clerk told us that no one was going to be at the hotel overnight. I thought he meant only *we* would be there. Yipes. But no, he actually meant no staff and said that if anything happened, we should call 112 (the European 911). That was unnerving, but I was somewhat relieved that, yes, other guests would still be there.

Tuesday, June 9

I felt better today and up for an excursion. Dale suggested a trip to Stechelberg, a wee town at the other end of the valley. We bought some sandwiches at the internet café, caught the bus right out front, and off we went. On the way, we passed Trümmelbach Falls, a waterfall that we had never seen, so we decided to stop there on the way back.

Stechelberg was not much more that an old, very small hotel and restaurant, a few houses, and a bus turnaround. We walked one of the paths to the bottom of the mountains. It was spectacular to be in that little V-shaped notch at the end of the valley surrounded by enormous peaks jutting straight up smack-dab in front of you. Amidst the grassy, flowery fields and watched over by those glorious, monumental stone formations, I was suddenly struck by how magical it all was. This was a first. I was probably too used to the mountains at home to be awed, but today I was suddenly captivated by them in an emotional way, like love! It was what I usually feel for cities (Paris and Lucerne) or, as Herman Melville said, for the true places that aren't down on any map.[1] I was utterly captivated by their gorgeousness and realized their ability to transport you to mystical realms. Or perhaps they suddenly became mystical realms to my eyes. Whatever, I was smitten.

We pottered around some more, me still marvelling at the wondrousness of it all, and then hopped on the bus back. A few stops later, we arrived at Trümmelbach Falls. We headed up a slope to the entrance gate, and suddenly, we were surrounded by masses of tourists from around the globe all keen to be first in line. Once inside, the path led to the bottom of a funicular where we were bundled into a cable car with about twelve other people. I was a bit anxious, but at least funiculars don't actually leave the ground. However, this one was unnerving. It went straight up the inside of the mountain through a dark, wet, narrow, cold, almost vertical tunnel.

The car started, and the ride was okay. At the top, we were let out through the other side of the car onto a platform near the falls. The tourists again charged and galloped and barrelled their way hither and yon. There were a lot of hithers and yons. We were at the midway point of the viewable falls, with many staircases leading up, down and sideways from there.

Dale and I started up. The noise of the falls became very loud, then roaring, then thundering. The water rushed down through hollowed tunnels and tubes inside the mountain. All were natural, and all were cleverly visible from a series of staircases and various platforms. The staircases wended their way through other person-made tunnels and afforded dramatic views of tumbling, gushing, pounding water cascading through the mountain. The engineering feat for these viewing areas was almost as impressive as the falls themselves. I was so impressed in fact, that I decided to go no further. Dale did go on. He told me later that the passageway got smaller and more cave-like, too claustrophobic even for him. It became surreal. He took some pix, but it was too dark to get good shots. He became even more uneasy and headed down.

I, in the meantime, had scooted out of there and gone down to the funicular platform where I waited for Dale. When he arrived, we eschewed the funicular and went down the pathway/stairs, past many more viewing sites of the raging, interminable torrent of water. It was a relief to get down on flat ground, but it had been an exciting, if rattling, experience. I later found out that the original walkways and bridges through the falls had been built by a local guy called Herr von Almen in 1877. These features were then expanded on by his son, who also discovered hidden caves behind the falls. Kasper, the grandson, then excavated another tunnel and, at seventy-eight in 2002, was still tending the area.[2] It was another testimony to the power of one, although three in sequence this time.

Dale walked back to town, and I took the bus to the internet café where I waited and read my Bryson book. I marvelled that, unlike Africa, it was very hard to be homesick here. It is so dramatic and spectacular that it takes all your attention, thus no brain cells are left to miss life at home. Dale arrived back, having had a good walk. We had dinner at the Jungfrau and then got organized for the move back to Chalet Horner tomorrow.

Wednesday, June 10

We found someone this morning to check us out of the Schützen, thank goodness. Back at the Horner, we were now in the Studio, a ground-level flat at the back of the house. It was larger that the Jungfrau flat and more private as it did not abut any other rooms. It also didn't have the dramatic view, being lower down and facing east instead of south, so it seemed like a regular flat anywhere instead of a viewing balcony of mountainous splendor with a small room attached to it, like the Jungfrau. However, the Studio did have an attractive patio outside the main door that faced the train tracks and Wengen, a mighty nice view in itself. The cute trains chugged past just below. Couldn't complain!

I was still exhausted and unwell so stayed put for the rest of the day. Dale set off on a big tromp, following a path up the west cliff to get a stunning view of Staubach Falls. Goethe was so impressed by this waterfall that he wrote a poem about it. Dale made do with just a walk and enjoyed it immensely, coming back looking very healthy, all bright-tailed and bushy-eyed.

We spent the evening congenially hanging out. I finished the Bryson book and felt sad, as if I had lost a little friend.

Thursday, June 11

I slept for nine hours last night and was quite a bit better this morning. It was gorgeously sunny on the patio and felt like we were at the beach lolling around and watching the little trains lap up against the shore. More cows came by on their way up to their summer resorts, and we rushed up to the road to see them. There were herds of them, all decked out in their huge bells (to slow them down apparently) and clanging their way along the street, sometimes trying to take a different path, like directly towards the tourists, like moi! I moved behind Dale. They were quickly prodded back on track by the herders.

After lunch, we decided to revisit Kleine Scheidegg and the Jungfrau, Mönch, and Eiger. I was a bit nervous (as usual) because those mountains were very big, and the train taking you up the winding railway was very tiny. But it was worth it. The mountains seemed like dear friends, not scary or intimidating at all, and perhaps were mildly happy to see us again. Dale hiked the Männlichen Trail towards Wengen while I waited for him on the bleachers and read. My recovery continued.

At about 8:30 this mid-summer evening, when it was still daylight in this northern country, we walked down to Staubach Falls. I love this time of day. Many people were out, a whole array of humanity, including Muslim families with the mums in burkas and veils, groups of high school kids walking together like giant amoebas, couples of all races, singles with their doggies, families of all races. Who knew a tiny Swiss village was such an international draw?

I loved this too. The blend was entrancing. I wished for more Africans to be there as well. I'm a big fan of transculturation, the mixing and melding of different cultures. I would love to wear a sari, for example, and would deeply hope not to offend anyone. They can take my blue jeans anytime. Oh wait, they have! A fellow in Vancouver started an annual mid-winter celebration combo for Chinese New Year and Robbie Burns Day. He called it Gung Haggis Fat Choy. It featured bagpipes and firecrackers. Genius!

Friday, June 12
This was another soothing day of me recuperating and now reading *Survival of the Nicest* and Dale doing a walk, this time back to Trümmelbach Falls. Each to their own and in this case, our owns were very good. The evening was warm and cloudless, and the sun didn't set until 9:20 or so. The dusk was bewitching. It had been a fine day.

Saturday, June 13

Our plan for today was to go to Murren, a little town atop the west cliff of the valley. We took a cable car up and then chugged across the top of the cliff in a little train to the town. The rides were unnerving as always. But I was okay, and the view was stunning, looking across to the Jungfrau, Monk, and Eiger almost at eye level with them. We didn't stay long. I was okay on the ride down too. All my work conquering my fear of flying had paid off handsomely in many ways.

In the afternoon, we meandered along a beautiful tree-lined path by the river. A gentle breeze was blowing, the sun was out, the air was warm and sparkling. Honestly, it was just too beautiful for words. Sometimes it seemed that Lauterbrunnen was so perfect that it could not be real. The Swiss Tourist Board (STB) had done an excellent job of putting together this ideal Swiss village, down to the yummy meals and cute little goats. It was perfection village-ified. Good job, STB!

We prepped and packed this evening because we were leaving tomorrow for Zurich. The contrast between Tanzania and Switzerland was staggering and shocking as always, and I was so grateful for the respite here. But it also tapped into my first-world guilt. Okay, I thought, I *can* still put some effort into the AVPA and would continue as I could.

Sunday, June 14

We had our granola and yogurt on the patio this morning, our last one here. I was glum to be leaving as this sojourn had restored my battered soul and ill body. We headed for the train station and decided to take the route through Lucerne, which was an hour longer than through Bern, because we wanted to see the spectacular scenery through Central Switzerland.

Well, the train was a zoo. It was crazy busy, jammed full of tourists, including us and other Caucasians, as well as many Asians and South Asians. I approved of this mightily as it felt quite like home. Dale and I sat across from each other in aisle seats. Beside each of us were two chatty Asian ladies who were holding animated conversations with their six family members in the seats on the *other* side of the aisle. The convo was right in my ear and very loud. Dale and I were our usual polite Canadian selves, whispering quietly to each other and even texting. I eventually got up my nerve and said a cheerful pleasantry to the ladies and though they didn't seem to speak much English, they looked quite pleased, and the din diminished somewhat.

Some bunch of punk rocker types were sitting on the floor of the entry way of the car. I was sitting a few feet away facing them and had an excellent view. They had scads of piercings and multi-coloured hair and an evil looking flag with a devil's skull giving the finger that they kept holding up at the doorway of the car so that we all could enjoy it. One guy was wearing a small cardboard carton as a hat. Seriously. Their T-shirts said things like "Fucked and left for dead" and "Bad to the bone." I began to think they were all a bit off, but actually, they were quite nice kids. They helped a portly lady get her suitcase off the train and apologized for one of their more outrageous companions. They were four guys and one girl, and the guy I thought was the most touched (with the cardboard hat) turned out to be the one who had the girlfriend and who had apologized for his friend in quite good English. It was rather sweet, some basically good kids, trying their hardest to be baaaaad! Goodness hides its charming face at times.

I later walked through the train, trying to find better seats (none), and discovered many more punk rockers. Apparently, there had been a rock concert in Interlaken over the weekend called Heaven Will Burn! Of course. They all got off at Lucerne and the train was suddenly much quieter.

Oh, yes, and the scenery was fabulous too.

We got to Zurich about mid-afternoon and went straight to the hotel. We decided not to move until we had to get up tomorrow at 4:30 a.m. to catch the plane to Paris and then home.

Monday, June 15

We caught the shuttle to the airport très early where we hopped onto the commuter plane to Paris with many, many suits. The flight took about one hour and twenty minutes. The Charles de Gaulle Airport was enormous and imposing, in keeping with the many other grand structures in that city, and it was a long walk to the KLM departure gate.

The flight to Vancouver was also long (ten hours and fifteen minutes). I watched *Dirty Dancing* for about the sixth time (I like to rewatch movies that I love). The music and the dancing are so good, what's not to watch again? The story is sweet also. At this point in the flight, I was just trying to pass time, but ironically, I actually *got* the movie this time. All the political stuff had seemed forced and wooden before, but for the first time, I got the class struggle. I understood what the working-class kids were talking about. I guessed helping in Africa and seeing firsthand the inequity in the world had opened my eyes. Everything else in the movie also made more sense, and it became richer and more profound, like seeing a completely new movie, but just as good. The parallel to helping in Africa was not lost on me: the difference in class between the rich and the poor kids in the movie, vis-à-vis the difference in nearly everything between the West and Africa. How sweet it was that, in the movie, they connected.

How lucky was I to have the chance to watch such fantastic movies for free (well, sort of) when I had tons of time on my hands.

We arrived in Vancouver about noon local time after a ten-hour flight, picked up our car, and caught the ferry home. At 6:30 p.m., I crashed, completely beat, in my own comfy bed, very happy to be there.

HOME

I did continue to work on the AVPA after our trip, and there were more email exchanges with the Okaseni folks over the rest of the year. In July, I emailed Melki asking him if he could get a sign for the dispensary like the one he got for the coffee nursery in 2007. In August, Melki replied that yes, he could get a sign like that. He also requested money to pay Tanesco, the hydro authority, for the power hook-ups. On August 21, I wired funds to the Kikilora account for the Tanesco charge, dispensary furnishings, and school fees. I requested receipts as soon as possible and thanked him for his work and dedication to the AVPA.

I did not hear from Melki about these funds or get any receipts from him, so on September 16, I emailed Salma and asked her to contact Melki about this.

In September, I received her reply:

I had a talk with Mr. Mushi and he promise to respond to you soon. He said, he couldn't get the chance to come to town for the internet because he was busy supervising electricians at the dispensary. They successful managed to put the electricity at the dispensary, so thrilled for this achievement.

Once again Sheena, THANK YOU A MILLION TIMES for making this dream come true. I am so moved by this success and I strongly believe is the same feeling everyone at Okaseni has it. Many thanks, Sheena, for your generosity! My special thanks to Dale too.

We were touched and pleased to have received this lovely message from Salma. On November 10, we received this email from her with another update:

Thought it would be useful to share with you a bit more about the progress for the dispensary. Few weeks ago we ordered the furniture for the dispensary as follows: two tables and two chairs for the medical practitioner. These two tables will have two to three [drawers] whereby the medical practitioner will be able to put their documents and tools. The plan is to receive the two tables and chairs before the end of this week, so, I will keep you more posted.

We have also ordered some medical equipment too, they run out of stock with some tools and waiting to receive another stock from Dar es Salaam. I will keep you more posted on this. Once, we are done with the first stage, we will use some of the remaining money to make two benches, which will be used for the patients' waiting area. We will also purchase four plastic chairs for the patient to use inside the doctor's room. Each room two chairs for the patients. I will make sure to send photos and all the receipts once this exercise is complete.

We are still waiting to hear from the DMO (district medical officer) about the possibility to get a clinical officer there. He said Mrs. Loveness [a local nurse who was volunteering part-time at the dispensary] is still continue with the new assignment and there is possibility that, she will need to continue there for a while. If that's the case, they will assign a new clinical officer at Okaseni. Not only that, they will also assign the health officer who will be able to come to the dispensary once every after three months to provide health education to the villagers. They will provide us with more detailed information after they are done with the dispensary inspections. Thanks for your always generous support on this!

We sent our thanks back to Salma and remained silently hopeful that the dispensary would eventually be staffed. Renovating the building had been slow and dependent on raising funds, but windows and electricity were finally installed, and the building finished. We received many messages of thanks from the villagers, saying that it was a dream come true for them and that they had never hoped Okaseni would have its own dispensary. Of all the projects we had done, the dispensary garnered us by far the most appreciation and gratitude.

The villagers approved our request to take us off the registry of trustees for the AVPT and fill our positions with villagers. In the fall, we received a copy of the registered trustees list dated August 19, 2015. Dale and I had been deleted, and Renatus and Mama Marietha had been added instead. You can imagine my joy at being turfed and also that the stars of our grants program were our replacements. The grants program itself was still doing well and creating jobs, which was what we hoped for.

In September, we received an update from Salma about the truck project.

I had a talk with Mr. Mushi about the truck and he agree that is important to form the committee soon and then discuss it in the village meeting in November. He also said is important to form the truck committee during the village meeting because they do have small farming groups in each sub village. The idea is to have the villagers' opinion as well as to decide on who should be selected in each small farming group to form a truck committee. The selected committee will then sit together and collect the ideas from the villagers and come up with the concrete plan on its implementation.

Generally, Okaseni grows lots of different types of bananas, avocados but there is also a possibility to grow other things such as peas, eggplants, and okra. These could be some of the things they will be happy to transport it to Dar or nearby regions. I am sure, we will get more ideas after they for the truck committee.

This all seemed rather convoluted. How complicated could it be to collect produce and rent a truck? However, it did seem like some progress was being made. This had been a year of unexpected AVPA successes, and for that we were grateful.

This year was also personally rewarding. My great house reorganization project continued. I organized and turfed masses of stuff, including four boxes of personal docs to be shredded. I even turfed Rotary. It had gotten less interesting, and I did not miss it one iota. I thought instead I might do more theatre events on Bowen so, to get some advice, I got in touch with Ian, a kindly, long-time, knowledgeable resident of Bowen. He was supportive of my idea, but by the end of our conversation, I realized that I would rather get off the island.

So I began to search on the mainland for fun and worthy things to do. I checked out several literacy programs with elementary school kids; one was great fun and I stayed for almost two years. An after-school program for high school kids was less successful and fizzled quickly, ditto an opportunity at a care facility. In September, I started going to the monthly meetings of First Call, an advocacy group for children and youth living in poverty. It was wonderful, full of people who cared. I realized there *was* a war on the poor. The group, however, was not active and did not do protests. They were more academic and scholarly, which was disappointing, but I loved the meetings and admired the members and attendees.

The most significant event for me this year was the death in September of a teenager called Alex Gervais. He had been in foster care and had just aged out of the system. (When they turn nineteen in British Columbia, foster kids are no longer eligible for government care from the Ministry of Children and

Family Development (MCFD). They are on their own, and many face dire circumstances.) Alex's death was likely a suicide. I was outraged, especially given that I had tried to find a young person like him to help, so I began a campaign lobbying the BC government to increase the age of support to twenty-four years of age.

I started a petition, first in Avaaz, the international social-activism organization, and then switched to change.org. Neither was a success. I wrote a detailed pamphlet about the difficulties and poor outcomes that ageing-out foster kids can experience, including mental illness, addiction, homelessness, abuse, and early death. I paid a local designer to help me with the format and design.

I wrote individually addressed letters requesting the government immediately increase the age of support and sent them with my pamphlet to various provincial government officials, including the premier, the MCFD minister, the leader of the opposition, and my local MLA representative. I also gave the letter/pamphlet package to Mary Ellen Turpel LaFond, the independent Representative for Children and Youth, who for years had recommended that the government support ageing-out foster kids. She never directly commented on my campaign, but I did receive a hint that she appreciated it. I also contacted Lori Culbert, a reporter at the *Vancouver Sun* newspaper, who had written excellent articles about foster kid issues. She was very kind and I kept in touch with her for the two years of my campaign.

At a First Call meeting, I gave out my pamphlet, hopeful that the attendees might join me in my campaign. They were not impressed, and only one person ever did participate. I sent my pamphlet and individual letters to the heads of the seventy or so organizations that were members of First Call asked for their support in my campaign. I heard back from one person. I forged on. I decided to hold a rally in February and started prepping for it. Despite the lack of support, it was invigorating to be taking action for a greater good. This year had started with a protest and then circled back on itself to another protest, another excellent opportunity for social activism. I seized it with both hands. Like my January "not afraid" action, it was at home, not halfway around the world.

My focus shifted even more away from the AVPA this year. The tedium of the day-to-day administration got replaced by easier, more rewarding ventures with (often) grateful and appreciative people. I made new friends and saw old friends more frequently, and I became more light-hearted and cheerful.

I was still on my activism mission though. On March 8, International Women's Day, we went to a party at Xenia, a retreat centre on Bowen. I wrote in my journal: "I gave a quick speech tonight at Mike's birthday party about heroes. The wondrousness of the male hero and how magnificent he is! How I saw the hero in men everywhere and how much I appreciated and respected them. And thanked them. We make a great team, men and women. But a woman's work is never done, so onward to improve women's rights!"

I wanted to give men a shout-out and celebrate their goodness. As well, I was remembering an African tragedy: the masses of heroic young males I saw in Tanzania with no outlet for that heroism. A stagnant economy, lack of opportunity, and the frustrated hopes and dreams of dynamic men who could contribute profoundly to society broke my heart. I wanted to acknowledge them as silently and hope for much better lives for them in the future.

Unlike that evening in the Lomé café in 1975, I did not have a pivotal moment about the AVPA. I knew in Tanzania in June that it would be our last trip to Okaseni, but when we left, I did not feel sad or have any sense of a forever goodbye. That departure was just like all the rest: I was leaving with a huge sense of relief and the sheer joy of going home. Perhaps my heart knew that I was done, but my mind was still engaged. I still had plans to help and do what I could. The dispensary, the grants, and the truck rental still interested me, and the future beckoned. As on my 1975 journey, I still had some way to go before the AVPA would finally be over.

CHAPTER 10

2016, AFRICA, THE MEDITERRANEAN, AND THE ANCIENTS

1975

After Ralph recovered from malaria in Lomé, we continued along the coast and crossed into Ghana. We visited a crumbling building on the waterfront that had been a holding area for African people who were to be shipped to the Americas during the slave trade. It was beyond me to grasp at the time the evil that was perpetrated there, but I remember the building well. We made our way along the coast to Abidjan, the capital of the Ivory Coast, and then north into Mali, a former French colony. We were heading for Dakar in Senegal, our departure point on the furthest western tip of the African continent.

In Mali, we were back in the Sahara. It was a sparsely populated country with few towns. We were picked up and invited home by a dentist, a thirty-ish man from France who was doing a two-year volunteering stint in Mali. The town he lived in was hot and dusty, and the roads were not paved. The garb was different from the coastal areas and more suited to a desert clime. There were some exotic, tall buildings made of mud with minimal ornamentation that had a kind of Gothic air. While we were there, a couple of other guys from France visited the dentist. They had a spirited conversation about which was the best road south to Abidjan, all in French. Travelling through Mali, the Cote d'Ivoire, and Benin, all former colonies of France, had exercised my own French, and I was delighted to realize I understood what they were talking about. Ooh la la, first time ever!

The dentist had a beautiful, young African woman living with him, and she didn't seem like a servant or maid. I wondered, were they married? Unlikely. He probably got together with her soon after his arrival and took her into his home for companionship while in this foreign country. I wondered what would happen when he left after the two years. Would he take her home? I was dubious. Would she be an outcast in her community? Find a local husband ever? Become independent and able to look after herself? I could not even guess. It seemed a grossly unfair situation although maybe I was missing something.

We continued north and eventually arrived in Bamako, Mali's capital city and the starting point of the train ride that would take us to Dakar. Bamako's population was only 363,000 people at the time, but it was a busy place as befitted the starting point of an important train line to the coast. We got our tickets and while waiting near the station, I noticed a man on the sidewalk with a small photography stand. His Polaroid camera was set up on a tripod and just in front of it was a chair in which a person who wanted their photo taken would sit and pose. A blind man was in the chair. He had a cane and seemed to be by himself. The photographer adjusted the camera, then walked over to the man and gently straightened out his collar, fussing a bit to make it look smart. Then he walked back to the camera and took the picture.

I was thunderstruck. I had never seen such kindness of one random person to another. I was touched beyond measure. The biggish city in which I had lived for twenty-five years was filled with people bustling here and there, to and from work, school, home, parties, shopping, and yet I had never witnessed such an action in public before. It seemed to me later that my culture perhaps lacked a kindness that this ancient continent had retained.

2016

When 2016 dawned, my heart was starting to win the battle over the AVPA. The joy and passionate sense of mission that had inspired me in 2007 was mostly gone. Nonetheless, I continued to do what I could to help Okaseni.

At the beginning of the year, Salma did a good job of keeping in touch with us about the dispensary, the business grants, and the truck project. On January 19, we received this email from her regarding the dispensary:

> For the dispensary, I have been started to work with the need list but is very unfortunately I am not quite sure the price for most of the things. However, I plan to go with

the list at one of the pharmacy and get the price of things. Once, I am done with it I will send it to you immediately. I will try to go to the pharmacy this weekend and will get back to you, Sheena.

The clinical officer will be needed at the dispensary, as foreign volunteers are not allowed to work at the dispensary themselves without the local staff due to lack of language barrier etc. The government have also been trying to support the community initiatives on health issues by educating more health practitioner, so they can be assigned to work in rural areas after accomplishment. Due to this, the government will be responsible for his/her payments. That's why Mr. Mush was following up with the District Medical Officer before the vaccination day to request for this possibility. If we will be assigned the government clinical officer, the expectation is for him/her to work full time at the dispensary. I will follow up with Mr. Mushi for this and check how far he has gone with it.

Another email arrived in January:

We have also purchased the equipment for the dispensary. I will take the receipt to town to scan it and send it to you shortly. Once again Sheena, thanks for your always support to the Okaseni people. The villagers are delighted with your generous support. They have been using the dispensary for the vaccine the small kids and also pregnancy women too attend the clinics there. I will keep you posted on the separate email.

We were delighted to get this news and hopeful that the Tanzanian government would eventually fund a clinical officer for the dispensary. Salma also let us know about the project to hire a truck to take village produce directly to markets in Dar es Salaam.

Sorry for not being in touch with you more often, things have been a bit slow lately but the village meeting finale happened and were able to select the committee which will be responsible for collecting products from the villagers and hire truck to supply these products to different markets. The committee will still need to meet and come up with the plan how best to implement this. I will let you know when they will be able to meet and I still hope to use that time as well to share the committee members about the AVPA expectations toward achieving this goal. I will keep you posted.

In February, we received more information from her about the truck project:

The villagers are very enthusiastic about this venture and already several actions have been taken after the selection of the truck committee. One of the reason why there were delays on this is because of the election [in November]. There were delays on conducting the first village meeting after the election because they were waiting for the leaders to be sworn. The ward executive leaders, village chairperson and other village leaders were sworn on December 12 and the first village meeting were conducted on January 5. And that's where they start to plan.

The truck committee met twice already and did a bit of research on the markets and the costs involved. Based on their research, the demand for their supplies are in Dar es Salaam markets. There is also a possibility for the market opportunity (banana products only) in Iringa. The Iringa market seems far and the demand is not high compare to the market in Dar. The villagers decided to focus on Dar markets for now and see the possibility in the future for supplying in other regions based on demand.

The costs to hire a truck for 7 tons from Okaseni to Dar per trip is Tsh 1,200,000 [about Can$1020 CDN] and for ten tons is Tsh 1,600,000. The chairperson of the committee already connected with the network of agents in Dar markets. These are official agents who are responsible at markets to order the products in the regions. The agent will order the product through the committee chairperson, who will share the news on the village meeting.

The other committee members will facilitate the collection of the products at the ward level, and each villager who has a products to sell will have equal rights. The registration of the products will take place at the village office in each ward. The registration will be based on the type of products each villager brought, the size and the price. So everyone knows how much they will get because the chairperson of the committee will confirm the price of each products before taking to the markets. Once they get the money to hire the truck, they will start the process of taking the first truck of products (banana and different fruits available in Okaseni) to Dar.

We appreciated getting this information of some progress, despite the delay of the elections. I assumed I would hear from her when the committee had ordered the products and were good to go. Oh, and one other little detail that Salma neglected to mention: Melki had not been re-elected as village chairperson.

Later in February, still unaware that Melki had been turfed, I mustered up the energy to begin the list of AVPA projects and their costs that I had promised him. Alas, this project was more complicated and involved more research than I had expected, and my motivation to do it evaporated. I was also unpleasantly surprised to discover how much money we had paid to Salma over the years: $5,000. Of all our projects, only the shipping container, dispensary, and water system had been more expensive. We were still paying her a stipend every month, donations were not coming in, and I could not stomach the thought of fundraising. We could not continue to pay her.

In March, I sent her the following message:

> We appreciate everything you have done for the Africa Village Project over these many years. You have been an

integral part of our organization, and we greatly value your contribution and your friendship.

The last financial year has been a very difficult one for the AVPA. We did not raise a lot of funds and were also unable to contribute ourselves. (We have always contributed our own funds annually since the beginning of the project.)

While we appreciate you very much, we cannot afford a large portion to you of the money we raise. As you mentioned in your January email, things have been slow in Okaseni. So to pay so much when there is so little work is beyond our capabilities as a small organization, especially since Dale and I take no money ourselves from the funds for anything, including our very expensive trips to Tanzania.

As well, we have had to cope with a major change in the exchange rate between the Canadian and American dollar. For the last few years, they have been almost the same. But in the last year, the Canadian dollar has fallen drastically. Our arrangement with you was to pay you in US dollars, but the increase is over 50 percent and beyond our capabilities to pay.

Again, please accept our heartfelt thanks for your great contributions to the AVPA.

On March 29, we wired her the final stipend payment for her help up to that date. She did not respond to any emails from us for months afterwards.

I did not do a good job of keeping in touch either. It became more difficult over this year to do anything on the AVPA. I was utterly sick of it. Sometimes I would give myself a pep talk and say, "Today I'm going to send Salma an email! It's been way too long. I can do this!" I would sit down at the computer, click into my emails, and a wave of nausea would wash over me. I would get up immediately and go do something—anything—else.

In the fall, I realized we hadn't heard from Salma about the truck project, so I did email her requesting an update. I received this answer:

I had the opportunity to talk in depth with Mr. Mushi about the truck project. The villagers didn't hire any truck to Dar yet. The chosen committee only sat and find out about the current needs in the Dar market. The plan was to have the funds to hire the transport to Dar first and then each ward leader will share the news with the villagers and set the date to collect the products. That's where the project stop because they couldn't have the funds to hire the truck to Dar.

Oh dear. I realized with a shock that they had been waiting for me to send them money since Salma's email in February. She had been vague about any further action, and I had not gotten her hint. She did not follow up and indeed did not answer any emails after I told her we had to cancel her monthly stipend. My continuing withdrawal also left me disinclined to follow up.

I immediately went to the bank and wired her enough money to pay truck expenses for two trips to Dar.

The business grants project rumbled along this year fairly well. Salma sent us applications in the fall from Mama Marietha and Renatus for grants to expand their businesses. Mama Marietha requested funds to purchase food to sell for human babies and domestic animals (cows, chickens, and such). Renatus wanted funds to purchase wood and scrapers for making crosses and gate decorations. I was glad to hear the news and sent Salma the funds in October. At year's end, I wired her funds for her help with these programs. Bless her, she snail-mailed us perfect receipts signed by Renatus, Mama Marietha, and all the eight members of the truck committee for all the money we had sent through her. (Alas, we never did hear how the truck program went but wished them well from afar.)

So the year continued with only sporadic work on the AVPA. We received only three donations this year and did no fundraising. My enthusiasm waned even more, if that were possible, but I still had to do the essentials, including the annual report for CRA. In September, I began work on the account expenses and could not reconcile the receipts we had received from Melki. No matter how many times I did the calculations, I wound up with a shortfall of about Can$400. This was a first. In the ten years we had been working with him, he had been good at getting us receipts, as far as we could tell.

I emailed Melki. He denied that there was money not accounted for and did not send the receipts. I eventually got in touch with Tumaini, who emailed Melki about it. Oh, and by the way, Tumaini let us know that Melki had lost the election last year for village chairperson.

Aha. Things fell into place with a thunk. The unfortunate meeting village last year came to mind, when the council members were surprised at how much money we had spent and had eyed Melki suspiciously. I remembered the sick expression on Melki's face when he told us the council had requested a list of projects and costs. The only conclusion that came to mind about the "missing receipts" was sticky fingers. At this point, Melki perhaps had nothing left to lose and was trying to get while the getting was still good.

When I told Dale all this, he said, "I guess you have been avenged for how Melki treated you." I politely refrained from doing a celebratory jig.

The missing money was, of course, unacceptable and a breach of our contract back in 2007. I had no choice but to formally shut down the AVPA. In October, I sent Tumaini and Peter Mchau the following message that said:

> I need to give you an update about the receipts. Melki has not sent us any receipts for the missing funds. Because of this situation, we cannot continue our relationship with Okaseni. Our partnership ends today. We are deeply saddened but have no other choice. Our ultimate responsibility is to the donors who trust us and the Canadian government to whom we have to report.
>
> Thank you very much for your extraordinary help throughout the years. It has been an honour and privilege to have worked with you and Okaseni. We wish we could have done more, but we are only two ordinary people, and we truly did our best.

If we received a reply from Tumaini, I do not remember it and did not keep a copy. Robert Minja got in touch and pleaded with us to stay. I replied that we were retired and had limited funds and sadly could not continue. We never heard from him again, or ever from Peter Mchau.

It was a relief beyond measure. My heart had finally prevailed. Yet I felt no exhilaration or a rush of released energy. My heart was already engaged elsewhere. Other ventures had captured my attention, and although at times difficult, were much more satisfying and rewarding.

One of the things I was most proud of this year was the work that I did on my foster kids campaign. I held two "rallies" and planned a third. The first was held in Victoria, the British Columbia's capital, in early February on the Family Day holiday weekend. I sent out announcements to TV and radio stations, government officials, friends, and all the associations who were members of First Call.

Dale and I went to Victoria the day before and stayed overnight in a hotel. In the morning as I was getting ready, I got a phone call from a person at CKNW, a Vancouver news radio station. She wanted to interview me about the rally and my campaign. Gulp. Not in any way prepared for this eventuality, I tried to answer coherently the questions she threw at me. At least I did know what I was talking about even though I seemed to stumble through the interview. (A couple of weeks later, an acquaintance told me she had heard the interview and said it was great. I keeled over in surprise.)

The rally was set for noon at the Legislature complex, so Dale and I got there about 11:30 to start setting up. The government buildings were regal and impressive and had been built in 1867 in the dome style of the period with copper finishings. There was a huge open walkway and lawn in front where we set up shop. My friends Pat and Cynthia turned up with Trevor, Cynthia's son. Their friendship and support meant the world to me. Doug Kinna, head of the union of social workers in BC, also joined us. He was the only person to ever contact me out of the seventy First Call organizations that I had reached out to. Later, a passer-by stopped to chat and complained bitterly about MCFD. I had my petition at the ready and a few random people signed it, for which I was very grateful. It being a holiday, there were not many people around, and I guessed it was a slow day for news because a couple of youngish guys from two different local television stations suddenly turned up with cameras and audio equipment to interview me. Another surprise. I was more awake by this time and managed to acquit myself reasonably.

I later watched the coverage on the websites of these two stations and was appalled at the difference. One fellow had asked me a lot of excellent questions and allowed me to explain the foster-kid situation and my mission. At the end, he said, "Wow, that was good." His report on the news that evening was several minutes long and showed me talking clearly and looking knowledgeable. The other fellow had not asked me any questions and made no comment whatsoever. His report on his television station was short, gave little info, and had been edited to show me as kind of idiotic. His clip also reported that the government said in a comment about our rally that foster kids ageing out of care actually *did not want support* from the government anymore. I could not believe my ears. Talk about fake news. The comment confirmed my opinion of the political party in power at that time. (Ugh.)

Anyhow, we had obviously made ourselves known to the government. Our next rally was outside the office of the MCFD minister. I scheduled it for October and sent out email invites again to everyone on my mailing list, including government officials. When we got to the office, it was closed, dark, and locked. I guessed the minister had fled. We got no media coverage, and only my loyal Dale and I and a twenty-something fellow who worked for First Call attended. However, the government had noticed us again perhaps?

I continued to make phone calls and send out letters and prepped for our next rally scheduled for January in the new year. I was optimistic about the future and anticipated nothing more than keeping up with my social activism, volunteering, and enjoying my pleasant life on Bowen. You might remember that old joke: How do you make God laugh? Tell him your plans.

In the years after I left BCIT and realized I did not want to devote all my time to the AVPA, I checked out or worked on about eighteen different ventures, including looking for a foster kid to help, starting my foster kid campaign, and working on the three theatre/music productions on Bowen. I looked into volunteering with kids, teenagers, a disabled person from Nigeria, a blind person, senior citizens, and folks in a care facility. Most were not for me, but several I stuck with for a year or two and enjoyed very much. All of them were a far cry from running a tiny NGO helping an impoverished village overseas.

The most significant thing I did, however, was take a Mediterranean cruise. As someone who had crossed the Sahara Desert and hitchhiked from Lisbon to Dakar, I was deeply unimpressed by cruises. But at a lunch with friends in February 2015, I was unexpectedly spellbound by a friend's description of her recent cruise through the Greek islands. Hmm, I thought, maybe I did want to take a cruise after all. I could see those gorgeous isles. Hey, I could also go to Rome, a city that had entranced me for decades. No hitchhiking! No waiting by the side of the road for kind souls to take me in! No anxious wondering about food and safety for the night! I was sold.

On April 11, Valerie, my loyal AVPA board member and friend, and I flew to Rome. We spent several days land-cruising the city, which was more gorgeous and dazzling than I ever imagined. On April 15, we boarded the *Koningsdam*, a Holland America ship on her maiden voyage, and set sail for Greek cities, Greek isles, and Turkey.

The cruise was everything my 1975 trip wasn't. I stayed in one place, had unlimited access to fabulous food and drink, and slept in the same comfy bed every night. I didn't have to lug around a hefty backpack or wonder how many miles I would cover that day. It was so easy and delightful that it felt almost sinful. (Was I betraying my adventurous youthful self?!) Yet while it was always the same on the ship, every day we visited some new place, some fabulous locale of beauty and history and significance. Athens, Crete, Rhodes, Olympia—just names in my head before—were now physically before my eyes in all their spectacular reality. I fell deeply and passionately in love. The ancient Greeks and Romans, their histories and civilizations, their mythologies, architecture, and art completely captivated me.

When I got back home, I decided to find out more and watched every television show I could find about the ancients. The first one I came across was *Troy*, starring Brad Pitt. Ooh, I thought, excellent start! Next was a series called *Ancient Worlds,* then a documentary on Roman art, then many more. I bought books galore. One afternoon, I was rhapsodizing to Dale about how much I loved it, and he said, "You should take a course." I thought, I can do that!

I registered for a Classical Studies course called Art and Archeology of Ancient Greece and Rome offered at Langara College in Vancouver. The course started in January, and I was mad for it to begin. I kept reading and watching fascinating shows. Little did I know that the faint cackling sound I heard in the background was the laughter of the (Greek) gods. I had no idea I was going to plunge deeply into the past and discover that the Greeks had done mostly everything already, that the Romans had soaked up everything Greek and then amplified and embellished it, using it as a marvellous step-pingstone and building on top of it. I was going to learn that these two monumental civilizations laid the groundwork for so much of our lives today that I began to feel we were just pale imitations of them, like hazy ghosts in their own future. We owe them so much. They are with us still every day.

When I started the AVPA, an acquaintance told Dale and me that we were trying to impose Western values and culture on the African people we were working with. I could not disagree more. We made a point *always* of asking the Okaseni villagers what they would like us to do, and then we did our best to do it. We had our own ideas (such as microcredit, the workshop for the teachers), but we always got the villagers' approval before going ahead. Surprise. They always wanted whatever we could do for them. In fact, they wanted what we had.

What Dale and I had was the benefits and boons of our culture. This is not to say that we are better than them or that ethnicity has any bearing on the worth of a civilization or a people. But why do Africans want to come to Canada? Those young men who approached Ralph and me wanted to get to Canada; we were not asking them for help to stay in Ghana. Many Africans die of malaria, do not have great diets, and have limited opportunities for education and careers. Their lives are hard, much harder than anything most of us in the West will ever have to cope with.

We take for granted our good fortune to live where we do. Our culture does a *very* good job of satisfying our needs for healthy, comfortable, safe lives. If you doubt it, please go visit an African village. You will see orphaned twelve-year-old children who look three or four years younger from an insufficient diet of bananas and maize, thin women lugging huge water pails on their heads along dusty dirt roads, and tiny houses made of cow manure and branches. You may think that, even so, these villagers have some hidden well of happiness that we lack. This is a belief in industrialized countries, that people in developing countries are happy, and that we over-privileged types are less so. I never saw that. If it were true, it's unlikely any African would want to leave for another country. The Sub-Saharan African people were kind and generous with what they had, but far too many of them faced enormous difficulties, and the constant struggle to stay alive another day did not provide for an abundance of joy. The Universal Happiness Report ranks annually the happiness of 156 countries around the world based on income, social support, freedom, trust, safety, and life expectancy. In 2023, Canada was ranked the fifteenth happiest country. Tanzania ranked 147th.[1]

It was hard for me to witness the privation in Okaseni and not feel a great sense of injustice. How did the West wind up with such a winning card in the poker game of life and Africa not so much? We can point to as causes the ills that befell Africa of slavery and colonialism. But how was it that Europe stomped all over Africa in the first place and not the other way around?

Jared Diamond has tried to find an answer to these questions. Currently a professor of geography at UCLA, he worked as an evolutionary biologist and studied birds in Papua New Guinea, living in the bush with people of "stone age" cultures on the island. A local politician who befriended Diamond asked him one day why the whites had so much "cargo," meaning the material goods of society, and the blacks so little.[2] Why indeed? thought Diamond. He decided to try to "understand what happened in history to cause such enormous variations in human societies."[3] How did Europe in particular wind up the tools of power and domination?[4] His book *Guns, Germs, and Steel* does a masterful job of tackling these questions. He states that "history followed different courses for different peoples because of *differences among peoples' environments,* not because of biological differences among peoples themselves."[5] (my emphasis)

Geography, he found, was of paramount importance. Environments differ greatly around the world, and some are better than others at providing the materials that can benefit human beings.[6] The earliest of these environs were the patches of verdant land around the world, including the Fertile Crescent in the Middle East, and areas in South China, Mesoamerica, the Andes, and the Eastern United States.[7] Our ancestors the hunter-gatherers in these areas shifted to agriculture and farming, and their success led to year-round settlements and stable supplies of food.[8]

Food production began to spread from the original areas, but it spread more easily in some places than in others,[9] again because of a particular geographical factor.[10] The continent of Eurasia is fat and wide, and its axis runs sideways: east and west. North and South America and Africa are slim and long, and their axes run up and down: north to south. Early food production moved more easily on the east and west axis of Eurasia[11] because places on the same latitude across the axis have similar seasons, climate, day length, temperatures and rainfall.[12] Places on the same longitude, however, share not much at all because they vary dramatically in length of day, growing seasons, etc.[13] As a result, the spread of food production was stymied in the Americas and Africa.

Along this latitudinal axis travelled not just food and farming, but also people, livestock/domestic animals, goods for trade, and most importantly, ideas and innovations. The Fertile Crescent was blessed with the Mediterranean climate and became hugely productive of food, enabling it to become a hot bed of cities, governments, bureaucracies, empires, and writing.[14] It begat stellar ancient cultures.

Over the centuries, writing, inventions, discoveries, ideas, and other boons spread back and forth across Eurasia. Europe became technologically advanced because it was on the most western point of the Eurasia axis and could gobble up all the local innovations brought there from China and places in between by travellers, traders, adventurers, and conquerors.[15] Steven Pinker, the psychology professor at Harvard whom we met briefly in chapter 7, has a rock-star take on this:

> The "culture" of any of the conquering nations of Europe, such as Britain, is in fact a greatest-hits collection of inventions assembled across thousands of miles and years. The collection is made up of cereal crops and alphabetic writing from the Middle East, gunpowder and paper from China, domesticated horses from the Ukraine. . . . But the necessarily insular continents of Australia, Africa, and the Americas had to make do with a few homegrown technologies, and as a result they were no match for their pluralistic conquerors.[16]

These greatest hits helped to give rise to my old chums, the Greeks and Romans, whose own brilliant civilizations created the cultural template for much of Europe and included a fabulous flourishing of art, architecture, and literature.

Pinker devotes a chapter to culture in his book *The Blank Slate* and notes "the most obvious cultural difference on the planet is that some cultures are materially more successful than others. People have needs and desires, and when they notice another culture is doing better than them, they shamelessly borrow what works best."[17]

Pinker points out that saying a culture is technologically advanced is *not* a moral judgement or that the culture is more deserving or superior.[18] Diamond calls racial explanations for the differences in cultures "loathsome."[19] Such arguments do not fly. Instead, it was geography that called the shots, and some areas of the world drew luckier cards than others.

But we cannot say that being technologically advanced is all good, all the time. Diamond points out that the New Guineans he hung out with seemed "more intelligent, more alert, more expressive, and more interested in things and people around them" than Westerners. They are on their toes because they have to avoid warfare, murder, accidents, and famine, while people in the West watch television and are passively entertained. The New Guineans also have the benefits of greater social and familial ties and support than we do.[20]

And more kindness too perhaps. I saw that kindness in Bamako when a street photographer gently rearranged the collar of his blind customer so that the guy would look spiffy in a photo he would never see. That gesture touched me deeply and has stayed with me, lo, these very many years. But even so, I know that my culture, despite its many faults, has what many people around the world would be ecstatic to have.

I completely understand. Before I went to Africa in 1975, I was a rebellious young person, a child of the counterculture, fierce for women's rights and freedom. I was passionate about what you could call *arete*, the word of those ubiquitous ancient Greek guys for "excellence," which in my case meant striving to make society better. But when Ralph and I came back to Canada from Africa, I was shocked and uneasy to see the affluence and material excesses of my culture. But I also saw the extraordinary bounties that the culture itself provided.

I realized what I had, what my culture had. I was humbled and grateful and told myself that I had no right whatsoever to complain about anything *ever* again. But I also knew I would keep striving for arete. I would strive as well to be as kind as possible, having learned that from a gracious and tender person in a culture very different from mine, and very far away.

CHAPTER 11

2017, FINALE

1975

The train ride from Bamako to Dakar was a joy. It was crammed with people, chickens, kids, and we had to sit in the vestibule until seats opened up. A fellow threw up in that area at one point, and we were close to the loo. But I was thrilled. This was the end stretch in Africa of our trip home. I love trains anytime so enjoyed watching the scenery flow by. We were still in the Sahel, and the landscape was arid and open to the sun and warmth. My spirits soared.

In Dakar, we bought our tickets and spent two days waiting for our flights on the back porch of a large stone building owned by a religious organization. They had grudgingly agreed to our request for shelter and were hostile and distinctly unchristian about it. We slept on the stone porch, and they left us safely alone. Our plane flights back to Montreal were uneventful, and we were finally back in Canada. Happy, happy day. We then hitchhiked across the country, getting back to Vancouver in about four and a half days. Home!

Our journey in Europe and Africa took about five months. In our almost complete circumnavigation of West Africa, we travelled approximately 7142 kilometres (4,438 miles). It was a very difficult trip. I lost 20 lbs. and came back home with stage one dehydration and the skin on my face ruined. Up to that point, it was the hardest thing I had ever done. But it brought me great gifts: eternal gratitude, a much wider vision of the world and humanity, and the satisfaction that I had lived the adventure and experience that I wanted. Africa stayed tucked away in my heart until the day I would go back and repay some of this goodness I received in 1975.

2017

On Wednesday, January 4, of this year, I attended the first class of the Art and Archaeology of Greece and Rome course that I had signed up for in the fall. It was by far the best thing I had done since leaving my job at BCIT. It was the beginning of a five-year Classical Studies binge that brought me so much joy, fun, and knowledge that I sent up prayers of thanks every day to Zeus and Aphrodite. We viewed a lot of statues of naked Greek men in this art course, which added an extra delight. I got an A.

In February 2017, the BC government allotted a sizable increase of funds to the MCFD in the annual budget!! I dared not hope: had it been us? I could not believe it. In June, that government was voted out of power, and the NDP got in with a majority. John Horgan, the new premier, promised while campaigning to raise the age of support for foster kids. (He had been one of the recipients of my pamphlet and letters.) I was so thankful for that and even more pleased he won the election.

The AVPA was almost at a full stop this year. We did not hear anything more about the truck project. Salma never responded to my emails. I hoped it was a success and continued over time. The dispensary was used sporadically for vaccination clinics, which was gratifying, but we never heard if it was regularly staffed. The government might have been unable or unwilling to pay for that, and my deep misgivings about doing buildings might have been justified. I hoped it would eventually be funded for its original purpose.

By spring, I had not been able to find an organization or church willing to take it on the AVPA. I did not want to cancel the CRA official charity status however, which I had worked long and hard to get. It had been good for us, giving us credibility and allowing us to issue receipts for tax deductions. Was there a person who might take *that* over (but not the village/AVPA too) to use as they wished? I started asking friends and neighbours if they knew anybody who might want it.

A Rotary chum told me about a young person on Bowen who volunteered in Africa and might be interested. She was. In September, she and I submitted documentation for the transfer to CRA and the BC Societies Registry from us to her. I was pleased but felt no sense of loss or sadness at this late date. It was just another chore that finally got done. I hoped that she made good use of that valuable charity designation.

We had about $800 in the bank that I needed to disburse to comply with CRA rules. In September, after no contact with Salma, I gave the money to Komera, another Bowen NGO that funded education for girls in Rwanda. In November, I did the last necessary task: closing the AVPA bank account at Vancity.

It was over. It was finally over. The AVPA had brought me so much joy and had been the vehicle by which I could do some good in the world. We did do some good, it seemed, but the difficulties finally did me in. The disrespect and contempt, the blatant misogyny, the interminable fundraising, the distressing suspicion that things were getting worse in the village all took the stuffing out of me. I lost heart and had to give up.

I marvel at my naïveté in 2007 and wonder why on earth I would ever have taken on such a project. I wanted to do good, but I could have written a check or three. Also, why did I try to find a foster kid to help? Why did I start a campaign to get foster kids the support they needed? Well, I had no idea what a monster the AVPA would turn out to be. Even so, it was a lot to take on, and I knew personally of only one other person who did something similar although on a much smaller scale.

I had been adventurous and intrepid as a young person although very shy. A child of the '60s counterculture, I never wanted a conventional life, eschewing marriage, children, and a long-term job, and instead embracing travel, an education, and adventure. I also blithely dismissed materialism, consumerism, and anything remotely resembling a career. My raison d'être was to find truth and beauty and experience the unfamiliar and exotic. Travel was the vehicle through which I could do this. And travel I did, most remarkably in that 1975 journey with Ralph across the Sahara and around the West African Coast. As you know, that journey forever changed me.

I never lost that youthful exuberance, but the desire to do good (not just rebel) took its own sweet time to show up. When I was about twenty, I read *Psychotherapy East and West* by Alan Watts, a British writer who wrote extensively about Buddhism and other Eastern religions for Western readers. As I remembered it, he talked in this book about the interconnection between good and evil and how they were two parts of a greater whole. No need to do good deeds then, was his message. Cosmic forces would likely negate them anyway.

Oh dear. I might have misinterpreted him, but unfortunately, this idea stuck, and I carried it with me until mid-adulthood. But once at BCIT, with my life going well, I began to challenge this misapprehension. In 2006, I heard about the school for girls that Oprah Winfrey was building in South Africa and realized that you could do good in the world without fighting against society, or the powers that be, or anything actually (another mistaken idea of mine). You could just go ahead and *do* something *positive*. OMG, I thought, I can do that!

So it was a long time coming, this desire to do good things. Better late than never. After that, all it took was to bumble along until Milton Wong's idea to adopt a village in Africa turned up. It was not a simple or easy task I took on. Neither were my foster kid ventures. All were frustrating and difficult. Again, why did I subject myself to such troubles? I have wondered about that.

I came across a possible answer in another book by Steven Pinker called *Enlightenment Now* in a chapter called "Happiness." He talks about the difference between people who have happy lives and people who have meaningful lives. Happy people are healthy, have money to live on, and enjoy themselves. "People who lead meaningful lives may have none of these boons."[1] Meaningful lives might actually *cause* unhappiness and lead to pain. The desire for meaning isn't masochistic, but it might be impelled by a vision or ideal that brings difficulties. "Finally, meaning is about expressing rather than satisfying themselves. . . . Happiness isn't everything. We can make choices that leave us unhappy in the short term but fulfilled over the course of a life, such as raising a child, writing a book [author's note: eep!], or fighting for a worthy cause."[2]

Well, two out of three ain't bad. I always wanted more than a typical life and instead wanted one more meaningful to me. The youthful passion I had for experience and adventure has remained with me, but it eventually flowered into the more mature dimension of wanting to do good in the world. My life has indeed had purpose and meaning. It has been difficult but also great fun and often filled with joy and a humble but gratifying sense of accomplishment.

Pinker adds another kick. He cites a 2018 study comparing happy lives with exciting lives. It turns out that more people (50 percent) found their lives exciting than found their lives happy (30 percent). "People who feel they lead meaningful lives are more susceptible to stress, struggle and worry. . . . They are not as happy as one would expect, perhaps because they have an adult's appreciation of life with all its worry and all its excitement."[3] Perhaps. Or maybe having a strong purpose in life *is* much more exciting than naught. My life has been exciting and immeasurably enriched by how I lived it and what happened to me, despite—or rather because of—the bumps, scrapes, and bruises. It has been what I wanted, and for that I am very, very grateful. I drew amazing trump cards.

It has been a journey, but then, I've always loved journeys. I subscribe to the Lawrence Durrell take on travel. "Let the tourist be cushioned against misadventure, but your true traveller will not feel he has had his money's worth unless he brings back a few scars." That's how I feel about life too.

EPILOGUE

1975

After Ralph and I got back to Vancouver in June and recovered from our trip, we bought a 1963 green Chevrolet truck we called Cami. Over that summer, Ralph built a little camper on it. It had no running water or electricity. He built a shelf along one side which I used as a kitchen counter to wash dishes and cook on a Coleman stove donated by my parents. Water containers, food, dishes, pots, and utensils were stored under this counter. We slept in sleeping bags on the floor and used as seats the wheel hub and stack of tires we kept on hand. In September, we left Vancouver for a ten-month long trip through Washington, Utah, Colorado, and Arizona, and California, on another difficult trip but another exciting adventure.

Ralph and I home from Africa and on to our next big adventure.

2023

Dale and I have never been back to Africa and never will go again. (Hmm . . . maybe I shouldn't say that. I swore in 1975 that I would never go back and then look what happened.) I was done with the AVPA, but even so, I kept all my AVPA materials: the binders of meeting minutes, projects, fundraisers and emails, and big manila envelopes stuffed with CRA and BC Society docs and more emails. I might write a book someday, I thought, while silently screaming NO WAY! It did seem like a worthy story to tell, but I could not stomach the idea of writing it.

Dale and I on our deck on Bowen Island at sunset March 2023.

In the midst of the pandemic shutdown, when I had taken all the Classical Studies courses I wanted at Langara, I unexpectedly had lots of free time. The thought came to mind: I just might start that book. Gulp. So in April 2021, I began. At first, I was depressingly negative about the AVPA, remembering only the pain, disappointments, and unpleasantness. I read through masses of my docs and other odd things, coming across an article Bill Gates had written defending Jeffrey Sachs and the Millennium Village Project. Billions of dollars had flooded to the MVP from countries around the world, and inordinate amounts of money were poured into a few villages with very modest results and very large payments to overseas academic consultants. But it had been worth trying, and Gates admired Sachs for doing so. Gates also said that in venture capitalism, a 30 percent success rate is considered good.[1]

I gasped. Hadn't my dear friend Mariana told me the same thing about international development? Here was Gates agreeing with her. Just trying is worth the effort.

The more I worked on the book, the more I saw the things we had accomplished. It was much more than I gave us credit for. Our infrastructure projects (water and electricity) were huge successes. So were the coffee plants. The shipping container was expensive, but it got there intact with a hefty amount of goods. The sewing machines were used to teach a marketable skill to young people. The bikes helped with transportation. The grants program was excellent, helping to provide jobs for more villagers. Kids stayed in school, and the school got some excellent teaching materials. The ad hoc dispensary room worked well for a while. The land purchase and renovations resulted in the dispensary building.

Other ventures were good, and I had hope for their futures. The dispensary was wildly popular and heartily appreciated and hopefully was regularly staffed. The poultry project probably managed to stay afloat. The milk goats likely improved nutrition and provided income for some people. The teachers' workshop perhaps helped raise the quality of primary school education a tad, ditto the volunteers. The truck project had the potential to be an ongoing success.

Less successful was the microcredit program, but it was worth a try. The grevillea tree project was a bust. Overall, I realized, our ventures had been far more successful that 30 percent.

So writing this book redeemed the AVPA for me. The kind words of Karen, the friend who was so supportive about Africa Night, came back to me: "Don't feel like you had an overly difficult group. From my perspective, you did a great job of pulling it together. It worked! You made money and it helped your endeavour. Good for you."[2]

I realized I could feel the same way about the AVPA.

Another friend cheered me recently by saying that I might never know the good that we had done in the long run. When I look back over the whole eleven years, one of the best things was helping Nuria. It was by far the easiest, most gratifying, and enjoyable venture, and absolutely worth the candle. She is our lifelong friend, and we will continue to help her as we can for as long as she needs it. I deem this relationship 100 percent successful.

Oh, and by the way, in 2022, the British Columbia NDP government said they would increase the age of support for foster kids to age twenty-seven.[3]

ACKNOWLEDGEMENTS

Of all the acknowledgements I can make about the years of working on the AVPA, the most important one is to my board. Dale, Charleen, Robert, and Valerie were the most supportive, dedicated, and thoughtful group anyone could hope for. They were outstanding. Thanks also to Sarah, Valerie's daughter, who came to board meetings, fundraisers, and to Moshi too. I appreciate you all more than I can say.

I am grateful for my friends, colleagues, and fellow employees at BCIT. It was phenomenal to have received so much support and generosity for our fundraisers and the shipping container venture. A special shout-out goes to Tunde and Melanie, Patricia, Jean, and the folks who supported us in Tanzania.

I also give many thanks to my Bowen and Vancouver friends and supporters for their help and goodwill. To everyone who gave so generously of their time, energy, talents, material goods, ideas, and money, you have my infinite appreciation. A special thanks go to Brooke, the Snug Café and shops on Bowen, Dr Hansen, Mariana, my dear high school chums, and my nephew Zack, who did our website.

Thanks so much also to everyone who supported me while writing this book. Carolyn, Angelyn, Bill, CeLinda, Karen, Michele, and Diane all read first drafts and gave me excellent feedback and good advice. Sam, Karolina, Una, Tia, and my sister Val were always so enthusiastic and kind. Without all their ongoing support, I would never have finished it. Thanks also to the Friesen Press folks for their always patient help. My gratitude goes to Ralph, my first husband, for sharing his memories of our 1975 Africa trip and answering my many questions. Our Zoom chats were fun.

My thanks go out as well to my lovely Bowen Island neighbors and walking chums who patiently listened to my progress reports and cheered me on: Ann C., Claire, Yoko, Dana, Ryan, James and Marilee, Sonia, Rick and Donna, Andrea and Rob, Ann B., and Mary, who told me not to write a smug cheerleader's manual, and Laurel, who said the story is always in the dark side.

Lastly, my love and eternal gratitude go to Dale, my dear husband. Not only did he live this story with me, but he also put up with me writing it. For two years, our house was filled with books, piles of papers, folders, notes, binders, and many drafts. I was often preoccupied and busy. But his fortitude was great, and his advice and insights much appreciated. He is a treasure, and I am, as always, very grateful.

Thank you very much for filling out this questionnaire. Its purpose is to give us an idea of how we may best help you. Please feel free to write your answers after each question below and take as much space as you need.

Please note that at this point, we are working at a grassroots level to adopt a village in Africa. The British Columbia Institute of Technology has not yet formally endorsed this plan. However, we would like to get an official BCIT program established to help Africa on an ongoing basis.

1. **Where is your village located? What is the nearest big city?**

Okaseni village is located in Moshi Rural District, Kilimanjaro Region, northeastern Tanzania. Local government administration in Tanzania consists of Village, Ward, District and Region. Okaseni village is in Mawella Ward. The nearest big city to the Village is Moshi town which is about ten (10) kilometers away. Okaseni has access to the town center at the Moshi central bus station through two roads. They do not have tarmac for most part. Both the roads are passable for most of the year with the exception of a few days during the rain season. Public transport from the village operates from 6 a.m. to 7 p.m. with a frequency of about one trip every two hours. Public transport service is operated by privately owned companies, using old and worn-out minibuses. The buses are normally overcrowded and people have to scramble to get into the buses. The limitations of public transport make it difficult for the service to be used effectively by villagers from Okaseni for business activities or taking kids to school.

2. **What is the closest international airport that has flights from Europe?**

The closest international airport to Moshi town is Kilimanjaro International Airport (KIA) which is about forty-five (45) minute drive from Moshi town. The airport is one of the two biggest in Tanzania. The other big international airport in the country is in the capital (Dar es Salaam), which is about seven hours drive from Moshi. KIA has direct flights to Europe.

3. **How would you describe the political climate of your country?**

Tanzania is known to be an island of peace in East Africa and the Great Lakes Region. Tanzania has been in the forefront in mediating conflicts in the region with peace negotiations conducted in Arusha. Peace in Tanzania is attributed to the fact that the country does not have big dominant tribes as the case with *Hutu* and *Tutsi* in Rwanda and *Luo* and *Kikuyu* in Kenya. Tanzania has about 120 small tribes and the country does not have a history of ethnic politics because that will not work in the country with many small tribes. Also, Tanzania has a low crime rate as compared to neighboring countries such as Kenya. The northern part of Tanzania has a strong presence of Christianity. Communities there are used to interacting with tourists from other parts of the world without any problem and visitors feel safe with locals.

4. **How many people live in your village?**

Okaseni village has a total of four thousand two hundred and ninety-nine (4,299) villagers. Okaseni is considered to be a big village as there are neighboring villages with about two thousand (2,000) people.

5. **Approximately how many elderly people, adults, and children live there?**

Out of the total number of people in Okaseni village, six hundred and ten (610) are elderly people, two thousand eight hundred and fifty-five

(2,355) are adults and one thousand, three hundred and thirty-four (1,334) are children.

6. **How many are female? How many are male?**

Okaseni village has two thousand two hundred and forty-four (2,224) females and two thousand and seventy-five (2,075) males.

7. **What is the primary food source? What crops are grown?**

Traditional cash crop in Okaseni and most of rural Moshi is Coffee. Villagers also grow banana, maize, beans, fruit trees, and some vegetables for food and selling. Moshi has the highest production of coffee and banana in the country and grows varieties of banana suitable for cooking and ripening. The area produces a lot of avocados for which Moshi is famous in the country. In 1980s production of green peas was introduced in Moshi, to export them fresh to Europe. Although this business was stopped due to export issues, the experience proved that Okaseni has a high potential to produce green beans for Europe. The area practices "zero grazing" in which case the livestock is kept in a house and fed there. Okaseni village has about 3,100 "modern" brands of bred cows and 2,500 indigenous cows. There are 5,600 goats and 2,100 sheep.

8. **Does the village have a school? How many children attend?**

Okaseni village has one primary school (called Okaseni Primary School) with a total of five hundred and forty-six kids. The village does not have a secondary school.

9. **Do the villagers have access to medical care? How far is the nearest hospital?**

Okaseni village does not have a hospital. For many villagers in Okaseni, the nearest hospital/health clinic is about four (4) to seven (7) kilometers depending on where one lives within the village.

10. Does the village have a health clinic? Who operates it?

The village does not have a health clinic.

11. What is the most pressing health problem the village faces?

Malaria is the most common health problem but recently, the village has been experiencing a high increase of deaths caused by HIV/AIDS which has created a problem of orphans. There are also problems with maternal and child health, stomach problems such as diarrhea and amoeba caused either by lack of access to clean water or poor toilets (pit latrines). Poor nutrition to small children increases their vulnerability to many diseases. The use of illicit liquor *(spirit called gongo)* by young and adults due to frustration, loss of hope, or simply addiction has led to deterioration of their health, making them susceptible to different diseased.

12. What is the primary power source? Does the village have electrical power?

The primary power source in Okaseni and other neighboring villages is hydro electric power. Only a few people (about 10 percent) have the ability to pay for the connection charges for electricity and the user fees. Many people with electricity have managed through support from their family and relatives living and working in towns.

13. What technology is available? Computers? Access to the internet? Cell phones?

Okaseni village do not have computer facilities or access to the internet. The use of cell phones is expanding fast and different wireless telephone networks can be accessed from the village. However, only a few people have afforded to buy cell phones and many have been given by their relatives living in the towns to ease contact with them. Also people need to have electricity to charge the phones and those without electricity at home decide not to think of owning one and those who get one have to ask a neighbor with electricity to charge the phones for them.

14. **What is the greatest challenge your village faces?**

Increase in poverty among villagers is the greatest challenge which Okaseni face. One of the reasons which led to the deterioration of the economic situation in the village and Moshi in general is the fall in the price of coffee in the international market and increase in production cost. The increase in the production cost of coffee was a result of removal of subsidies by the government of Tanzania as one of the conditions to receive aid from the IMF/World Bank. Communities in Moshi and Okaseni have not been able to find an alternative economic activity. This has led to a problem of high unemployment among the youth. The possibility to find alternative economic activities in the village through, for example engaging in agriculture for other alternative cash crops, has not been exploited. The potential to use the land to grow vegetables has not been fully utilized, the possibility to process the ripe banana into juice for export has not been exploited and fruits such as avocadoes which are massively produced in the village and region end up transported only to neighboring regions within the country. Due to poverty, people cannot pay for the pipes to have access to water in their homes which makes them vulnerable to disease. The ability of communities to build better houses and toilets is also limited, making them susceptible to diseases. Kids from families with electricity at home have the ability to study and do their homework at night and proceed to further studies but many villagers don't have the ability to have electricity at home. To ease the need for income, people have resorted to cutting down trees which have grown in the area for ages hence continuing to jeopardizing the environmental situation of the village, the region and the country. This compound to the existing problem of melting of the snow on top of Mount Kilimanjaro, which is currently receding at an alarming speed due to global warming. Also associated with the problem of poverty is the scourge of HIV/AIDS as many poor women engage in unsafe relationships through prostitution or for the need to meet their daily livelihood through support from men. Normally, the government support communities to build road, hospitals, and health centers but it is easier to get support if local communities are already mobilized with resources and then ask for support. This is however difficult in a situation where people are more concerned in sustaining their day-to-day lives.

15. **What is the most critical help we can give you?**

The well being of communities in Okaseni village will be improved through the following kinds of support:

i. *Skills building to young men and women living in the village:*
Often, educated people relocate from the village to towns to live and work there. When uneducated and unskilled people migrate to towns, they are unwelcome there and end up doing unreliable jobs, petty businesses, prostitution, or crime. Therefore less skilled and uneducated people in the villages need to be empowered to have the competence and skill to manage their lives in the village without thinking of migrating to towns. For example, young men and women can be taught on how to start up and run together micro projects such as building, carpentry, welding skills, local tour guide, vegetable gardens, environmental conservation, to name but a few.

ii. *Access to technology as a tool connect the community in the village to the outside world, awareness raising and incentive for youths to live in the village:* Having designated places in the village ("Village Communication Centers") where people can get access to the internet will allow both students and non students to be connected to the world, acquire new skills and enhance their know how on different spheres of life. TV/Video in the centers with educational media for subjects such as fight against HIV/AIDS, maternal health and environmental conservation would be helpful and would create a place where villagers will positively use their free time instead of loitering around and drinking alcohol. The feeling by the youths that they are not underprivileged in social life as compared to their fellows in towns will act as incentive to make them stay in the village.

iii. *Access to clean water:* It is not possible to provide tape water to every household as this needs a big investment but support for creation or more water tape points where people don't have water source in their vicinity will be very useful. This will decrease the potential for outbreak of diseases and save the time which women and children use to fetch water from tapes far away. Building reserve tanks to store water will alleviate people's suffering to a great extent.

iv. *Support to launch tree planting campaigns:* Communities in Okaseni and Moshi rural in general depend on the availability of rains and the snow on top of Mount Kilimanjaro as a water source. Communities in the area exacerbate the environmental threat to the mountain by cutting down trees without planting new ones. The establishment of tree nurseries in primary schools for free distribution of seedlings to villagers will be extremely useful.

v. *Support for the community to develop alternative sources of income through tourism:* Considering its accessibility to Moshi town with tourists coming to Moshi to climb Mount Kilimanjaro and see wildlife there is a potential for Okaseni to attract tourists by establishing a small "Museum of *Chagga* Heritage." This kind of initiative which will be the first if its kind in the region will not only preserve the heritage of Okaseni and *Chagga* but will also attract tourists and provide for an alternative income generating activity to the village.

vi. *Support for health and educational services:* The creation of a small dispensary at a location which will be easily accessible to the villagers will help to alleviate peoples' suffering and save lives. A small house with about four rooms and toilets can serve this purpose. Normally, the government would provide and pay the personnel. The other alternative would be improving the existing health services provided in the nearby villages where Okaseni residents go for treatment so that they offer better services. Support for educational services to the village can be in the form of equipment such as computers and books to the existing primary school, training of the teachers to be able to teach computer technology to the kids, renovation of buildings and toilets and possible, building more classes.

Although the community in Okaseni is in dire need to have better houses and toilets, roads, additional schools, access to water and power in their houses, the suggestions above have taken into account the reality of costs involved in fulfilling peoples' expectations.

Okaseni village very much appreciates the decision of the British Columbia Institute of Technology (BCIT) to extend an invitation to the Village to complete this questionnaire. We look forward to your positive consideration and working with you.

Sincerely,
Melkizedeck Mushi, Chairman, Okaseni village
Tumaini Minja, Lawyer and Peace Activist, Resident of Okaseni village
24th June 2007

NOTES

Introduction

1. Mary Janigan, "Making a Difference." *Macleans,* December 1, 2003, https:/archive.macleans.ca/article/2003/12/1 /front-2.
2. Joni Mitchell, "Coyote," track 1 on *Hijera,* Asylum, 1976, CD.

Chapter 1

1. Nathan Nunn, "The Long-Term Effects of Africa's Slave Trades," *The Quarterly Journal of Economics* 123, no. 1 (2008): 4, http/The Long Term Effects of Africa's Slave Trades | Nathan Nunn (harvard.edu).
2. Nunn, "The Long-Term Effects," 1.
3. Nunn, "The Long-Term Effects," 4.
4. Nunn, "The Long-Term Effects," 5.
5. Nunn, "The Long-Term Effects," 1.
6. Basil Davidson, *Africa in History* (New York: Simon & Schuster Inc., 1995), 308–309.
7. Davidson, *Africa in History,* 312.
8. Davidson, *Africa in History,* 312.
9. Jeffrey D. Sachs, *The End of Poverty: Economic Possibilities for Our Time* (New York: Penguin Group Inc., 2005), 189.
10. John Reader, *Africa: A Biography of the Continent* (New York: Alfred A. Knopf Inc., 1997), 663.
11. Sachs, *The End of Poverty,* 189.
12. Sachs, *The End of Poverty,* 190.
13. Sachs, *The End of Poverty,* 81.

14. Stephen Lewis, *Race Against Time* (Toronto: House of Anansi Press Inc. 2005), 6.

15. Sachs, *The End of Poverty,* 189.

Chapter 4

1. David Sedaris, *Me Talk Pretty Some Day* (Boston: Little Brown and Company, 2000), 164.

Chapter 5

1. "Vancouver Stanley Cup Riot," Wikipedia, accessed March 30, 2023, https://en.wikipedia.org/ wiki/2011_Vancouver_Stanley_Cup_riot.

2. "From Our Village to Yours," *Bowen Island Undercurrent*, October 11, 2011, 16.

3. Karen Williams, email to author, October 30, 2022.

Chapter 6

1. Leonard Pitts Jr., "Dear White Conservatives: Here's What Else Dr. King Said," *The Seattle Times,* January 16, 2022, https://www.seattletimes.com/opinion/ dear-white-conservatives-heres-what-else-dr-king-said.

2. Martin Farrer, "Historian Berates Billionaires at Davos over Tax Avoidance," *The Guardian,* January 30, 2017, https://www.theguard-ian.com/business/2019/feb/01/rutger-bregman-world-economic-forum-davos-speech-tax-billionaires-capitalism.

3. Matt Coyle, "Was It Something I Said?" *The Sun,* January 21, 2020, https://www.thesun.co.uk/news/10786956/ historian-rutger-bregman-davos-world-economic-forum/.

4. Rachael Sandler, "How MacKenzie Scott Has Given Away Billions— And Is Still One of the World's Richest Women," *Forbes,* May 30, 2022, https://www.forbes.com/sites/rachelsandler/2022/04/05/

how-mackenzie-scott-has-given-away-billionsand-is-still-one-of-the-worlds-richest-women/?sh=3479522f36ac.

5. Sandler, "How MacKenzie."

6. Elizabeth Redden, "A Fairy Godmother for Once-Overlooked Colleges," *Inside Higher Ed,* January 4, 2022, https://www.insidehigher-ed.com/news/2021/01/04/mackenzie-scott-surprises-hbcus-tribal-colleges-and-community-colleges-multimillion.

7. Redden, "A Fairy Godmother."

8. Emily Glazer, "Melinda Gates No Longer Pledges Bulk of her Wealth to Gates Foundation," *The Wall Street Journal,* February 2, 2022, https://www.wsj.com/articles/melinda-french-gates-no-longer-pledges-bulk-of-her-wealth-to-gates-foundation-11643808602.

9. Bill Chappell, "Dolly Parton Gets $100,000,000 from Jeff Bezos to Spend on Charity," *NPR,* November 14, 2022, https://www.npr.org/2022/11/14/1136454716/dolly-parton-jeff-bezos-imagination-library.

10. Ramishan Maruf, "MacKenzie Scott Announces Another $2 Billion in Donations," *CNN,* November 15, 2022, https://www.cnn.com/2022/11/14/business/mackenzie-scott-donations/index.html#:~:text=Since%20her%20divorce%20from%20Bezos%20in%202019%2C%20Forbes,1%2C500%20organizations.%20Her%20most%20recent%20donation%20totals%20%241%2C990%2C800%2C000.

11. Iglika Ivanova, "Have Taxes Changed All That Much over the Past Half-Century? *Canadian Centre for Policy Alternatives,* April 21, 2010, https://policyalternatives.ca/publications/commentary/have-taxes-changed-all-much-over-past-half-century.

12. Arwa Mahdawi, "The Rich Haven't Just Got Richer—They've Also Gotten a Lot More Selfish," *The Guardian,* April 23, 2022, https://www.theguardian.com/commentisfree/2022/apr/23/us-billionaires-taxes-elon-musk-week-in-patriarchy.

Chapter 8

1. Joseph Hanlon, Armando Barrientos, and David Hulme, *Just Give Money to the Poor: The Development Revolution from the Global South* (Sterling, VA: Kumarian Press, 2010), 2.

2. Hanlon, *Just Give Money,* ix.

3. Hanlon, *Just Give Money,* 18–19.

4. Hanlon, *Just Give Money,* 3.

5. Hanlon, *Just Give Money,* 74.

6. Hanlon, *Just Give Money,* 74.

7. Hanlon, *Just Give Money,* 5.

8. Hanlon, *Just Give Money,* 5–6.

9. Hanlon, *Just Give Money,* 72.

10. Hanlon, *Just Give Money,* 2.

11. Hanlon, *Just Give Money,* 6.

12. Hanlon, *Just Give Money,* 10.

13. "Tanzania Denies Huge MP Payoff," BBC News, February 6, 2014, https://www.bbc.com/news/world-africa-26075155.

14. "Tanzania Monthly Wages in Private Sector," Trading/Economics, 2015, https://tradingeconomics.com/tanzania/wages.

15. Kathleen Harris, "Outgoing MPs Can Expect Financial Windfall, Even If They Plan Their Exit," *CBC News,* September 9, 2015, https://www.cbc.ca/news/politics/canada-election-2015-severance-package-1.3211474.

16. "Income of Individuals by Age Group, Sex, and Income Source, Canada, Provinces, and Selected Metropolitan Areas, 2015," Statistics Canada, accessed March 21,2023, https://www150.statcan.gc.ca/t1/tbl1/en/tv.action?pid=1110023901&pickMembers%5B0%5D=1.1&pickMembers%5B1%5D=2.1&pickMembers%5B2%5D=3.1&pickMembers%5B3%5D=4.1&cubeTimeFrame.startYear=2015&cubeTimeFrame.endYear=2015&referencePeriods=20150101%2C20150101.

17. Hanlon, *Just Give Money,* 1–2.

18. Hanlon, *Just Give Money,* 15.

Chapter 9

1. Ralph Stern, email to author, August 5, 2022.

Chapter 10

1. J. F. Helliwell et al., eds., *World Happiness Report 2022*. New York: Sustainable Development Solutions Network, 2022, *https://worldhappiness.report/ed/2022/*.
2. Jared Diamond, *Guns, Germs, and Steel* (New York: W. W. Norton, 1997), 14.
3. Diamond, *Guns, Germs, and Steel*, 18.
4. Diamond, *Guns, Germs, and Steel*, 23.
5. Diamond, *Guns, Germs, and Steel*, 25.
6. Diamond, *Guns, Germs, and Steel*, 408.
7. Diamond, *Guns, Germs, and Steel*, 98.
8. Diamond, *Guns, Germs, and Steel*, 35.
9. Diamond, *Guns, Germs, and Steel*, 177.
10. Diamond, *Guns, Germs, and Steel*, 176–78.
11. Diamond, *Guns, Germs, and Steel*, 186.
12. Diamond, *Guns, Germs, and Steel*, 183
13. Diamond, *Guns, Germs, and Steel*, 135–136.
14. Diamond, *Guns, Germs, and Steel*, 135.
15. Steven Pinker, *The Blank Slate: The Modern Denial of Human Nature* (New York: Penguin Group, 2002), 68.
16. Pinker, *The Blank Slate*, 68–69.
17. Pinker, *The Blank Slate*, 66–67.
18. Pinker, *The Blank Slate*, 67.
19. Diamond, *Guns, Germs, and Steel*, 19.
20. Diamond, *Guns, Germs, and Steel*, 20–21.

Chapter 11

1. Steven Pinker, *Enlightenment Now: The Case for Reason, Science, Humanism, and Progress* (New York: Viking, 2014), 267.
2. Pinker, *Enlightenment Now*, 267.

3. Pinker, *Enlightenment Now,* 267.

Epilogue

1. Bill Gates, "Why Jeffrey Sachs Matters," *Project Syndicate,* May 24, 2014, https://www.project-syndicate.org/commentary/bill-gates-explains-why-the-millennium-villages-project--though-a-failure--was-worth-the-risk.

2. Karen Williams, email to author, October 30, 2022.

3. "Historic Help for Youth from Care Will Support Strong Transitions to Adulthood," BC Gov News, March 15, 2022, https://news.gov.bc.ca/releases/2022CFD0009-000353.

BIBLIOGRAPHY

BBC News. "Tanzania Denies Huge MP Payoff." February 6, 2014. https://www.bbc.com/news/world-africa-26075155

BC Gov News. "Historic Help for Youth from Care Will Support Strong Transitions to Adulthood." March 15, 2022. https://news.gov.bc.ca/releases/2022CFD0009-000353.

Bechtel, Dale. "Life Springs from Trummelbach Falls." July 1, 2002. /www.swissinfo.ch/eng.

Bowen Island Undercurrent. "From Our Village to Your Village." October 7, 2011.

Chang, Ja-Joon. *23 Things They Don't Tell You About Capitalism.* London: Penguin, 2010.

Chappell, Bill. "Dolly Parton Gets $100,000,000 from Jeff Bezos to Spend on Charity." *NPR,* November 14, 2022. https://www.npr.org/2022/11/14/1136454716/dolly-parton-jeff-bezos-imagination-library.

Coyle, Matt. "Was It Something I Said?" *The Sun,* January 21, 2020. https://www.thesun.co.uk/news/10786956/historian-rutger-bregman-davos-world-economic-forum/.

Davidson, Basil. *Africa in History.* New York: Simon & Schuster Inc., 1995.

Diamond, Jared. *Guns, Germs, and Steel.* New York: W. W. Norton, 1997.

Farrer, Martin. "Historian Berates Billionaires at Davos over Tax Avoidance." *The Guardian,* January 30, 2017. https://www.theguardian.com/business/2019/feb/01/rutger-bregman-world-economic-forum-davos-speech-tax-billionaires-capitalism.

Gates, Bill. "Why Jeffrey Sachs Matters." *Project Syndicate.* May 24, 2014. https://www.project-syndicate.org/commentary/bill-gates-explains-why-the-millennium-villages-project--though-a-failure--was-worth-the-risk.

Glazer, Emily. "Melinda Gates No Longer Pledges Bulk of Her Wealth to Gates Foundation." *The Wall Street Journal,* February 2, 2022. https://www.wsj.com/articles/melinda-french-gates-no-longer-pledges-bulk-of-her-wealth-to-gates-foundation-11643808602.

Hanlon, Joseph, Armando Barrientos, and David Hulme. *Just Give Money to the Poor: The Development Revolution from the Global South.* Sterling, VA: Kumarian Press, 2010.

Harris, Kathleen. "Outgoing MPs Can Expect Financial Windfall, Even If They Plan Their Exit." *CBC News,* September 9, 2015. https://www.cbc.ca/news/politics/canada-election-2015-severance-package-1.3211474.

Helliwell, J. F., et al., eds. *World Happiness Report 2022.* New York: Sustainable Development Solutions Network, 2022. https://worldhappiness.report/ed/2022/.

Ivanova, Iglika. "Have Taxes Changed All That Much over The Past Half-Century?" *Canadian Centre for Policy Alternatives,* April 21, 2010. https://policyalternatives.ca/publications/commentary/have-taxes-changed-all-much-over-past-half-century.

Janigan, Mary. "Making a Difference." *Macleans,* December 1, 2003. https:/archive.macleans.ca/article/2003/12/1/front-2.

Lewis, Stephen. *Race Against Time.* Toronto: House of Anansi Press Inc., 2005.

Mahdawi, Arwa. "The Rich Haven't Just Got Richer—They've Also Gotten a Lot More Selfish."

The Guardian, April 23, 2022. https://www.
theguardian.com/commentisfree/2022/apr/23/
us-billionaires-taxes-elon-musk-week-in-patriarchy.

Maruf, Ramishan. "MacKenzie Scott Announces Another $2
Billion in Donations." *CNN,* November 15, 2022. https://www.
cnn.com/2022/11/14/business/mackenzie-scott-donations/
index.html#:~:text=Since%20her%20divorce%20from%20
Bezos%20in%202019%2C%20Forbes,1%2C500%20orga-
nizations.%20Her%20most%20recent%20donation%20
totals%20%241%2C990%2C800%2C000.

Mitchell, Joni. "Coyote." Track 1 on *Hijera.* Asylum, 1976. CD.

Nobel Prize. "Elinor Ostrom: Facts." Accessed March 20, 2023. https://
www.nobelprize.org/prizes/economic-sciences/2009/ostrom/facts/.

Novogratz, Jacqueline. *The Blue Sweater: Bridging the Gap Between the Rich
and Poor in an Interconnected World.* New York: Rodale Books, 2010.

Nunn, Nathan. "The Long-Term Effects of Africa's Slave Trades. *The
Quarterly Journal of Economics* 123, no. 1 (2008):139–176. http/The
Long-Term Effects of Africa's Slave Trades | Nathan Nunn (harvard.edu).

Nutt, Samantha. *Damned Nations: Greed, Guns, Armies, and Aid.* Toronto:
Signal Books, 2011.

Pinker, Steven. *The Blank Slate: The Modern Denial of Human Nature.* New
York: Penguin Group, 2002.

Pinker, Steven. *Enlightenment Now: The Case for Reason, Science, Humanism,
and Progress.* New York: Viking, 2014.

Pitts Jr., Leonard. "Dear White Conservatives: Here's What Else Dr. King
Said." *The Seattle Times,* January 16, 2022. https://www.seattletimes.
com/opinion/dear-white-conservatives-heres-what-else-dr-king-said.

Reader, John. *Africa: A Biography of the Continent.* New York: Alfred A.
Knopf Inc., 1997.

Redden, Elizabeth. "A Fairy Godmother for Once-Overlooked Colleges." *Inside Higher Ed,* January 4, 2022. https://www.insidehighered.com/news/2021/01/04/mackenzie-scott-surprises-hbcus-tribal-colleges-and-community-colleges-multimillion.

Sandler, Rachael. "How MacKenzie Scott Has Given Away Billions—And Is Still One of the World's Richest Women." *Forbes,* May 30, 2022. https://www.forbes.com/sites/rachelsandler/2022/04/05/how-mackenzie-scott-has-given-away-billionsand-is-still-one-of-the-worlds-richest-women/?sh=3479522f36ac.

Sachs, Jeffrey D. *The End of Poverty: Economic Possibilities for Our Time.* New York: PenguinGroup Inc., 2005.

Sedaris, David. *Me Talk Pretty Some Day.* Boston: Little Brown and Company, 2000.

Statistics Canada. "Income of Individuals by Age Group, Sex, and Income Source, Canada, Provinces, and Selected Metropolitan Areas, 2015." Accessed March 21, 2023. https://www150.statcan.gc.ca/t1/tbl1/en/tv.action?pid=1110023901&pickMembers%5B0%5D=1.1&pickMembers%5B1%5D=2.1&pickMembers%5B2%5D=3.1&pickMembers%5B3%5D=4.1&cubeTimeFrame.startYear=2015&cubeTimeFrame.endYear=2015&referencePeriods=20150101%2C20150101

Trading/Economics. "Tanzania Monthly Wages in Private Sector." 2015. https://tradingeconomics.com/tanzania/wages

Watts, Alan. *Psychotherapy East and West.* New York: Vintage Books, 1975.

Wikipedia. "Vancouver Stanley Cup Riot." Accessed March 30, 2023. https://en.wikipedia.org/wiki/2011_Vancouver_Stanley_Cup_riot.

Printed in the USA
CPSIA information can be obtained
at www.ICGtesting.com
JSHW042053050324
58451JS00008B/16